WHAT KIND OF READER ARE YOU?

Do you find yourself reading only one word at a time? Do you frequently go back over a passage to get its meaning? Do your lips move when you read "silently"? Do you take more than a minute for a page of an average novel?

No matter what your present difficulties, this book will help you! It will help you if you're a very slow reader or even a fairly fast one, whether you understand a lot of what you read or now miss most of it.

Through a series of short, easy-to-take self-tests, *Faster Reading Self-Taught* will show you *exactly* what's wrong with *your* reading. Then—once you know your weaknesses—it gives the simple five-step plan that will eliminate your bad habits forever.

Overnight this book will open the door to a whole new world of pleasure for you at home and immense profit for you in your career. It will make you the reader you have always wanted to be!

Books by Harry Shefter

Faster Reading Self-Taught
How to Get Higher Marks in School
How to Prepare Talks and Oral Reports
Shefter's Guide to Better Compositions
Short Cuts to Effective English
Six Minutes a Day to Perfect Spelling

Published by POCKET BOOKS

FASTER READING

Self-Taught

HARRY SHEFTER

**Professor of English
New York University**

PUBLISHED BY POCKET BOOKS NEW YORK

FASTER READING SELF-TAUGHT

POCKET BOOK edition published September, 1958

12th printing......February, 1973

Faster Reading Self-Taught was originally published under the imprint of WASHINGTON SQUARE PRESS, a division of Simon & Schuster, Inc.

This POCKET BOOK edition is printed from
brand-new plates made from newly set, clear, easy-to-read
type. POCKET BOOK editions are published by POCKET BOOKS, a division
of Simon & Schuster, Inc., 630 Fifth Avenue, New York, N.Y. 10020.
Trademarks registered in the United States and other countries.

L

ACKNOWLEDGMENTS

For permission to reprint material controlled by them, the author thanks the following authors, publishers and agents:

AMERICAN EDUCATION PUBLICATIONS for "Is Woman's Place in the Home?" published in *Every Week*, a weekly newspaper for high school students, American Education Publications, Columbus 16, Ohio.

ARKANSAS GAZETTE for "Traffic-Choked Main Street Outmoded," by Gene Foreman, from the June 11, 1957, issue.

ASSOCIATION OF AMERICAN RAILROADS for "Railroads" and "Unloading a Box Car" from *The Stories Behind the Pictures*.

ROBERT BIRD for "How to Write Successful Ads." Reprinted by permission of the author.

CHICAGO DAILY NEWS for "But Can You Stay in Love?" by Sydney J. Harris.

B. J. CHUTE for "New Words for Old," which appeared in the March, 1957, issue of *Inside the ACD* under the title "How Dictionaries Grow." Reprinted by permission of the author.

EDWARDS & DEUTSCH for "Academy Awards"; "Jai Alai . . ."; "The King's Hunter"; "120—And Like It!" by Jack Mabley; "Slow, Slow—Quick, Quick," by George Duke; and "Spills Thrill!" from the Oldsmobile owner magazine, *Rocket Circle*.

ESQUIRE, INC., for "The Anatomy of a Sneeze," by Madelyn Wood, reprinted from the August, 1956, issue of *Coronet,* copyright, by Esquire, Inc. 1956; "The Incredible Crab," by Reed Millard, reprinted from the January, 1957, issue of *Coronet,* copyright, by Esquire, Inc. 1956.

THE FLORIDA TIMES-UNION for "Peck of Trouble Looms in Abandoning Bushel," an editorial from the June 11, 1957, issue.

GUIDE PUBLICATIONS, INC., Plymouth, Massachusetts, for "Clever Young Man from Old Chatham," "Fables and Foibles" and "Kids, Goats, and Bees" from the July 13, 1957, issue of *Cape Cod Guide*.

THE HALIFAX HERALD, LTD., for "The Day of Decision," an editorial from the June 10, 1957, issue of *The Halifax Chronicle-Herald*.

LOS ANGELES TIMES for "Kitten Saves Actor from Rattler Bite" from the June 12, 1957, issue.

THE MUTUAL BENEFIT LIFE INSURANCE COMPANY for "Causes and Cures of Snowblindness," "Crank Her Up Again," "Down Your Alley," "For a Polite Dog," "Got a Match?" "It Doesn't Come Out in the Wash," "Misguided Missiles," "Only a Medium of Exchange," "Sea Farmers," "The Story of 30,000,000 Christmas Trees," "They Call 'Em as They're Taught to See 'Em" and "To Shave or Not to Shave" from *Good Property*.

NEW YORK POST for "The Terror of Muse, Pa., Has a Very Busy Day" from the June 17, 1957, issue. Reprinted by permission from New York Post. Copyright 1957 New York Post Corporation.

THE NEW YORK TIMES for "Boy in Well Rescued After 24 Hours" from the May 18, 1957, issue of *The New York Times;* "How Much for a Home?" by Walter H. Stern, from the June 2, 1957, issue of *The New York Times;* "Sticker Styles," by Oscar Godbout, from the March 14, 1957, issue of *The New York Times Magazine;* "Topics of The Times," by Lewis Nichols, from the July 15, 1957, issue of *The New York Times;* "'Town Meeting' of the Stockholders," by A. H. Raskin, from the May 12, 1957, issue of *The New York Times Magazine.*

ANGELO PATRI for "Our Children" from the June 6, 1957, issue of *The Idaho Daily Statesman.* Reprinted by special permission of The Bell Syndicate, Inc.

PLAYBILL, INC., for "Traveling with a Camera," by John Ryan. Reprinted by permission of the author and Playbill Magazine.

THE READER'S DIGEST for the excerpt from "New Weapons Against Heart Disease," by Francis and Katharine Drake, from the May, 1957, issue of *The Reader's Digest,* copyright, 1957, by The Reader's Digest Association, Inc.

SAN FRANCISCO CHRONICLE for "Smoke Scare" from the June 9, 1957, issue of *This World* magazine of the *San Francisco Chronicle.*

THE SATURDAY REVIEW for "Everyone Writes (Bad) Poetry," by John Ciardi, from the May 5, 1956, issue of *The Saturday Review,* copyright, 1956, by Saturday Review Associates, Inc. Reprinted by permission of the author.

HOWARD N. SELTZER for "The Letter." Reprinted by permission of the author.

STEPHEN M. SELTZER for "Death." Reprinted by permission of the author.

THE TIMES-PICAYUNE PUBLISHING COMPANY for "Chance for Gas Bill," an editorial from the June 11, 1957, issue of *The Times-Picayune.*

FRANKLIN WATTS, INC., and POCKET BOOKS, INC., for the excerpt from *The Science Book of Wonder Drugs,* by Donald G. Cooley. Copyright, 1954, by Franklin Watts, Inc.

To the Boss

Table of Contents

FASTER READING
Self-Taught

CHAPTER I

Why Better Reading Pays Off

ON A SUNNY October morning not long ago, a twin-engined plane took off from Mitchell Field in New York and headed south. On board were twenty-five educators who had been invited to spend three days touring the Air Force University at Maxwell Field, Alabama. I was privileged to be a member of that group.

When we landed we were greeted by Lieutenant Colonel Minietta, who was to be guide and companion to us during our stay. By the time we were ready for our return flight, we had seen and heard enough to convince us that a really remarkable job was being done to prepare Air Force officers for positions of leadership. It gave us a deep sense of security to observe the high caliber of the students who would someday be entrusted with the task of maintaining and extending United States air power.

Of course, none of us will ever forget the thrill of zipping through the skies in jet fighters, while we feverishly reviewed the steps required to eject us from the plane, seat and all, if we had to leave in a hurry. Yet, as teachers, we found it almost equally exciting to witness the amazing devices used to train these hand-picked candidates. We enviously inspected and tried out the concealed microphones used by instructors to reach large groups with a minimum of voice strain. Our eyes popped as we saw, sliding in and out of walls, maps and charts complete with magnetized markers for easy demonstration. It was fun experimenting in sound-proofed booths equipped with recording and playback machines, designed to help a student literally give *himself* language instruction. But it was the presence of an elaborately appointed reading clinic that startled me!

"You mean," said I to Colonel Wood, who was briefing us on this phase of the program, "that some of these captains, majors, and colonels—almost all college graduates—have reading problems?"

"We have a few brigadiers coming here, too," he replied with a smile. "Most of these fellows read well enough for ordinary purposes. However, at this place there is such a mass of stuff they have to plow through in a short time—books, pamphlets, magazines, reports—that average speed just won't do. Our men must learn to read at least 500 words a minute in order to keep up with their class assignments. That's why many of them come in to be helped. They know that better reading ability will pay off, will earn them advancement."

The story of these highly capable and intelligent officers is dramatic proof that superior reading skill is an important part of any plan for self-improvement. It also shows that you are not the only one who has found it necessary to do something about his reading habits. As a matter of fact, it has been estimated that about 60,-000,000 Americans, in their jobs or professions, or even at home in their kitchens and workshops, have learned that better reading would pay off. It would help some to keep abreast of the latest ideas in their fields, give others the confidence to discuss current affairs freely with friends or business associates, enable still others to be more successful in their school work, and be a boon to many home owners, who could take full advantage of the wonderful material now available in book form on do-it-yourself projects. The main point is that everyone who doesn't read well has at least one good reason to

2

want to read better. It is for those people who have the reason *and the desire* to improve that this book has been written.

Can a book take the place of a reading laboratory or trained instructor? Let there be no mistake about it. If you can afford the time and money to get individual help in solving your reading problems, by all means do so. That's the best way.

But the job can be done by you yourself! Arthur I. Gates, prominent reading authority from Teachers College, Columbia University, made some significant remarks in this connection at the conference held by the International Reading Association in May, 1956:

> . . . there should be provided newer types of manuals to place directly in the hands of the pupils, manuals in which the major purpose is to tell and demonstrate to pupils the good techniques of reading, describe for them the activities that should be pursued to acquire them, in brief, to guide them in the process of learning. The purpose of these little manuals should be to make clear the kind of reading skills that are needed and to induce the youngster to try to learn by himself.

> No amount of instruction by the teacher or practice by the pupil is adequate unless it increases the pupil's insight and his interest and skill in trying to learn by himself. He should learn to read in school by trying to discover by himself the nature of the good techniques, by endeavoring to diagnose and direct his own learning, and by getting pointers from his peers and teachers. That is what the apt learner does on the baseball grounds.

A reasonable conclusion one can draw from the comments of Professor Gates is that self-training has highly desirable features in a program of reading improvement. The officers we talked about are shown how to go about developing better skills, and then they proceed at their own speed and under their own power. But unlike these Air Force officers you don't have a reading clinic practically in your back yard. You may live many miles from the nearest university reading center. Even if reading classes are available to you, a busy daily schedule may prevent you from attending. What you do have at your disposal is some free time almost every day that you could put to good use in improving your reading ability, *if you knew how*. This book will show you how.

It will show you *how* to read with greater speed, to read with better understanding.

But please get this straight at the very outset! To make any progress at all, *it is you* who will have to do the required exercises. *It is you* who will have to master the techniques. *It is you* who will have to follow a consistent training program. The job cannot be done *for* you. The job must be done *by* you.

If you do not have the self-discipline needed to make an honest try, you'd better forget the whole idea. Neither a laboratory nor a book will do you any good.

However, let's suppose you are determined to rid yourself of your bad reading habits.

Are you willing to spend 15 minutes a day to practice improving your skills?

Are you prepared to accept the fact that it won't always be easy to push yourself?

Do you think that a substantial increase in your reading speed and comprehension is worth accomplishing—in as little as 5 or 6 weeks for some people?

Would you like to increase your reading ability eventually by 25 to 50 per cent?

If you can truthfully say *Yes* to these questions, then you have already won half the battle. The rest of the victory will be achieved after you have faithfully applied yourself to the pages that follow.

CHAPTER II

Good Readers and Bad

"A little learning is a dangerous thing."

—ALEXANDER POPE

THE EIGHTEENTH-CENTURY English poet who said this knew what he was talking about. Every one of us has sometimes jumped to a conclusion that is not supported by sufficient facts.

For example, consider Mrs. A. She has thumbed through a few "home medical advisers," has exchanged symptoms of assorted ailments with her friends, and has become frightened after reading a magazine article. One day she feels a sharp pain and proceeds to diagnose herself. Mrs. A. starts to worry, and before long she is certain she is very ill. When she finally decides to seek professional advice, Mrs. A. has worked herself into such a state that the doctor *does* find something wrong with her blood pressure and her digestion. The original pain has long since disappeared.

Too little knowledge used in connection with one's reading habits can be equally harmful. For instance, many people believe in certain wise sayings, such as:

Haste makes waste.
Slow but steady wins the race.
Don't bite off more than you can chew.

Certainly there is good sense to these expressions when applied to many situations. But if your reading habits have been influenced by them, you are just like the wom-

6

an who tried to be her own doctor. You may have created your own difficulties because of foggy notions you have formed about what is good or bad to do in reading. Clinical studies have shown that in so far as reading is concerned, reasonable haste does not make waste, the slow will almost always lose the race, and a larger bite of words can be chewed by most readers.

Let's examine statements made by people who have created their own reading problems. Let's separate fact from fancy. Then we can take a look at the *real* causes of poor reading.

"But if I go fast, I'll miss everything."

This is just not true. All evidence points to the seemingly illogical conclusion that the faster most people read, the better they understand. About fifteen years ago, at my suggestion and under my supervision, a remedial-reading project was introduced into a high school where I was chairman of the English department. About 125 *exceptionally* slow pupils were grouped for extra help in reading. More than 70 per cent of them showed progress after a few months. There was a minimum increase of more than 20 per cent in speed—and during the same time better than a 12 per cent improvement in comprehension scores. Countless other experimental groups have demonstrated similar results in recent years. Even our Air Force officers, despite the amazing speed that they attain (more than 500 words a minute), show an average increase of 3 to 5 per cent in comprehension.

"How can you expect me to read better? I wasn't taught as well as students were years ago. Some experts have recently proved it, too."

Three separate studies, made in 1949, 1952, and 1954, proved that modern students not only are taught as well as their grandparents were, but understand more of what they read. This is remarkable when we consider the fact that high schools have almost doubled their attendance since the turn of the century and are now teaching many youngsters who formerly would have dropped out in the lower grades because of discouragement over their poor learning progress. In short, the average reading ability today is better than ever even though the job of teaching is harder. So-called experts who argue this point simply haven't studied the facts. Don't blame your troubles on your teachers!

"What's the use of trying to change now? I've been doing it wrong for such a long time that it will take years for me to develop better reading habits."

Again we have a statement that is not borne out by the evidence. Assuming the ability to improve is present, the time it will take you to read better depends entirely upon your willingness to do the hard work required to break bad habits. College clinics have been able to get their students to double their reading speed in a matter of weeks. I have personally known members of special reading classes to make a gain of more than two years in their reading level in less than six months. In fact, later on I'm going to prove to you that you can increase your reading skill to some extent in less than 5 minutes!

"Every time I come across a new word in a book I'm reading, I stop to look it up in a dictionary. After a while I become confused—but I can't just ignore the words I don't know."

Yes, you can and should ignore those words. If you have been stopping to look them up, you have been using what is perhaps the worst method of improving your vocabulary. And what's more, you have been ruining your concentration and thus weakening your reading skill more than ever. We'll talk about the right way to learn new words in Chapter IX. For the moment it is sufficient to say that you probably forget the meanings of such words almost as fast as you look them up. Rarely does the sense of a paragraph depend upon a word or two. The skilled reader skips frequently without losing anything of the main idea. You can learn to do this, too, and still be able to master many of the strange words that crop up now and then.

"I read novels and short stories at a pretty good pace. But I can't seem to train myself to read just as quickly when I tackle scientific or historical stuff, or when I have a batch of math problems to work on."

The false idea here is the notion that you ought to read all material at the same speed, regardless of the content. Authorities are in agreement that there are different levels of speed one should employ, depending upon the difficulty of the subject matter. A student learning to play a musical instrument progresses from easy note patterns to the more complicated. After the basic skills have been mastered, light, carefree pieces can be learned during one practice session, but the more difficult selections will still require a much slower pace and greater concentration. Your recreational reading will go the fastest; a serious editorial should take you longer for the same number of words; a scientific study of the functions of the bodily organs might cut your rate of speed in half. That's fine. That's as it should be. There is really no such thing as a uniform reading speed.

"I've been told that anybody can be taught to read and understand 300 to 500 words a minute. My kid brother's been taking reading lessons for two years now, and the teacher hasn't done a thing for him."

In the first place, it would be wise to find out whether the boy should even have been accepted as a remediable

9

case. Unfortunately, not everyone can be taught to improve. Nature, as you probably know, is not completely democratic. Some of us are born with less mental ability than others. Somewhat more than 2 per cent of the population of this country cannot learn to read under any circumstances. This amounts to almost 4,000,000 people. There are additional millions who are mentally retarded and who cannot ever hope to be able to read better than a third-, fourth-, or fifth-grade elementary-school pupil. The best methods and teachers in the world could not enable the latter to read at an average rate, between 300 and 350 words a minute. Of course, it is sometimes possible to help one who is retarded and who does no better than 125 words or so a minute to increase his speed by 20 per cent or more. Quite frankly, however, such a person would not be able to handle the material in this book by himself. He would need patient individual attention from a skilled instructor.

If, therefore, a youngster or an adult makes no progress despite instruction, he may be doing the best he can. He should not be driven beyond his limits. A personality problem is often at the root of a reading deficiency. Indeed, even with those of average intelligence and above, as we shall see later, emotional difficulties and reading ability are often very closely allied. "Do the best you can with what you have" should be the guiding principle in any situation involving reading improvement. Fortunately, the bulk of the population, more than 100,000,000 of us, can be taught to read at least 350 words a minute, and millions can push themselves to well over 500.

We have demonstrated that there are false notions about this business of learning to read well. Now we can turn to the real causes of poor reading. We'll examine a few case histories of people who have required help with their reading problems. It's very likely that you will find some of their troubles similar to your own. Once you understand what is holding you back, we'll be able to work together to effect a permanent improvement in your reading skill.

Eleanor T., College Student

Eleanor had her earliest reading lessons at home. Her doting mother thought it would be a fine thing if her little girl entered school "ahead" of the other children. Unfortunately Mrs. T. stressed the pronunciation of words so much that her daughter got into the habit of saying every word, whether she read orally or silently. By watching her one could easily tell that she had become a lip reader.

It wasn't so bad in high school. Because her rate of reading was so slow, Eleanor never had the time to finish the novels and biographies for which reports were required. But the other kids were always around to lend her their papers. She actually thought she was getting away with something. She once boasted that she had not read a whole book in her entire high-school career. Of course, she had trouble with her history assignments, couldn't do math problems, and admitted that the chem textbook was all Greek to her. However, with faithful Mother's help, she managed to pull through.

Now Eleanor's in trouble. Her college professors make so many demands on her reading time and are so quick to detect unoriginal work that the days of faked reports are over. Even Mother can't help. Either Miss T. must learn to keep up with her assignments by herself or the diploma will elude her. Chapters V through IX would be particularly helpful to this troubled young lady.

George K., Mechanic

Life wasn't easy for this young man when he was a boy. He quit school early because his part-time jobs weren't bringing in enough to enable his family to meet the weekly bills. George never had much time for homework, and when he did force himself to look at a book he usually gave up in disgust. He would laboriously work out one word at a time and discover that at the end of an hour he had covered nine or ten pages. It was doubly frustrating not to understand even the few pages he had read. With almost a sense of relief he had exchanged classroom attendance for working papers on his sixteenth birthday.

George is not without ambition. He'd like to get out of the rut he's in. But his bad reading habits have been standing in his way. He suspected this when he had to take the written test for his driver's license three times. He became convinced of it when he flunked a few civil-service examinations. It was useless to pretend that the questions were *dopy*. His word-by-word reading had done him in, he had to admit privately.

George is a good man. His boss tells him so. But a mechanic who wants to get ahead should be able to handle shop manuals without an interpreter and be able to gather information for a report the way Tom Clemens, the foreman, does. Young Mr. K. has to start from scratch. He should give Chapters V through IX the full treatment, and concentrate especially on Chapter VI, if he really does want to climb up the ladder.

Victor G., M.D.

Dr. G. has been a successful general practitioner for eleven years. He still remembers those tough days in medical school when he spent countless hours struggling through heavy, thick textbooks. He had to be very careful about his reading because one can't just waltz through a chapter on anatomy and expect to learn the location and function of the various organs of the body. When Victor was graduated, he became much too busy during his internship and early years of building up a practice to worry about his habit of reading everything as if it were to be memorized. Now that he can stop to take a leisurely breath occasionally, he has come to realize that his slow rate of reading is very annoying. He would like to keep up with the latest in his field and would also enjoy going through a best seller now and then. But reading still takes so much time! He knows that he no longer has to concentrate on every word, but his old habit still haunts him. Dr. G. has all the mental equipment needed to become a skilled, rapid reader. All he needs is a push—and he'll get it if he follows the suggestions outlined in Chapters V-VII.

Philip M., Businessman

You, too, would become irritated if you watched the correspondence pile up on your desk day by day and wondered helplessly when you would ever get to the bottom of it. Mr. M. envies a few of his associates who seemingly can glance at a letter and dictate a reply simultaneously. Philip reads fast enough, but he has to reread a letter or report several times before he is certain he has grasped the central point.

His wife sometimes complains about his sense of humor. She once said something about his not being able to see the forest for the trees. He didn't quite understand her then, but one doesn't admit such things to one's wife. Later he realized that she was referring to his habit of paying such close attention to the details of a story that he often missed the punch line.

Philip M. needs some training in rapid reading for main ideas. He can get this from Chapters VI and VIII.

13

Catherine R., Private Secretary

The honeymoon with her new position is over. Catherine had always dreamed of being a girl Friday to a big executive. And nice Mr. Faredon is vice-president of his company.

But how was she to know that men like him talk worse than college professors. Those words he uses! He should have hired a walking dictionary. Besides, how can a girl look up a word if she can't even spell it?

Catherine is worried that she will lose her present job for the same reason that that young lawyer stopped seeing her last summer. She had known then that her limited vocabulary embarrassed the two of them when they got into a conversation. Now she would be embarrassing Mr. Faredon if she messed up some of his dictation.

She had been promising herself for years that she would start reading something better than picture magazines and comic strips. On an impulse she had even registered for an evening course in great books the previous fall but had dropped out after the first two weeks. Chapter IX could do wonders for Miss R. She should stop bemoaning her poor stock of words and make a concrete effort to improve her vocabulary.

Carol W., Housewife

Only last week Carol recalled how she used to put one over on her old health-education teachers when they conducted the annual eye examinations. She would memorize the eye charts in advance, and when her turn came she would rattle off the letters the same as students who had twenty-twenty vision. This was an old trick she had been practicing ever since the seventh grade. It was then she had discovered that she was having difficulty recognizing even her friends until they were a few feet away from her.

She had dreaded being exposed and forced to wear *spectacles,* as she sneeringly referred to them. She had completely agreed with the sentiments expressed in the widely circulated witticism "Boys seldom make passes at girls who wear glasses." Carol had literally stopped reading because the eyestrain and resulting headaches made the experience painful. Anyway, dates and parties were more important than graduation from high school.

Now that Carol has been married for a few years and has moved into a new community, she has been subjected to a rude awakening. She has learned how easily some of her neighbors can detect a nonreader and how hard it can be to make and keep social contacts. Her husband has been arguing with her for some time to forget her vanity and regain her sight. Unless this foolish woman submits to a complete eye examination very soon, her domestic and social problems will continue to pile up. None of the chapters in this book can do the slightest good for her until she has honestly and sensibly removed the physical block to progress in reading. Glasses come first!

Frederick J., Teen-ager

Fred is younger by twelve years than any of his four brothers and sisters. Of course, he was babied outrageously from the start and became accustomed to everyone's undivided attention. He learned very early that he was certain to become the center of attraction if he refused to eat, pretended to be terribly hurt when he fell, or cried when he couldn't do something as well as the older boys.

His first days in kindergarten convinced Freddy that he wasn't going to like school. There was too much competition. Those other kids wanted as much of the teacher's time as he did. He'd fix 'em. He wouldn't learn! Then the teacher would have to give him more attention. The folks at home would be worried, too.

When their son seemed to make far slower progress in reading than his classmates, his parents deluded themselves into thinking that he would snap out of it. However, the situation became worse. He subconsciously began to fight the idea of becoming a satisfactory reader. His handicap enabled him to duck homework assignments and prompted him to pretend illness when test days came around. This got him more attention than ever.

Lately a change has come over Fred. It occurred shortly after he returned from a hunting trip with his favorite uncle. The boy is fourteen now and for the first time has expressed a desire to succeed in school. He wants to become an engineer, just like Uncle Charlie. But what is he going to do about his reading deficiency?

Even before he starts a book, he believes he will have trouble understanding it. His mind begins to wander after he has read a few pages, and much as he wants to now, he can't seem to concentrate. A feeling of restlessness seizes Fred when he comes upon what he calls "deep stuff," and he lives in constant fear that he will remember nothing of what he reads. He puts off doing his lessons with one excuse or another until it is too late to begin. His school work continues to be a mess.

Like Carol, who won't wear glasses, Fred cannot be helped at this stage by any of the chapters in this book. He needs to solve his emotional problems first. His parents would do well to take him to some youth consultation center that specializes in straightening out teenagers who have deeply rooted personality difficulties. Not until his emotional block has been removed can our young friend start a planned program of reading improvement.

16

The seven people you have just met illustrate the basic and real causes of poor reading. Let's review for a moment:

1. Certain physical obstructions, like lip movements during silent reading, can hold back one's speed.

2. Word-by-word reading leads to lack of proper understanding as well as slowness.

3. Some people read slowly simply because they lack the drive to force themselves to break old bad habits.

4. Failure to differentiate between minor details and main ideas creates confusion for many readers.

5. A poor vocabulary is a serious problem for anyone who wishes to improve his reading ability.

6. Poor eyesight, either ignored or undetected, can make progress in reading almost impossible.

7. Emotional problems can block any attempt to increase rate and comprehension of reading.

The last two reasons, in addition to mental retardation, must be eliminated from consideration in so far as our purposes here are concerned. An oculist or a psychiatrist must be consulted first. Certainly if Carol took care of her poor vision and Fred stopped fighting his desire to improve his reading, we would welcome them among our readers. Until then we must confine ourselves to readers like you, who need help and who have *the will* and *the ability* to accept it.

You know what's wrong with George, Catherine, and the other five cases about whom we are going to concern ourselves. Although some of their difficulties may have struck a responsive chord, you would still like to be sure of just where you stand. A good way to find out is to perform a self-diagnosis. The next chapter will offer you the opportunity to do this. You will know after you have taken the various tests what your major shortcomings are. This knowledge will direct you toward the remedial techniques in this book that are best suited to your needs. Although you may eventually find it necessary to spend most of your time on only specific chapters, I strongly urge you to examine the entire book. You may pick up some pointers that will strengthen still further those skills of yours that are already satisfactory.

CHAPTER III

What Kind of Reader Are You?

A SELF-TEST

You WILL NEED a pad of paper, some pencils, and a watch with a second hand. If you have or can borrow a stop watch, so much the better. Select a place where you can work undisturbed, seat yourself comfortably, and make certain you have adequate light.

The object of this self-analysis is to reveal your strengths and weaknesses in reading as they exist at this moment. Make no special effort to do well unless the instructions request you to do so. The idea is to perform as naturally as you can so that you can get a true picture of your abilities.

TEST I

As you read this, please do exactly as I say. Place your fingers lightly on your lips. Now continue to read this paragraph. Are your lips moving? Now concentrate your attention on your tongue. Is it absolutely at rest, or is it attempting to sound out the letters of the words you are supposed to be reading silently? Now place two fingers on your Adam's apple. Do you feel any vibration? Are you unconsciously using part of your voice mechanism?

The next part of this test is rather difficult. You will have to try to read and at the same time figure out what

19

your mind is doing. Ready? Good. As you read this sentence, determine whether your mind is repeating to itself *one word at a time*. That is, are you still actually reading aloud in your mind, even though not a sound is coming out of your mouth?

If you answered *Yes* to any of the questions, you are in the habit of placing mechanical obstacles along your path of reading. In Chapter V, I will tell you what you ought to do about them. Our purpose in this test was to help you decide whether you, like many other people, are guilty of interfering with your potential ability to read faster by setting up these roadblocks. Now please go on to Test II.

TEST II

Before you take this test, it is important that you understand clearly exactly what I want you to do. Holding your head absolutely still, look first to the left and then to the right. Only your eyes should have moved, not your head. Now keep your eyes absolutely still and move your head up and down. My purpose here is to remind you that your head and your eyes can move independently of each other.

In the selection that follows, you are to keep your eyes absolutely fixed (but don't strain) and allow only your head to travel down the page. You must try to take in the entire group of words on each line in one glance. Do not let your eyes jump from left to right, from one word to another. You may find this extremely difficult to do, but if you concentrate and exert your will power you should be able to read the selection as you have been directed. Try your very best to do this, and even if you have a lot of trouble don't stop until you have finished this selection.

The Incredible Crab

BY REED MILLARD

In the blue-green depths
of the Indian Ocean
a strange battle
seemed certain to come
to a swift, deadly end.
For one of the opponents
was a two-foot fish
with razor-sharp teeth,
the other a small crab.
The helpless crab's shell
was not very hard,
its delicate claws weak.
It could not even
move rapidly enough
to escape.
Yet, within seconds,
the sharp-toothed fish
was fleeing wildly.
For this little
Indian Ocean crab
had done something incredible—
something almost unheard of
in nature.
He had picked up a weapon
and used it
against his adversary.
This crab's weapon
was a sea anemone,
a curious marine animal

which looks like a flower
and is equipped
with powerful stingers
capable of shocking
and partially paralyzing
many animals or fish
they touch.
In each of his claws,
which are not affected
by the plant's sting,
the crab had seized
one of these
natural hand grenades
and had hurled them
at his foe.

Were you able to control your eye movements? If
you were, you have an asset that is the most important
factor in any effort to increase your reading speed. If you
found it impossible to prevent your eyes from hopping
from one word to the next, you will need extensive drill
in the material presented in Chapter VI, which is designed to eliminate word-by-word reading. Now please
try Test III.

TEST III

You will recall that I said it would be possible for you
to improve your reading speed to some extent in less than
five minutes. This third test, therefore, has a twofold purpose. It will enable you to determine how your speed
compares with the average (300 to 350 words per minute)
and will demonstrate how you can read faster than you

generally do without any more instruction than the suggestion that you *try* to do so.

Here is an article selected from a magazine. You will
read it in two parts. In the first half which follows, read as
you normally would, but time yourself as you do. Count
the actual number of minutes and seconds it takes you to
complete reading the paragraphs.

Remember, read this part of the article at your normal
reading speed. As soon as you're ready to time yourself
you may start.

The Anatomy of a Sneeze

BY MADELYN WOOD

When a 13-year-old Virginia girl started sneezing, her
parents thought it was merely a cold. But when the
sneezes continued for hours, they called in a doctor. Nearly two months later the girl was still sneezing, thousands
of times a day, and her case had attracted world-wide
attention.

Hundreds of suggestions, ranging from "put a clothes-
pin on her nose" to "have her stand on her head," poured
in. But nothing did any good. Finally, she was taken to
Johns Hopkins Hospital where Dr. Leo Kanner, one of
the world's top authorities on sneezing, solved the baffling
problem with miraculous speed.

He used neither drugs nor surgery for, curiously
enough, the clue for the treatment was found in an ancient superstition about the amazing bodily reaction we
call the sneeze. It was all in her mind, he said, a view
which Aristotle, some 3,000 years earlier, would have
agreed with heartily.

23

Dr. Kanner simply gave a modern psychiatric interpretation to the ancient belief that an excessive amount of sneezing was an indication that the spirit was troubled; and he proceeded to treat the girl accordingly.

"Less than two days in a hospital room, a plan for better scholastic and vocational adjustment, and reassurance about her unwarranted fear of tuberculosis quickly changed her from a sneezer to an ex-sneezer," he reported.

Sneezing has always been a subject of wonder, awe and puzzlement. Dr. Kanner has collected literally thousands of superstitions concerning it. The most universal one is the custom of invoking the blessing of the Deity when a person sneezes—a practice Dr. Kanner traces back to the ancient belief that a sneeze was an indication the sneezer was possessed of an evil spirit. Strangely, people the world over still continue the custom with the traditional, "God bless you," or its equivalent.

When physiologists look at the sneeze, they see a remarkable mechanism which, without any conscious help from you, takes on a job that has to be done. When you need to sneeze you sneeze, this being nature's ingenious way of expelling an irritating object from the nose. The object may be a speck of dust, a dash of pollen or a growth of microbes in the nose which nature is striving to remove from the nasal membranes.

A study of the process reveals that the irritation sets up a series of reactions with incredible swiftness. At the instant of irritation, the tongue moves against the soft palate and the air pressure, built up, unable to escape through the mouth, blasts its way out through the nose. A sneeze is thus quite literally an explosion of air.

(450 words—app.)

24

Jot down immediately the total time it took you to read this portion of the selection: _____

(minutes)—(seconds)

Now check your time with the data presented in the chart below. First, locate the time it took you in the first two columns at the left; then read the number in the column to the right and you will have the words-per-minute score:

WORDS-PER-MINUTE CHART

Minutes	Seconds	Wds/Min	Minutes	Seconds	Wds/Min
1	0	450	1	50	245
1	5	415	1	55	235
1	10	385	2	0	225
1	15	360	2	5	215
1	20	335	2	10	205
1	25	315	2	15	200
1	30	300	2	25	185
1	35	285	2	35	175
1	40	270	2	45	165
1	45	255	2	55	155

(Approximate)

If you finished the passage in less than 1 minute, you are reading at a rate that is far above the average and you have little to worry about. However, if it took you more than 3 minutes, you are reading exceedingly slowly —at less than half the average rate. You will have a lot of work to do to increase your speed.

Now, in the second half of the article I should like you to do the following as you read:

Decide, now, that you are going to read as fast as you can *even if you miss a word or two here or there!*

25

Try not to look at each word separately, but keep your eyes running rapidly across each line, scooping up the words in bunches.

Push yourself. Remember, you are racing against the second hand on your watch. Of course, don't go so fast that you fail to understand what you are reading.

Get your watch set! GO!

The MIT sneeze detectives found that the violent explosiveness of a sneeze can project up to 4,600 particles into the air at "muzzle velocities" of 152 feet a second. Some particles were expelled at even greater speeds—perhaps as high as 300 feet a second. The velocity is often sufficient to hurl heavier particles a distance of 12 feet.

The moisture sheath around an expelled particle evaporates, leaving a tiny nucleus which remains floating in the air. English researchers have found as many as 4,000 such particles floating there half an hour after the occurrence of the sneeze which precipitated them.

These particles are not simply harmless drops of water or inert matter. Investigators found that out by setting up, opposite a sneezer, a vertical plate coated with a culture medium favorable to the development of bacteria. By a count of bacteria growing on the plate, a single droplet has been found to create 19,000 colonies of bacteria. Thus a single sneeze can distribute more than 85,000,000 bacteria. No wonder medicine is convinced that the sneeze plays a major role in the spread of disease.

Historically, it is known that the excessive amount of sneezing involved in the influenza epidemic of 1918 helped make it the horror that it was. The Great Plague of the Middle Ages, which wiped out whole populations overnight, was helped in its spread the same way. Bubonic-plague-infected fleas, carried by rats, bit people whose lungs became infected with the pneumonic form of the disease. Then these people sneezed, spreading the plague with shocking swiftness.

Medical men say there should be a change in the way we cover a sneeze. Put your hand over your mouth, for instance, and what happens? Some of the particles, as shown by the high-speed photographs, shoot out beyond the hand, or are deflected upward to be left floating in the air. A handkerchief or tissue works far more effectively, if you have time to get one out and in place before you sneeze.

But, with or without handkerchief, the advice of an official publication of the AMA is: "When you feel a sneeze coming on, turn your head and sneeze downwards." Some authorities contend that, if we bent not only the head but the whole body in a deep bow, much of the harm done by sneezes could be avoided.

The explanation is revealed by those tell-tale photographs. The particles expelled by the sneeze are hurled toward the floor, to which they adhere, and never get a chance to become airborne and thus inhaled by others.

Sneezing in this scientific way may not provide a cure, but it could be an important weapon in medicine's battle against the common cold.

(470 words—app.)

Now jot down immediately the total time it took you to read this part of the selection: _____

(minutes)—(seconds)

Before going any further, let's make sure you understood what you read, even though you tried to go faster than you generally do. From the following statements, select the one in each group that you think accurately reflects an idea mentioned in the selection:

I. ___ a. Sneezing cannot spread disease.

___ b. Sneezing can spread disease rapidly.

___ c. There is no evidence that sneezing can or cannot spread disease.

II. ___ a. Particles lose their effect in less than a minute.

___ b. Particles remain in the air as long as a half hour after they have been expelled.

___ c. Particles quickly travel upward and out of reach of other people in the area of the sneeze.

III. A single sneeze can distribute as many bacteria as:

___ a. 8,500

___ b. 85,000

___ c. 85,000,000

IV. ___ a. No matter how you sneeze, the effects are the same.

___ b. The best way to sneeze is to hold your hand over your mouth.

___ c. The least danger occurs when you sneeze with a deep bow, head down.

ANSWERS: I. b, II. b, III. c, IV. c.

Check your time and speed in the chart below.

WORDS-PER-MINUTE CHART

Minutes	Seconds	Wds/Min	Minutes	Seconds	Wds/Min
1	0	470	1	50	255
1	5	435	1	55	245
1	10	400	2	0	235
1	15	375	2	5	225
1	20	350	2	10	215
1	25	330	2	15	210
1	30	315	2	25	195
1	35	300	2	35	180
1	40	285	2	50	165
1	45	270	3	0	155

(Approximate)

Now let's take stock. The second selection is about 20 words longer than the first, but you probably read it as much as 25 per cent faster because of your strong effort to do so. And if you got the answers right, you also proved to yourself that you lost very little in comprehension. Let me point out that the questions are not easy ones but represent what you would normally be expected to derive from the contents of the article.

If you were unable to read the second selection faster than the first, there is no need for discouragement. Work hard on Chapters V, VI, and VII. Then come back to this test. You will probably read both parts with greater speed than you did before.

TEST IV

Now we come to a test of your ability to separate main ideas from details. The short paragraphs below have been taken from typical New York State Regents examinations in English Four Years that are given to candidates for the high-school diploma. To the right of each paragraph you will find questions. In each set the first question is based on the main idea and the others on details.

Read each paragraph carefully and then answer the questions. Note that 2 points are assigned to "main idea" and 1 point to "detail" answers. The total is 20 for the six paragraphs.

a. The modern end in football must be fairly tall so he can catch forward passes. He must be shifty and clever if he is to get into a position where he can catch the passes. He must be fast and elusive if he is to cover punts well. He must also have enough ruggedness and power to enable him to play his regular offensive position in the line and to play his defensive position satisfactorily. An end who is too short is handicapped in catching passes.

The title below that best expresses the ideas in this paragraph is
1. How to catch forward passes
2. A clever football player
3. Offensive and defensive tactics in football
4. Players' handicaps
5. Qualifications of an end ....( )

Vigor is essential to the end for
1. catching punts
2. receiving forward passes
3. playing in the line
4. intercepting passes
5. throwing the ball ( )

b. Spun rayon is no more than the continuous filament rayon cut into short lengths similar to wool or cotton fibers and spun into yarn, as either wool or cotton is spun. The resulting yarn looks and feels like wool. Fabrics made wholly or partially of it can not

The title below that best expresses the ideas in this paragraph is
1. How spun rayon is made
2. How to distinguish between rayon and wool

be distinguished from all wool except by experts—and not always then. It creates novel and attractive fabric effects, and, since its production cost is far below that of good wool, it should offer a practical new item in our consumer price structure. But consumers everywhere are asking: Does it behave like wool? Has it the inherent characteristics of wool?

3. Spun rayon fabrics
4. Novel fabric effects
5. Spun rayon for wool
.... ( )

Spun rayon differs from wool in that it is
1. more attractive in appearance
2. spun into yarn
3. cheaper to make
4. smoother to the touch
5. rougher to the touch
.... ( )

c. Propaganda is the most terrible weapon so far developed. It is worse than poison gas. If the wind is in the right direction, gas may kill a few and injure others; but the possibilities of manipulating the public mind by withholding or discoloring the facts are appalling. One is so helpless in the face of it. No one can think intelligently without knowing the facts; and if the facts are controlled by interested men, the very idea of democracy is destroyed and becomes a farce.

The title below that best expresses the ideas of this paragraph is
1. Propaganda or poison gas
2. The threat of propaganda
3. Control of facts
4. How to detect propaganda
5. Propaganda in a democracy .... ( )

Manipulating the public mind by controlling the facts is a denial of
1. interest
2. intelligence
3. democracy
4. directions
5. help .... ( )

d. Though the pain from a scorpion's sting is intense and may endure for several hours, there is little danger of serious and lasting injury. The scorpion is a sinister-looking creature, with an armored, segmented body supported by eight legs. It possesses numerous eyes, yet for all practical purposes it is devoid of vision, with only monstrous, fingerlike pincers to guide it. These pincers are powerful weapons with which the scorpion seizes and crushes its prey. The jointed tail, with its poison needle point, can be wielded with deadly accuracy if the pincers are not effective. Sinister as is the scorpion in the insect world, there is no reason why it should be feared by man. Its enemies are principally insects that destroy grain fields, and in killing these pests the scorpion serves a beneficent purpose.

The title below that best expresses the ideas of this paragraph is
1. How the scorpion fights
2. Enemies of the scorpion
3. A forbidding ally
4. The scorpion's sting
5. Why men fear scorpions ....( )

The scorpion's primary threat to its enemies lies in its
1. range of vision
2. speed of motion
3. armored body
4. pointed tail
5. pincers ....( )

e. Are we getting more than our usual share of snow in this part of the country, or less? It's hard to say one way or the other. Only within recent years has there been enough interest in snow, especially from the sport angle, to bring about careful recording of snow depths. Most weather records lump snow and rain under the noncommittal head of "precipitation." We do know that, because of a general trend toward higher temperatures over the last half-century or so, the winter precipitation in this part of the world has had an increasing tendency in recent years to take the form of rain. Whether this trend will continue this winter and in future winters is anybody's guess. The process of sublimation that leads to the

The title below that best expresses the ideas of this paragraph is
1. A possible trend in weather
2. Popularity of winter sports
3. Snow and winter sports
4. Weather prediction
5. What meteorological records show ......( )

We do not know whether or not we are getting more snow than usual because
1. formerly snowfall and rain were not reported separately

precipitation of snow is one that man can not at all control and one that man has only a limited ability to predict.

2. weather reports are inaccurate
3. winters are getting warmer
4. we can not predict weather accurately
5. winter sports are relatively recent ....( )

During the last 50 years there has been
1. an increase in average annual snowfall
2. more interest in winter sports
3. an increase in precipitation
4. less snow and more rain
5. a tendency toward colder winters ....( )

f. Escape of coffee aroma vapors and gases does not in itself impair the flavor of coffee, according to new researches reported in Industrial and Engineering Chemistry. Oxygen is the chief culprit in staling. Tests showed that roasted coffee is best preserved in tightly sealed vacuum cans. If oxygen is present the coffee deteriorates even though the sealing is tight. The tests were made with the aid of professional coffee tasters. Samples hermetically sealed in a vacuum remained fresh throughout the test period of 48 days. Coffee swept continuously for 55 days with dry nitrogen remained comparatively fresh

The title below that best expresses the ideas of this paragraph is
1. Methods of storing coffee
2. The chemistry of coffee
3. Deterioration of coffee
4. Research in coffee
5. Experiments in keeping coffee fresh ..( )

Coffee will retain its flavor best when
1. oxygen is excluded
2. it is kept in tightly sealed containers
3. it is kept in a vac-

and showed that the evolution of gas has no detectable effect on flavor.

uum for more than 48 days
4. the gases are not allowed to escape
5. it is roasted ....( )

In a special experiment coffee was kept fresh by means of
1. oxygen
2. nitrogen
3. coffee gases
4. airtight containers
5. constant testing ..( )

ANSWERS (Remember—2 points for the "title" or main idea and 1 point for the "detail" answers):
a. 5, 3; b. 5, 3; c. 2, 3; d. 3, 5; e. 1, 1, 4; f. 5, 1, 2.

Your score: _____ points

COMPREHENSION CHART	
Score	Classification
0-10	Unsatisfactory
11-13	Borderline
14-15	Average
16-17	Good
18-20	Superior

Your score should tell you how much attention you will have to pay to the exercises presented in Chapter VIII. It is almost like stating the obvious to say that the basic objective of all reading is to understand what has been written. Sheer speed without comprehension is completely valueless.

You can't do a satisfactory job without the proper tools. One of the most valuable tools in the job of reading is a good vocabulary. Let's see how you rate in this respect.

Below you will find a paragraph in which certain words have been omitted. Next to each blank space the definition of the missing word has been inserted in parentheses. From the list at the top of the paragraph, select the word that matches the definition and write it into the space provided. The object here is to test your vocabulary, not your powers of guessing, so select only those words that are familiar to you. There's no sense in cheating yourself.

derision   abate
elation   admonition
decorum   docile
brusque   altercations
antagonists   diminutive

An _____ (warning) to Jimmy to refrain from engaging in further _____ (fights) with the boy next door had brought little results. It is difficult to _____ (check) the fury of young _____ (opponents), each eager to prove he is superior. A _____ (harsh) order to observe _____ (model behavior) is rarely effective with _____ (small) battlers. Accordingly, both fathers decided to use some psychology. They would greet future conflicts with _____ (scornful laughter) and praise the more _____ (gentle) of the lads. It was with _____ (great satisfaction) that the parents noted gradual progress.

ANSWERS (in order of appearance): admonition, altercations, abate, antagonists, brusque; decorum, diminutive, derision, docile, elation.

Your score: _____ right

Did the words seem too hard? Well, they were taken from a list judged to be suitable for high-school students. The same words and others like them can be found daily in newspapers, magazines, books, television programs— in almost any medium in which educated people talk or write. If you scored under 7, you can be sure that your limited vocabulary is a handicap to your efforts to achieve reading skill. You will need to work very carefully with the suggestions made in Chapter IX.

Now that you have participated in this series of self-diagnostic tests, you should have at least an inkling of the causes of your particular reading weaknesses. You should also have some idea of which techniques you must stress in your study program and which you have fairly well in hand. You should be about ready to get to work. But first let me answer one more question that may be troubling you. How *long* will it take you to improve?

CHAPTER IV

How Long Will It Take You
to Improve?

A FRIEND OF MINE recently told me how he became a good golfer. He had been blundering his way along the fairways for several years. Like many of us, he had spent much of his time chopping out huge chunks of grass or wandering about in the brush looking for a lost ball. One day a startling thought struck him.

"It occurred to me," said Louis, "that golf is one of the very few games played with the ball in a stationary position and untouched by the opponent. That annoying white pellet just sits there on a tee or piece of sod and dares you to hit it. Take handball, baseball, tennis—I've tried them all—your success depends a lot on what someone else does with the ball. But in golf you're on your own. If you dub the shot, you're the only one responsible. You can't blame it on anyone else; you have no alibi. So if you want to become a good golfer, what you have to do is to find out how to swing a club properly and then practice and practice by yourself until it becomes a habit."

The next morning Louis bought a book on golf. According to the author, a player should at first limit himself to the five-iron. Behind this suggestion was the very sound idea that the fundamental techniques of grip, rhythm, and timing should be perfected with one club. Then they can be applied, with slight variations, to all the others.

My friend followed this advice. For months he used nothing but a five-iron. Every chance he had, even if it was for only a few minutes, he practiced the proper swing. He tried it out on driving ranges, in his back yard, and sometimes on his living-room rug with a cotton ball. He wasn't satisfied until he could land the ball within a few yards of a spot he had selected in advance. Eventually he was able to give the same treatment to the woods and the other irons. It turned out to be a successful plan. This fellow today casually shoots in the low eighties—and he's a week-end golfer, at that!

You may be wondering what all this has to do with becoming a good reader. There is really a remarkable connection. Just as a company manufactures a ball and makes it available to be hit properly, so do writers make words available to be read properly. Just as what a golfer does with a ball depends entirely upon him, so do the speed and understanding with which you handle words depend upon your own reading habits. Just as a player can become proficient with many clubs by concentrating on one until his swing is correct, so can you train yourself to read all kinds of material efficiently by acquiring the skills involved in reading anything at all. And just as consistent practice is the only way a golfer can master approved form, so can short, daily practice sessions help you develop the correct habits of reading rapidly and intelligently.

You have already had a preview of the major causes of poor reading ability. In the next five chapters, you will find a step-by-step analysis of each one and you will be told how to eliminate any bad reading habits you still have. When you have finished Chapter IX, you will be familiar with the procedures you should follow when you practice. The entire program is designed to provide you with a five-step drill for your daily sessions, each of which should require no more than 15 minutes of your time.

We'll come back to this schedule in Chapter X and give you the details. By that time you'll know what to practice and how to go about it.

Is that all there is to it? you say. No, not really. We must be honest with each other. The 15 minutes each day will be the warmup, the practice period. Just as our golfer friend could never have become a topflight player by merely practicing and never trying out his skill on a regular course, so you won't make much progress if you don't apply your improved reading habits to an ever-increasing range of materials. You will have to become a *reader,* with all that is meant by the word when it is said with emphasis—a reader of books, newspapers, magazines. You will have to learn to "use every club" correctly.

This branching out of your reading interests will, I hope, take you longer than 15 minutes a day. But remember this. There is so much more fun to a game when you play it well. The lasting pleasures many people derive from reading can be yours, too, if you are willing to spend 15 minutes a day practicing faithfully—and then participate in the joy of reading willingly because you do it well.

Here's another question you might reasonably ask: *You say 15 minutes a day. But how long will it take before there is permanent improvement?*

In my own classes I have observed students make good progress in as little as 5 weeks. You will recall that I suggested this as a possibility in the first chapter of this book. Further evidence is provided by Dr. Irving A. Taylor, Supervisor of the Reading Development Program at Pratt Institute, as reported in his article "Breaking the Reading Barrier," in *Career Briefs,* a publication of the institute.

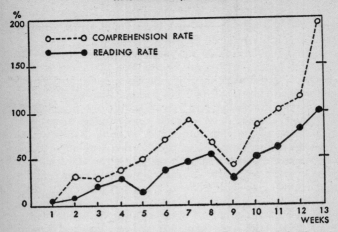

The accompanying Table and Figure indicate the results in a typical group. The first few weeks are reserved for discussion and preparation. After thirteen weeks of laboratory training and practice in comprehension the group rose from an average of 229 to 447 wpm [words per minute], an increase of 218 wpm or 95 percent. A more important measure, however, is that of rate comprehension. This measure is obtained by multiplying the percentage of the material comprehended by the reading rate. If a student reads 300 wpm, for example, and obtains an achievement score of 50 percent, his rate of comprehension is 150 wpm. This type of score is better than rate of reading since it combines both speed and comprehension. It is misleading to use speed alone to reflect reading level; increase of speed without a corresponding increase in comprehension is obviously useless. The class represented in the Table and Figure increased in rate of comprehension by 192 percent. One student was able to improve rate of comprehension 340 percent. (The marked decrease during the ninth week of training was produced by

anticipation of the Easter re-
cess which immediately followed.) Follow-up tests given
six months after showed nearly
75 percent of the gains retained.

TABLE

Weekly Increases in Reading Rate and Comprehension

Week	Rate of Reading		Rate of Comprehension	
	WPM	% increase	WPM	% increase
1	229	0	142	0
2	234	2	181	27
3	271	18	175	23
4	283	24	184	30
5	255	11	209	47
6	287	25	239	68
7	305	33	260	83
8	336	47	225	58
9	284	24	182	28
10	342	49	251	77
11	373	63	281	98
12	409	79	293	106
13	447	95	415	192

Before you decide that these are college students and
therefore it is easy for them to improve but it won't
be for you, let me tell you this: There isn't necessarily any
high correlation or connection between educational background and reading ability. There is a very strong correlation between native intelligence and reading potential. Thus if you have the ability to improve at all, you
can do it whether it is in a college classroom or in the
quiet of your own room. And at home you have the
advantage of being able to proceed at a pace best suited
to your circumstances, with no obligation to meet the
requirements of a large group.

Now let's look at additional conclusions that can be
drawn from the figure and table, and let's see how they

apply to you. You will note that progress is not necessarily regular. At one point you may make a big jump, and at another a small one or even none at all. This means that you must not be discouraged if you are not getting results as fast as you think you should. No doubt interferences from your home or business life may interrupt your schedule of improvement. These are to be expected, but you must not allow yourself to offer them as reasons to give up in disgust. You will have your low periods, just as the students did when they were anticipating a holiday and didn't feel like working very hard. You can be encouraged by observing the sharp jump in achievement that occurs after each dip on the figure.

Another point you should bear in mind is that after the new habits have been firmly established—by the 10th week in this study and sometimes sooner if you work by yourself—there follows a very rapid rise in both speed and comprehension. This fact, too, should be good news to you.

Finally, you can observe proof to support one of the most important ideas presented in this book and accepted by every authority in the field of reading improvement. Except with very difficult material, as your speed increases so does your comprehension. This is basic. Remember it well.

All right. You know what is ahead of you. Follow closely the suggestions that will enable you to eliminate your bad reading habits. Learn how to set up your daily 15-minute practice session. Do your practicing and follow-up work, and the rewards you reap will be worth more than you can measure.

You are ready for Step 1 of your 15-minute-a-day plan. Let's knock out those roadblocks!

The Five-Step Plan

CHAPTER V

STEP ONE:

Knock Out the Roadblocks!

Do you remember the handicap events that sometimes formed part of the program for school field days? In one of the most common races the contestants stepped into large gunny sacks and then hopped frantically to the finish line. Or perhaps you remember the spoon-and-potato race, in which the contestants almost went mad struggling to pick up and balance the elusive vegetables.

Certainly you will agree that even the slowest and clumsiest runner would've won if *he alone* hadn't bothered about sack or potatoes. However, because it was a contest, all deliberately assumed these handicaps.

When you read, you are not participating in a handicap event. You want to go as fast as you can. Yet an odd fact about some readers is that they set up obstacles as they try to follow the printed word. Unknowingly they interfere with their own speed as much as the runners who allow gunny sacks and potatoes to check their progress. We shall call these obstacles to better reading "roadblocks," because they block your road to rapid and meaningful progress from one thought to the next on a page. We shall examine typical roadblocks in detail, but first a point that applies to all your reading skills must be made clear.

Despite what the magician tells you, *the hand is not*

faster than the eye. Nor is the lip, tongue, or finger. What your eye sees is interpreted by your mind, and mental activity is much faster than any physical activity you can perform. Therefore, in reading, whatever you do that forces the mind to keep the same pace as a physical movement slows it up and creates problems.

For example, some parents become worried when their three- or four-year-olds begin to stammer and stutter after learning to talk in sentences. Generally, there is little reason to be concerned unless some deeply rooted emotional problem is involved. With most children the condition is brought on by the fact that their minds are racing far ahead of their speech organs, and the words come tumbling out in a disorganized fashion. Soon the youngsters learn that they cannot form sounds as fast as they can think them. Almost instinctively most of them adjust their speed of thought to their rate of producing understandable spoken language.

There is no need to slow up your mind in silent reading. Indeed it is essential that you do not, if you don't want to cut down your speed. The less interference you give your mind as it tries to understand what your eyes are looking at, the faster and better it operates.

Now let's see what reading roadblocks are, where they come from, and how you can eliminate them. It is possible that your reading problems do not stem from any of the obstacles we are going to discuss. Or you may discover that you have been handicapping yourself with only one or two of them. As soon as you have read the description of a particular roadblock and are convinced that it isn't one of your bad reading habits, forget about it. As a matter of fact, you should skip those portions of the chapter that refer back to it. You can spend your time more profitably in practicing the elimination of a weakness you do possess.

I. What Are Some Common Roadblocks?

A. TECHNICAL TERM: **VOCALIZATION** AND **LIP READING**

If you are faced with these problems, you tend to make the *sounds* of the words in your throat (vocalization) instead of reading them silently, or you move your lips voicelessly (lip reading) as if you were reading aloud to yourself. Thus you force your mind to absorb the material at a pace no faster than you can speak. That is not nearly fast enough for efficient silent reading.

B. TECHNICAL TERM: **CRUTCHES**

Crutches are used by people who unfortunately need extra supports. There are mental crutches, too. Suppose that as you read you are in the habit of pointing your finger at each word, or sliding a straight edge, like a ruler, from one line to the next. If so, you are using a mental crutch. You are attempting to give your mind an extra support in its efforts to concentrate. But you are also holding back your speed! To repeat, your hand cannot possibly move as fast as your mind.

C. TECHNICAL TERM: **FAILURE TO USE PERIPHERAL VISION**

Look directly at any object in the room you are now occupying. Let's say it is a lamp. You see the lamp, but about ten feet to the right of it your eye has also absorbed the image of perhaps a chair, and far to the left, possibly a picture on the wall. You definitely see all three objects, even though your eyes are focused on only one of them. This ability of yours to see out of the corners of your eyes, so to speak, is what is known as peripheral vision.

Moreover, if you wanted to make a more detailed study of the chair or picture, there would be no need to move your head. By moving only your eyes you could shift their focus to any object within the limits of their peripheral vision.

A further illustration of this point can be found in observing people at a tennis match. For those seated directly facing the center of the court, the ball passes out of peripheral vision so quickly that they must move their heads from side to side continually to watch the play. Those seated behind the players have no need to indulge in a mass exhibition of neck twisting because their eyes can take in all the action.

Similarly, a line of print very easily falls within the limits of your peripheral vision. It is true that you have to shift the focus of your eyes as they move across the line, *but you should not move your head.* Otherwise, you are setting up a roadblock as bad as finger pointing. Since your head cannot keep pace with your mind, you are decreasing your reading speed.

D. TECHNICAL TERM: REGRESSIONS

If you have this bad habit, you don't seem to be able to go from the end of one line to the beginning of the next without frequently going back (regressing) to the one you have just read. All of us, of course, do this sort of thing occasionally when we wish to reread a particularly good sentence or when our minds have been elsewhere and we have not been concentrating fully on what we were supposed to be reading. Regressions, however, become a serious problem if you find yourself unable to control them. Surely you can see how difficult it is to move ahead quickly on a page if you keep covering the same ground twice.

E. TECHNICAL TERM: SUBVOCALIZATION

This is another fault that can be found with almost everybody's reading habits. There is no movement of lips or sounding of words as in vocalization, but if you *say the words in your mind* (subvocalization) you are engaging in what might be termed mental speech. And as we've said, anything that resembles reading aloud holds back the mind from realizing its full speed potential. It is admittedly not very easy to eliminate this tendency altogether, nor is it absolutely necessary. However, if you can cut down your subvocalization, obviously your reading speed will increase.

F. TECHNICAL TERM: **REVERSALS**

Does *not* ever read *ton* to you, or does *saw* become *was* sometimes? Does what you thought was *won* turn out to be *now?* These are *reversals,* actually caused by a momentary reading from right to left, rather than the normal left to right. Such errors lead to confusion and in themselves create some of the other roadblocks we have mentioned above. It's pretty much like dropping the potato off the spoon and having to go back to pick it up again.

II. Where Do These Roadblocks Come From?

Lip reading, vocalization, crutches, head movements, and subvocalization usually result from failure to overcome habits formed in childhood. Your earliest reading experiences were largely oral. Great stress was laid on saying words aloud, getting the feel of the sounds with your tongue and lips, and pointing to familiar objects as you identified them. This is all very good practice in the primary grades, where the effort is made to train the students to associate sounds with meaning. However, some children do not progress easily into the silent-reading stage. Whether it is caused by feelings of insecurity or by reading selections that are too difficult for them, or just by habit, they continue to read aloud, actually or mentally. They follow the words with their fingers or their heads because they don't trust their eyes and want to make sure they don't get lost. In this way they build up the obstacles to speed that plague them when they grow older.

Regressions stem, to a large extent, from lack of confidence. The reader is constantly worried that he has missed something and is, in a sense, fearful of going forward. For instance, people who are always concerned about losing things (although they rarely do) are apt to be regressive readers. They simply must go back to check.

Reversals may be caused by brain injury or some visual defect. But if these factors are not present, the problem can be traced to a lack of familiarity *in the mind* with the structure of the word, a failure to have the "feel" of it. The design or image of the word rings the wrong bell.

III. How Serious Is the Problem of Roadblocks?

Fortunately, this is the area of reading disabilities where progress can be made most rapidly. For one thing, not every one of the roadblocks needs to be or even can be eliminated entirely. We've already noted that many readers are guilty of subvocalization. If you can substantially reduce the amount of mental speech you indulge in when you read silently, good. If you don't seem to get very far, do the best you can and don't worry about it. Do everything else right, and you won't be sacrificing much.

There is no question about lip, finger, or head movements, or any of the other physical interferences that have been mentioned. You must get rid of every one that is still holding back your reading speed. You can do that easily, too, as you will shortly see.

In general, you will have to experiment. Once you have convinced yourself that you aren't bothered by a particular roadblock, don't waste time practicing its elimination. Instead, practice the exercises designed for the removal of a specific hindrance that *is* a problem to you. At the very worst, if you spend a few minutes a day over a period of 2 or 3 weeks you should have no trouble conquering the bad habit.

IV. How Are Roadblocks Eliminated?

After each suggestion below, you will find sample exercises for practice. I'm sure you realize that it would be impossible to include in any book all the material you will ultimately need for your full program of practice. The idea is for you to set up additional exercises following the examples given. In most instances, this will mean that you pick at random paragraphs from newspapers, magazines, or books that will provide you with the necessary drill. You will also follow this procedure when you want to apply your newly developed skills.

A. VOCALIZATION AND LIP READING

First, vocalization. To make sure you know where the sounds are made in the throat, do this now. Place one finger on each side of your Adam's apple. Blow air steadily through your lips. No vibration? Right. Now hum any tune. Do you feel the buzzing effect? *That's what you want to eliminate in silent reading.* As you read the following passage, make certain there is no vibration of any kind in your throat. If you have trouble controlling the sound, keep your fingers on your throat and blow *air* out as you read.

For a Polite Dog

Every dog can be trained to be a well-behaved pet and an obedient one.

Your first problem is housebreaking. The owner of the famous "Lassie" accomplished it by using a large box as her home. When he couldn't watch her, he barred the exit. She soon learned if she used her living quarters improperly her keen sense of smell made the situation unpleasant. By allowing her out after every meal, her owner soon began to adjust her needs to those times. A gentle pat on the head and a tidbit told her she had done the right thing.

❊   ❊   ❊

There are several ways of eliminating lip movements. Try these suggested procedures and select the one that suits you best.

1. Place between your lips, *not your teeth*, some object heavy enough to force you to exert pressure to hold it as you read.

2. Press your lips tightly together, and at the same time push your tongue firmly against the roof of your mouth.

3. Although I certainly don't recommend this as a permanent habit, try chewing gum with exaggerated jaw and lip movements, something like the very tough characters seen in gangster pictures.

4. Purse your lips in a whistling position and blow air out, *but make no sounds*.

Of course, you understand that you use these artificial controls only as long as you think you have not yet habitually removed the roadblocks. This applies to any of the "cures" described in this chapter. In the passage below, test out each of the above recommendations, one for every two or three sentences, until you can decide on the one method you will use for later practice sessions.

For a Polite Dog (continued)

Chewing, although a natural instinct, is also one of the early problems. Transferring the dog's attention to a ball or toy while keeping other objects out of the way soon cured Lassie.

Dogs leap at people to show their affection, but it annoys most people. The best way to cure it, according to Lassie's owner, is to pick up their front paws and step lightly on their back paws. By associating a leap with sore toes, your pet will soon stop.

Running after cars was one of Lassie's worst faults. She was finally corrected by tying her to a post near the street. After lunging at several cars with the resulting pull on her neck, she soon learned her lesson.

B. CRUTCHES

The advice here is so simple that it may sound ridiculous to you. However, there are lots of things we do wrong only because we aren't aware that we can correct them by an obvious device. For instance, if someone told you that you make too many gestures when you talk to people, you might cure the habit very easily by putting your hands in your pockets when you speak until you have learned not to bring them forward unnecessarily. To cure finger pointing or using a ruler to guide your eyes, all you need do is hold the book, newspaper, or magazine you are reading *in both hands* until the undesirable habit is under control. Thus you fight the problem by making it impossible to arise. Before you practice, try this as a warmup. Select objects in various parts of the room. Describe their positions aloud, but remember to keep your hands at your sides. Now for the exercise. *Hold the book in both hands.*

For a Polite Dog *(concluded)*

You'll also want your dog to come when called. To train him on this point, walk him around the yard on a leash. Call him by name with "Come" and a gentle tug on the leash. When he reaches your side, praise him and give him a tidbit. But never command your dog to come and then scold him. Go to him to do that.

Whenever he misbehaves, a few light strokes with a rolled-up newspaper and a stern "No, no, no" let him know your disapproval. That is the only punishment a dog should ever receive. Hurting him will ruin the chances of winning his cooperation—let alone his affection.

When your dog has acquired these elementary lessons, you can give him a "high school" course at one of the many obedience schools. Then if you have the patience and time to devote to him almost completely, there is "college" to teach him such tricks as Lassie performs.

C. FAILURE TO USE PERIPHERAL VISION

We are concerned here with the elimination of head movements as one part of training yourself to see more than one word at a time. I'll have a lot more to say about this skill in the next chapter, when I show you how to read words in groups. Therefore, do not treat this exercise lightly. The extent to which you can learn to use peripheral vision will determine the increase in speed of reading you will eventually achieve.

Do the following exercises carefully so that you build up to the very important skill that will be discussed later on. Again it is suggested that you experiment with the techniques recommended for practice and pick the one you prefer.

1. Place one finger on either side of your jaw.

2. Put one hand on your chin as a man does when he feels his beard.

3. Place a finger on the tip of your nose.

The important thing is to check any movement of your head as you do the exercises.

WARMUP 1

Look directly at the center number on each line below, holding your head still as suggested, and try to read all three numbers as if they were a total. For example, in the first set your mind should register "one hundred thirty-nine," not "one, three, nine."

1	3	9
7	6	2
8	4	7

2	2	5
4	5	3
6	9	1
3	1	4
5	7	6
9	8	8
1	7	8
2	1	7
8	2	4
6	3	5
9	3	6
4	2	5
9	1	7
8	9	2
7	5	3
1	4	6
8	8	8

Now do the same with the following word groups. The first one you would read "Three Blind Mice," as the title of the well-known song, not as three isolated words. In short, try to get meaning out of the phrase, which you have probably seen many times before. Caution: keep

your eyes moving down the center column, but keep
your head still.

WARMUP 2

THREE	BLIND	MICE
MY	FRIEND	FLICKA
THE	THREE	MUSKETEERS
HOME	SWEET	HOME
TOM	DICK	and HARRY
DOWN	THE	HATCH
FRIENDS	ROMANS	COUNTRYMEN
TINKER	EVERS	CHANCE
TICK	TACK	TOE
SLIDE	KELLY	SLIDE
STAR	SPANGLED	BANNER
MISSED	THE	BOAT
TIME	MARCHES	ON
MY	DEAR	SIR
YOURS	VERY	TRULY
GO	TEAM	GO
RED	RED	ROSE
RAISE	THE	ROOF
TIE	THE	KNOT
SMOOTH	AS	SILK

Now read the following newspaper column. If anything moves across each line, it's your eyes, mind you, not your head.

Kitten Saves Actor From Rattler Bite

Actor Steve Cochran is thankful that his 9-week-old stray kitten, Terrible Touhy, is so truculent.

Otherwise, he said yesterday, he instead of the ferocious little feline might be nursing a rattlesnake bite himself.

Cochran said he was walking through a geranium patch Monday afternoon behind his home in Beverly Hills, helping workmen to lay out a new swimming pool. Terrible Touhy was at his heels.

The actor said he had killed a 4-foot rattler on the premises a few hours earlier, but didn't see the 6-footer that lurked in the geraniums a few feet ahead of him.

"Suddenly Touhy dashed past me and pounced on the snake," he related. "At the same time I heard the whirr of the rattles and Touhy was knocked back several feet as the snake struck."

Cochran said he picked up Touhy and called his secretary, who rushed the kitten to a pet hospital. Meanwhile, he got his 45-caliber pistol from the house but the rattler had slithered away.

At the pet hospital, Touhy was administered drugs and blood was sucked from the wound between the eyes. Veterinarians said the head was swollen to twice its size Monday night but it was back to normal yesterday.

Cochran said he named the kitten for the notorious gangster because the first thing it did after he took it into his house was to attack his large dog.

"Two weeks ago I found out Terrible Touhy is a female," he said. "But I still think the name fits."

D. REGRESSION

Perhaps the most important recommendation I can make here is that you have a frank talk with yourself. You must try to stop worrying about having missed something in a previous portion of a paragraph. Keep moving ahead steadily, regardless of any strong desire you may have to turn back, to regress. Added confidence will help you eliminate this tendency. Train yourself, also, as you come to the end of a line, to use your peripheral vision to sneak a look at the beginning of the next line (through the corner of your left eye).

In the following selection you will find a mass of statistics. Read them, but resist the desire to go back to check each figure. When you have finished, you should have an appreciation of the bigness of railroad transportation, but there is absolutely no need for you to be able to quote any figure that is offered to make the point.

STRAIGHT AHEAD—NO REGRESSIONS!

Railroads

The railroad story is, in a large sense, the story of America—its history and its people. It is a story of achievement and progress that brought about the greatest transportation system in the world.

Nearly 221,000 miles of railroad line stretch between our cities and towns. Much of it has two, three, or more parallel tracks. Another 117,000 miles of track are in yards and sidings. Altogether this trackage adds up to 369,000 miles—enough track to span the continent 100 times and more.

Over this track run the nearly 40,000 passenger-train cars and over 2,000,000 freight cars in operation on America's railroads, hauled to their destinations by more than 33,000 locomotives.

Helping to make this movement of freight and people safe and efficient are a million railroad workers, employed in hundreds of railway occupations from accountant to yardmaster. Together, they perform this big job of transportation, moving people to places, raw materials to factories, and goods to market—a coordinated operation that has made America's railroads the greatest single form of mass transportation.

*   *   *

If you now know that railroads use thousands of miles of tracks and millions of pieces of rolling stock to transport people and materials back and forth across the country, you have gotten from the article enough of the main idea. The writer was trying to give you some concept of the hugeness of railroad operations in America. Your understanding of this concept would not have been increased if you had gone back several times in your reading to verify a particular statistic.

For more direct practice, you can do any of the following:

1. Type several paragraphs, leaving 3 spaces between lines for the first few sentences, then 2 spaces, then 1, and finally no space. Subsequently, reading these paragraphs will aid you in developing a rhythmical sweep across and back from line to line:

To Shave or Not to Shave

Considering the implements they had, it's a wonder the

ancients ever thought of shaving.

The Chimus, who came before the Incas, pulled out

their stringy beards with solid gold tweezers as each new

hair appeared. When they died, the tweezers were laid

in the coffin.

Shavers in Africa had an even more barbarous method.

Warm oil first softened the whiskers; then a "razor" in

the hands of a barber literally chiseled the whiskers off.

Indians of Central and South America faced the problem in practically the same way except they used nut shells or bamboo knives on the oil-softened beard. Other natives in Africa daubed resin on their face, let it remain for a few minutes, then took resin, whiskers, and probably a little skin off with an oyster or clam shell.

2. Type another paragraph, this time with normal spacing, but alternate small letters for one line and all capitals for the next.

To Shave or Not to Shave *(continued)*

Some hardy gentlemen of olden times re-
MOVED HAIR FROM THEIR FACES BY CHEMICALS WHICH
burned rather than cut. A bone knife scraped
OFF THE RESIDUE.

Shaving came into modern use in France in
THE REIGN OF LOUIS XIII, BUT IT WAS NOT UNTIL
the 18th century that shaving the whole beard
BECAME COMMON.

A note for the future. A college professor
RECENTLY PREDICTED THAT A NEW BEARDED AGE IS ON
the way in the next decade or two!

3. Take another column, preferably from a newspaper, and underline every other line before you read it.

Traffic-Choked Main Street Outmoded

BY GENE FOREMAN

A noted architect warned the
National Citizens Planning Con-

ference yesterday that the onrushing tide of automobile traffic had made Main Street "an absurdity with no sound basis for existence."

Victor Gruen, Los Angeles architect and author of the Fort Worth plan for downtown redevelopment, issued the warning at the outset of a three-day meeting designed to plan the ideal "Main Street, 1969."

Gruen told the more than 700 delegates at Hotel Marion that the typical Main Street today was being choked by "hordes of mechanical monsters."

It can be saved, he said, by separating flesh and machines—by taking automobiles out of the downtown shopping district and making this vital area a reservation for pedestrians.

"We have held onto a pattern of our cities and towns which is basically identical to the one we had 200 years ago," he said. "We have completely disregarded the fact that an entirely new population group has immigrated into these cities and towns. This new group is the automobile populace of 60,000,000 mechanical beings."

4. An important point to remember in your efforts to control regressions is that it is not necessary to know the meaning of every word in a paragraph or even to get

every small detail in order to understand the main idea. Move straight ahead. I'll tell you later what to do about particular words you may want to look up.

E. SUBVOCALIZATION

It is true that most good readers subvocalize (read aloud in their minds) to some extent. It is next to impossible to eliminate this habit entirely. Nonetheless it is also a fact that there need not be mental pronunciation of any kind. Some years ago experiments were conducted with deaf-mutes. They were taught to read acceptably, and yet they didn't even have the physical equipment that makes subvocalization a problem.

At any rate, added speed of reading will bring improvement in this respect, too. To test yourself, in so far as deciding whether you will be able to reduce subvocalization, try any of the following devices with the selection below.

Traffic-Choked Main Street Outmoded *(continued)*

BY GENE FOREMAN

1. Keep repeating the word *no* as you read—*no* for no subvocalization.

As a result of this planning lag, he pointed out, the city streets are clogged by hopeless traffic congestion. The appearance of Main Street has become complex with addition of traffic signals, parking meters, warning signs, billboards, wires, and cables.

"If we want to create peaceful conditions of co-existence between the natives and the newcomers," Gruen declared, "we will have to create reservations for the human race and automobile race.

2. Try to busy your mind with a picture of what you are reading, a picture without words.

"We have to give to each of them the environment which is natural to their needs and likes. For the automobile, there is the freeway with its many lanes and landscaped buffers. For the human, there are the pedestrian courts and malls of varying size and shape."

Gruen expressed confidence that an over-all plan of this type could be sold to the public.

He predicted that Main Street in 1969 would not be a street "in the sense of today's vehicular [streets] at all.

"It will be a humane and human kind of . . . town market place."

3. Go so fast that at best you have time to subvocalize a word here and there.

Edward D. Stone of New York City, an Arkansas-born architect, deplored the lack of art and color of modern buildings in addressing the conference yesterday morning.

"We architects should return to the idea that we are artists," Stone declared. "Nowadays people shy away from the architect who talks glowingly about creating 'a masterpiece of art.' But let's not be satisfied with drab structures when we can create beautiful buildings and plazas that will be a heritage for the generations to come."

Stone . . . said the architects and planners should revitalize both residential areas and the downtown districts.

"We ought to give up the practice of building houses that look like boxes on little plots," he said. "This is a field where new ideas and community planning are needed."

F. REVERSALS

To handle reversals, you can use a method that is also very effective in strengthening spelling skill. Keep a list of words that cause you trouble. From time to time spend a few minutes using the tracing technique.

Suppose you constantly seem to read *net* for *ten*. Write the word *ten* out on a scrap of paper. Place your *finger*, not your pen or pencil, directly on the word. Now trace the letters as you say each one aloud. Do this three times. Then turn the paper over and write the word rapidly as you pronounce your name or some other phrase. You must be able to write the word entirely automatically, without thinking about it at all. Authorities who have experimented in this field agree that if you can experience the form of a word through your sense of touch you are less likely to confuse it in your mind. For a more detailed description of the tracing technique, see my book *Six Minutes a Day to Perfect Spelling*, published by Pocket Books, Inc., in a CARDINAL edition.

So much for the roadblocks. Let me caution you once more. If you are sure that some of these obstacles to rapid reading bother you only occasionally, don't spend too much time on them. Concentrate on the one or two that need serious attention—and then only 2 minutes a day, according to our schedule, which we will explain in detail in Chapter X. After a few weeks, when you probably will have removed a particular roadblock, use the practice time on one of the other steps mentioned in the chapters that follow.

CHAPTER VI

STEP TWO:

Stretch Your Span!

NOBODY SHOULD ATTEMPT to fix an engine unless he knows how it works. This principle can be applied to the mechanism that runs a car or lawnmower as well as to the "engine" that makes it possible for you to read. The "parts"—your eyes, mind, and emotions—are few in number, it would appear, but they function in a much more complicated manner than most people realize. For this reason, then, it is essential that you have a thorough knowledge of how the reading machine works before you make an effort to repair it.

How do your eyes function when you read?

The typewriter, as you know, is designed to punch out words letter by letter. Every time a key or the spacing bar is struck, the rubber-covered cylinder, called the *carriage*, jumps slightly to the left. If you were typing the following sentence, for example, you would cause the carriage to jump 34 times (27 letters, 1 question mark, and 6 spaces):

Can you count the number of stops?

If you wished to increase the size of the jumps, you could set up column stops. These permit the carriage to slide to a given point (skipping the intervening spaces), accept the imprint of a number or two, slide to the next point, and so on, as below:

| 1 | 12 | 15 |
| 7 | 9 | 18 |

Thus it is possible to have as many as 80 stops to a line, or fewer than 10, depending on the nature of the material being typed.

You may be somewhat surprised to learn that when you read, your eyes behave much like the carriage of a typewriter. They do not travel across a line of print in one continuous sweep, but move in the stop-and-go fashion of the machine. You can prove this immediately by getting someone to help you for a few minutes.

Ask your friend to hold a book or magazine selection about a foot in front of and above his head. Place yourself so that you can watch his eye movements. Now ask him to begin reading—but tell him to read *only the letters, one after another*, not the words. You will be observing a human "typewriter" in action. You will see the eyes leapfrog from letter to letter; they will not sweep smoothly along. You will actually be able to count the stops after a little practice.

Now ask your reader to concentrate on *words, one by one*. You will notice that the stops decrease in number and that the eyes slide a bit before they pause.

Finally, tell your friend to read as fast as he can. If he is an average reader, you will observe his eyes stop only three or four times per line. They will be operating exactly as the carriage of the typewriter does when a typist is using the column stops.

You should be convinced then that the eyes *do* stop periodically as they move across a line of print. You should also accept the fact that the more stops there are per line the slower is the rate of reading. Now that you know how the eyes behave in reading, let's turn to the mind.

How does your mind function when you read?

Let us return to our typewriter comparison. We know that when a key is struck, the letter or symbol is printed on the paper at the moment contact is made with the carriage, and that each time an impression is made there is a split-second stop. Similarly, every time the eyes of a reader pause, they send an impression to the mind, which interprets it and gives it meaning. That's why, even though it sounds impossible, we say that you read while your eyes are *not moving*. If you need further evidence of this point, think of what happens when a fighter feints his opponent out of position. It isn't so much that the latter lets his guard down, but that his eyes are *moving* to watch the pretended blow with the left hand and they actually don't see the right that lands on the jaw. Just as no letters can be typed while the carriage is in motion, so no images can be sent to the mind while the eyes are moving. You can readily understand that the more stops there are on a line, the more the total picture is broken up, and consequently the more difficult it is for the mind to interpret it. Surely it is easier to study a photograph if it is presented in one piece than if it is cut up jigsaw-puzzle style.

Now, your reading mechanism has one very significant advantage over a typewriter. If you've ever watched a champion typist in action, you have seen her ten fingers fly over the keys so rapidly that the carriage sweeps steadily to the left without any visible pauses. Even the skilled office worker, though she is not quite so fast, manages to operate in bursts, like bullets from a machine gun, and only three or four definite pauses are noticeable on a line. Only when you watch the "hunt and peck" artist laboriously bang out one letter at a time can you clearly see the numerous stops. The typewriter cannot be made to print whole words, however, as a printing press does. Regardless of the speed, it is impossible to strike two or more keys simultaneously without jamming the machine. Thus the speed typist creates an optical illusion when she goes so fast that the carriage seemingly slides along without stopping. The stops are there, whether you see them or not.

But the reader *can take in a word or more at a glance.* There is no fixed limit to the size of the image your eyes can send to your mind. Only those almost hopelessly retarded in reading stop at every letter. Even the very slow reader can manage at least a word at a time. Good readers consistently pass from one phrase to the next. A few read so fast that if you watched their eye movements you would notice hardly any pauses at all. Moreover, there would be no optical illusions here. The stops would not be present because they had not been made! So you can see how tremendous an advantage your reading mechanism has over the typewriter. It is the key that unlocks the secret of how to improve your reading speed.

You are not held back by the limitations of a machine. Your mind will absorb as much as you can give it within reason and within its basic ability to interpret. You are the master here. If one way to train yourself to read faster is to decrease the number of times your eyes stop on a line, it is within your powers to do so! Your problem, therefore, is not whether you *can,* but *how* to do it.

Before we tell you how, let's continue with a few more observations on how the mind operates in the process we call reading. You have learned that you read when your eyes pause and that your mind interprets what you see at that time. How much do you have to see in order for the mind to derive meaning? Experiments have demonstrated that only the general outlines of words and phrases are necessary for recognition. Just as you can recognize some member of your family merely by hearing his walk or seeing the back of his head, so the eyes don't need the letter-by-letter picture of a word to identify it. A glance at but one or two prominent letters may be enough. For instance, in *departmental* the *d, p, t,* and *l* may suffice to complete the signal to the mind.

In fact, it has also been clinically proved that we don't even need the whole letters to make our identification. We tend to recognize the upper parts of letters more than the lower. Take a card of some sort. Cover the lower half of the letters in a line of print. Then try reading it. Follow this by covering the upper half. You will note that you can read more easily using the first method.

If, then, the mind does not need every letter of a word to recognize it, doesn't even need the complete designs of the ones it does use, it is reasonable to conclude that there is rarely the need to look at every word to extract the meaning of a phrase. The mind can employ the pattern technique here, too. A quick glance and the image is interpreted! Indeed, the minds of people who read a thousand words or more per minute are able to handle 10 or 12 words at a time. However, we'll leave this super-speed group for another chapter.

So much for how the mind functions. Now, a brief word about the role emotions play in the act of reading.

How do your emotions function when you read?

As was said earlier, it is not the intention of this book to delve into the psychiatric mysteries that make poor readers out of people who have all the physical equipment to become superior ones. I leave that problem to the men and women who are professionally qualified to treat such cases.

However, the reading speed and comprehension of every one of us is affected by our emotional state from one time to the next. If you've had a quarrelsome day at the office, you are not likely to be able to concentrate very well on a book or magazine. A draftsman or a jeweler may have strained his eyes so much during the day that he is not inclined to expose them to additional exertion at night. Even if he does, he will not be able to use them very efficiently. The person who has chronic uncorrected troubles with his eyes is not very much interested in engaging in an activity that exposes his weaknesses.

It is extremely necessary that you realize that reading is not only a physical and mental process. When you can't figure out why the interest that caused you to read this book is no longer there, look to your emotions. When you can't put your finger on what is responsible for your failure to make more progress in your practice sessions, look to your emotions. And when you feel like dropping the whole business of improving your reading ability, get hold of your emotions.

Your emotions can influence how your mind interprets words, too. If you don't like the author of a particular piece, if you think the material is too deep for you, or if you have no intrinsic interest in the subject matter of an article, you will have difficulty understanding it. You may say, "Why read something I don't care about?" Occasionally you have to. At such times you must control your emotions so well that they don't interfere with your getting the meaning of what has been written. The person who boos a speaker rarely takes the trouble to listen to him.

71

The preceding explanation of the reading mechanism should have helped you realize that although it is complicated, it is not beyond your abilities to learn how to operate it efficiently. Treat it as the craftsman does his tools. He uses them with confidence, care, and understanding. Only then does he do good work.

How can you begin to improve your reading mechanism?

Your first job is to train yourself to increase the size of the image your eyes send to your mind. The number of words a reader habitually identifies *during a particular pause* is known as the RECOGNITION SPAN. Thus, if your eyes stop only three or four times in reading a 12-word line, each recognition span can accommodate from 2 to 5 words, depending upon the length of the individual words. For instance, in the following passages the diagonal lines indicate the approximate width of the recognition spans of the type of reader being illustrated.

• The actual eye stops do not occur at the diagonal lines but somewhere between them, sometimes on a word and at other times on the space between words. Material on both sides of the stop is absorbed.

• The eyes have a tendency to cover more words or letters to the right of a given stop than to the left. Thus the stop does not occur at midpoint in the recognition span but is overbalanced to the left.

• Since every reader gradually develops a basic rhythm in his eye movements, the stops assume a more or less uniform pattern across the lines. For the purpose of our exercises, we will show the recognition spans in a uniform pattern, although you must understand that it *may not necessarily fit yours.* If you have to make adjustments as you practice, that is as it should be. It is impossible for anyone to predict how your eyes will behave. No two readers are exactly the same.

• As you will see by the examples, there is not too great a difference between the average and the fast reader. It amounts to little more than a reduction of about one stop per line.

Word-by-Word Reader

There/ is/ no/ telling/ how/ many/ different/ "local/ times" there/ were/ in/ the/ United/ States/ prior/ to/ the/ adoption/ of Standard/ Time/, but/ we/ do/ know/ that/ before/ 1883/ there were/ something/ like/ 100/ different/ times/ in/ use/ by/ the railroads/ of/ this/ country.

Average Reader

A traveler/ going from Maine/ to California,/ if anxious to have correct railroad time,/ was obliged to/ change his watch/ some twenty times/ during the journey.

In the railroad station/ in Buffalo,/ there were three clocks— one set to New York time,/ one set to Columbus time,/ and the other set/ to local Buffalo time.

Fast Reader

In Kansas City/ each of the leading jewelers/ furnished his own "standard time"/ and no two agreed./ Sometimes the difference was as great as twenty minutes./ Each jeweler/ took his own readings./ He had his own customers/ who set their watches by his regulator and/ were willing to wager/ on the correctness of his time.

The situation/ became so notorious/ that an astronomer was hired to untangle the mess./ On his recommendation/ the problem was solved/ by the city's adoption/ of a "time ball" system.

Super-speed Reader

These time balls, now almost forgotten,/ were a great institution in their time./ Each day at official noon at a particular location, a large ball, sometimes three or four feet in diameter,/ so as to be visible for several miles,/ was dropped from a lofty mast. As the ball fell,/ the people—watching from many vantage points— set their timepieces at noon,/ and thus everyone in the city was provided with uniform time.

Did you notice that the word-by-word reader has more than twice as many stops per line as the average reader? One can manage no better than 125 to 150 words a minute, whereas the other can proceed at a speed of 300 to 350 words a minute. You noticed, too, that the super-speed reader averages about two stops per line. Some of these extraordinary people can read *down a newspaper column* (averaging 5 or 6 words a line) with no left-to-right stops at all! If you can learn to do this some day, you will be in the top 2 per cent of all readers.

* * *

We can now begin your training program for increasing your recognition span. Let me prove to you first that you already have considerable experience in this area. Note the following:

167

In the split second it took your eyes to glance at this number, your mind promptly registered it as *one hundred sixty-seven*. Whether the number was used to refer to someone's weight, the seating capacity of a restaurant, or the total miles to a distant city, your mind would have reacted to the whole image—one hundred sixty-seven— not to a *1* and a *6* and a *7*.

Even though the dollar sign and the decimal point have been added, your glance produces the picture of *one dollar and sixty-seven cents*. The *1, 6,* and *7* are again lost as individual numbers in the process of creating a typical expression of monetary value.

The New York Yankees

What happened when you read this phrase? Did your mind carefully and slowly decide that *The* means one? Did it then go to *New* and conclude that this must be something of recent origin? And did it wonder about the fine old English origin of *York?* And did it finally get to *Yankees* and recall the interesting terms that grew out of the Civil War? I'm sure it did not. You took a quick look and immediately thought of a famous baseball team.

Even if you are a slow reader, there are thousands of other number combinations and word groups that you recognize instantly without examining their piece-by-piece construction. The meaning of these familiar expressions comes in a flash because you have seen them before. Under such circumstances your recognition span automatically increases to 3, 4, and even 5 words. You've had experience with them. You react to them as you do to houses or trees or similar well-known objects. You see the house as a Colonial, ranch, or split-level type, not as a collection of studs, rafters, and nails. The tree is an oak or birch, not individual branches, leaves, and bark.

All this means that your recognition span is acceptable sometimes. To become a skillful reader, you need to train yourself to include about 3 or 4 words in your eye stops habitually, whether the phrases are familiar or not.

There is something else. In our discussion of *The New York Yankees,* you had concrete evidence of a point suggested briefly before. Not only is it faster to read the phrase in one gulp, so to speak; it is also better for your understanding. You had a good example of the confused notions that are possible for a person who reads one word at a time. He fails to see the total picture; he fails to "see the forest for the trees." We'll have more to say about this principle in Chapter VIII.

One more remark offered in review and then we can go on to the exercises. What you now know about the disadvantages of reading word by word should make doubly clear to you why roadblocks must be eliminated. If you point, mumble to yourself, move your head, or do any of the other undesirable things that were mentioned in the previous chapter, you are forcing your recognition span to limit itself to a single word at a glance. How harmful this is to speed and comprehension cannot be repeated too often.

EXERCISES

Your objective in the following exercises is to train yourself to see and understand groups of words at a glance and to develop rhythmic eye movements so that you can read comfortably and quickly. Under no circumstances are you to attempt to cover all of the following suggested material in one sitting. Our eventual schedule will call for no more than 3 minutes a day for practicing this skill once you understand how to go about it. Be thorough, but be patient. You will gradually discover, as with the roadblocks, that certain exercises do you more good than others. When you have decided upon your favorites, concentrate on these.

I. Flash Cards

This is one of the oldest drills used in the field of reading improvement, yet it is still very effective if properly done. There is need for some effort on your part to set it up, but if you are serious the effort will pay a rich dividend.

You will find a list of word groups below. Get a supply of index cards. If at all possible, *type* each phrase on a separate card; otherwise, write it out neatly in a small hand. On the first 50 cards, center the material, thus:

A.

```
                  on a Sunday morning
```

On the next 50, place the phrase at the bottom of the card, thus:

B.

```
                  several years ago
```

FIRST 50

a flight of bombers
none of the boys
almost equally exciting
many of the pilgrims
the rest of them
the light fantastic
eluded the police
mowed the grass
quickly disposed of
in a passionate embrace
the British Parliament
first fall planting
in an hour or so
The United States of America
toys, books, and crayons
result of a survey
Taming of the Shrew
by word of mouth
the thousands cheered
first on the program
plan of attack
behind the window
down the middle
plunged into the water
lifted the package

totally wiped out
down the garden path
several days later
put into gear
thrown out at home
wall to wall carpeting
for sentimental reasons
totally different ideas
slowly but surely
a remarkable job
a feeling of guilt
behind the rocks
a flight of bees
with great force
who had voted
seven league boots
sworn to secrecy
gales of laughter
lazy days of summer
with Joe and Bill
a restful night
a roar of delight
not for very long
I'll be glad to
not on your life

SECOND 50

superior reading skill
to many home owners
clearly and distinctly
developing better habits
master the techniques
Girl of the Golden West
from Spain to Portugal
be equally harmful
chop down the tree
for the majority

tall, dark, and handsome
with a loud shout
The Star-Spangled Banner
in your back yard
a thousand times *No*
that deadly routine
to send it home
as a matter of fact
has been written
amount of instruction

78

busy daily schedule
half the battle
spoke rather rapidly
too little knowledge
not too early, Joe
roast turkey and gravy
at the end of the month
on the front cover
a transcontinental journey
and you, too, Tom
four years at college
no, of course not
rather seriously hurt
split down the middle
a mass of stuff

panes of glass
trying to learn
prepared to accept
handful of peanuts
home medical adviser
long since disappeared
yes, I think so
a very flat tire
with reasonable pride
slippery as an eel
under clean sheets
much less, I think
I hope I can
a strong swimmer
over the counter

Flash-Card Exercise A (Use cards with phrase in center.)

Collect the cards into a pack, face down, so that when you lift a card the words will be right side up. Now lift a card, facing it up just long enough to place it at the bottom of the pack. The idea is to grasp the entire phrase in a glance as it flashes before your eyes. Start with whatever speed is comfortable to you. With practice, of course, you will be able to increase the speed of the flash-look. You can use the pack at least a half dozen times before you become too familiar with the word groups. You can then set up new cards by copying some of the numerous phrases that you will find in the exercises that follow. When you can go through a whole set of 50 cards as fast as you can flip them, you will not need to do this exercise more than once a month, and eventually not at all. If you can get someone to do the flashing for you, so much the better.

Flash-Card Exercise B (Use cards with phrase at bottom.)

This technique is a variation of the one we have just presented. From the second pack of cards, select a half dozen or so. Now take an average-size book. Place it on a table with the wide side facing you and with the binding at the rear. Insert the cards at intervals between the pages of the book. Make certain that the cards are face up and that the letters are right side up. Place one thumb beneath the last page and toward the center of that page. Now place the remaining four fingers on the center of the first page. You now have the text of the book grasped in your hand. Using the same thumb to flip the pages, proceed until you come to the first phrase card and go slightly past it. Here again the idea is to absorb the word group within a single recognition span in the split second it is visible before it is covered by the pages. Continue flipping pages until you have identified all the cards, and then replace them with others. After you have become skilled in this method, you will be doing with the pages of a book what is done in reading laboratories with very expensive mechanical equipment.

II. Span-Stretching Exercises in Columns

Various exercises will now be presented with the contents broken up into word groups and arranged in vertical columns. Your objective will be to follow the sense of the paragraphs as *your eyes move down the page and absorb the individual phrases in single stops.* There is to be no right-to-left movement of the head or eyes at any time. At the end of each article there will be a test to determine whether you have gotten the important ideas from your reading.

Spills Thrill!

Spurred on
by many vacationers
who have imported it
to their home lakes,
water skiing has become
America's fastest growing
water sport.
This has been encouraged
by the phenomenal growth
of small boat ownership
in the last ten years.
Exceedingly easy to learn,
water skiing is
one of the few
"one lesson" sports.
You can learn
the basics of
the "take-off"
on dry land,
then transfer the knowledge
to a deep water start—
which you make
from a sitting position
in water which
reaches your shoulders.
As the tow boat
gradually increases speed,
you rise slowly
until you are standing

with back straight
and knees slightly bent.
You are now skimming
along the water's surface
at about 20 miles per hour.
You take the turns
on the outside,
so as not to slacken
the ski rope;
you bend your knees
to absorb the slight shock
of passing across
the boat's wake—
you gather confidence,
even daring,
and raise one arm
to wave toward the shore.
By the end
of a long weekend,
you may have ventured
a few tricks—
and had a few spills.
Stick to it.
You'll soon be skiing
at greater speeds,
jumping,
even carrying a partner
on your shoulders.
Water skiing brings out
the daring in nearly everyone,
because its basics
are so simple—
and so much fun!

COMPREHENSION TEST

Another title for this selection could be

A. Elbows, arms, and legs

B. A rumbling speedboat

C. Water tricks

D. A popular water sport

ANSWER: The fourth letter in the alphabet.

COLUMN EXERCISE B

To introduce variety, the material will now be printed in two columns. Continue as before; read *down* one column, and then the other. *One glance, one stop, one word group! Stretch your recognition span. Go faster than you think you should!*

But Can You Stay In Love?

BY SYDNEY J. HARRIS

I turned on
the car radio
to get the news,
and was assaulted
by a vocal duet—
a recording
of a boy and a girl
bleating in unison,
"We're so lucky
to be young
and in love,"
or words
to that effect.
Yet, what is so
"lucky" or unusual
about being young
and in love?
Sometimes this nation of ours
seems pathologically devoted
to the adoration
of juvenile romance.
Being in love
(or thinking you are,
which amounts to
the same thing)
when you are young
is an exhilarating experience,
but it is also
easy and commonplace.
I was in love
half-a-hundred times
during my adolescence.

There is no
trick to it.
A pretty face,
a turned-up nose,
a fetching figure,
is often all it takes.
Sometimes even less
than that—
sometimes just a glimpse
of a golden girl
turning a corner
in the dusk,
and you know
it is She, The One.
Being in love
is a natural
and inevitable
state of youth.
In those years
we are only half-alive
when we are
out of love.
We live in a condition
of perpetual self-delusion,
intoxicated with
our dreams.
But to be older
and in love—
to be in love
for a long time—
to be in love
as middle age approaches,
and responsibilities
bear down, and
vexations crop up—
this is worthy of celebration
in song and story.
And this
we have little of

in our popular recordings
and our movies
and our magazine serials.
Our national culture
is crazed with juvenilia;
and so, is it
any wonder that
our young people,
carefully taught that
they are the most important
and glamorous segments
of the population,
begin to act
as if the world
were created by
and for them alone?
Love is worth nothing
until it passes through
the fever of infatuation,
until it settles down
to a steady
day-by-day routine,
until the golden girl
begins to fade
around the edges,
and the lithe, lean boy
begins to fatten
in the middle.
Anybody can be young
and in love;
it is hard
not to be.
But only those
graced by the gods
can persist in loving
when the chill of autumn
begins to set in.
For love is
an act of will,

not a sentiment;
it may start
in the blood,
but it can
only be sustained
by the mind
and the spirit.
Where are the singers
of this song,
the tellers of this tale?

COMPREHENSION TEST

Another title for this selection could be

A. Boy and girl
B. Young people in love
C. Love is true when it lasts
D. Middle-aged people lose love

ANSWER. The third letter of the alphabet.

COLUMN EXERCISE C

In this exercise there will again be two columns. However, you will not find a dividing line. The word groups will follow one another, two to a line. You will have to make *two stops per line*, left to right, and then on to the next line. This is actually preliminary eye-rhythm training, more of which will follow later. NO ROADBLOCKS! NO REGRESSIONS! MOVE RIGHT ALONG! SPEED! SPEED! SPEED!

Got a Match?

In the flick   of an eye
it takes you   to read this line,
16,000 matches   are being struck
in the United States.   Of the 500 billion matches
manufactured a year,   200 billion
are book matches.   Book matches were invented
in 1892   by Joshua Pusey,

a Philadelphia lawyer.
he made an economical
match book.
accidental flare-ups
the igniting ingredients
of the match,
inside the cover.
50 matches
and called
"Flexibles."
his book matches
because sparks
often ignited others.
which had bought
put the striking surface
and printed
on the flap.
book matches
in the millions.
as they come
You can try a test.
goes out in one breath,
too easily extinguished
useless outdoors.
it is dangerous,
to be thrown away
Two quick puffs
for ordinary breezes
Book matches
to advertise everything
to the need
during World War II.
four million packages
"I Shall Return"
Political candidates
The White House has them
Thousands of Americans
as a hobby.

After many tries
and comparatively safe
He eliminated
by putting part of
in the head
part in the striking surface
Then he stapled
into a cardboard book
his new product
The public regarded
as dangerous,
from a lighted match
Finally the match company,
his invention,
outside the book
"Close cover before striking"
From then on
began to be ordered
Paper matches are tested
from the machine.
If the match
it is
and would be
If it takes three puffs,
for it is likely
while lighted.
are just right
and are called safe.
have been used
from chewing gum
for an apartment
General MacArthur dropped
bearing the prophecy
over the Philippines.
use them.
for the Presidents.
save book matches
A man in Fort Worth

is said to have
over 50,000.
perhaps by now
the first match book
distributed in 1896
Its hand-lettered cover
powerful cast—
get seats early,"
of the star trombonist,

the largest collection—
Orchestra leader Lopez
has found the rarest prize—
to carry advertising,
by the Mendelssohn Opera Co.
reads: "Cyclone of fun—
pretty girls—
and has a hand-pasted photo
Thomas Lowden, on it.

COMPREHENSION TEST

Write T (true) or F (false) next to each statement below.

_____ Book matches at first were dangerous.

_____ Paper matches are rarely tested.

_____ Only liquor is advertised on match covers.

_____ Many people collect match covers.

_____ Advertising on book matches is only a very
recent addition.

ANSWERS: T, F, F, T, F.

COLUMN EXERCISE D

Here's another exercise exactly like the previous one.
Follow the same instructions, but this time try to read
even faster. Don't worry about the meaning; you'll get
it!

Down Your Alley

A bowler may be
skinny or fat,
man or woman.
the blind and
were among the 20,000,000

big or little,
young or old,
Three-year-olds,
people in wheel chairs
who rolled the

87

"big black apple"
and enjoyed
of the ball
Bowling is a game
all-out proficiency
No opponent can
and an occasional bowler
a higher score
But it's far
Skill puts the ball
the ten pins regularly.
luck combines with skill.
has duplicated the feat
who had rolled
and delivered
for a strike.
split in half lengthwise
and stood up
That's the only case
bowled 299½ out of 300.
bowling started
in Europe about 300 A.D.
for defense
To dramatize religion,
stand their clubs
and roll large stones
which stood for sins.
was a sin overcome,
was a sin
Nine pins,
by the Dutch,
in the early days
banned it
The law definitely
A little later on
and the game
with no law
By 1900
had started bowling

last year
the satisfying sound
crashing down the pins.
that doesn't demand
in order to enjoy it.
frustrate your best shots,
can add up
than an expert.
from being all luck.
where it will down
Sometimes though,
For instance, no one
of an unknown bowler
a series of perfect frames
his last ball
But one of the pins
and one half bounded back
in about its original spot.
where a bowler
Records state that
as a religious ceremony
Peasants carried clubs
even to confession.
priests had the peasants
in a corner
at the clubs
A club knocked down
one left standing
to be conquered.
brought over here
became so popular
that the authorities
to prevent gambling.
stated "nine" pins.
someone added another pin
became ten pins
to prevent its enjoyment.
the American Bowling Congress
on its way

to an Olympic sport.
at the 1936 Olympics
could roll a hook ball
was other than
The ABC soon
the Americans' skill,
had devised a scale
of the ball
and thus guard against
a "loaded" bowling ball.

An opposing bowling team
wondered how the Americans
unless their ball
the regulation one.
convinced them it was
for the congress
to weigh one quarter
at a time
any attempt to use

COMPREHENSION TEST

Again write T (true) or F (false) next to the following statements.

_____ Only a handful of Americans enjoy bowling.

_____ Bowling is a combination of luck and skill.

_____ Bowling started more than 1,000 years ago.

_____ Originally the game was nine pins.

_____ It is possible to hook an unloaded ball.

ANSWERS: F, T, T, T, T.

The limitations of a book make it impossible to provide you with all the exercises you will need to stretch your recognition span permanently. As was said before, you can use the word groups that appear in the column exercises to arrange additional flash-card drills. To supplement your supply of column drills, it is suggested that you get some copies of magazines like *Coronet* or *The Reader's Digest*. The average column in one of these contains 5 or 6 words. Simply draw a line arbitrarily down the center of a column and use this as a rough guide. Read with no more than two stops per line and let the vertical marker act as your reminder. Even though it cuts right through words, you will find that your eyes adopt a rhythm and adjust to the word phrases regardless of where the line cuts them off. You will recall that it is not necessary to see every letter of every word in order to identify it. The important thing is to move right along speedily and to resist temptations to linger over individual words.

Let me remind you again here, as I shall do periodically, that you are not to attempt to race through all the exercises in one sitting. You have enough material in this chapter to keep you busy for weeks. Become familiar with the objective of each chapter, try an exercise or two, but wait for the details of the Daily Plan in Chapter X to explain how you can intelligently proceed to improve your reading ability in 15 minutes a day.

III. Combined Span-Stretching and Eye-Movement Exercises

The flash-card and column exercises are very helpful in increasing the number of words you can handle at a glance. However, merely stretching your recognition span and assuming you will transfer your new habit to a regular line of print is taking too much for granted. To become a rapid reader you will have to learn to make no more than about three stops per line. The exercises that follow, therefore, will help you develop a three-stop-per-line rhythm of eye movements. So that the exercises will approximate what you actually do when you read, comprehension questions will be added to some of the drills. There would be no point, certainly, in confining your practice to a mechanical stretching of your recognition span without attempting to determine whether meaning was being derived.

RHYTHM EXERCISE A

You will notice that a series of dots (point of eye stop) will be placed on lines (limit of recognition span). Focus on the dot and use your peripheral vision to absorb the limits of the line at either end. Then let your eyes slide to the next dot, and finally to the last on the line. Make your return sweep and proceed with the next series of dot and line symbols. The purpose of this exercise is to set a likely or typical pattern for your eyes so that the conscious effort to make about three stops per line will develop into a habit. The position of the dots on the lines will vary, as do your eye stops when you are reading. Increase your speed gradually. Do not do more than one set of symbols in any one session.

A

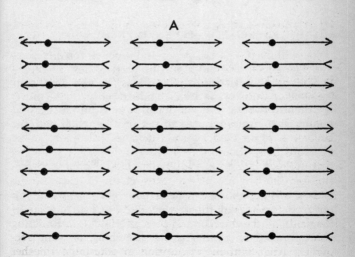

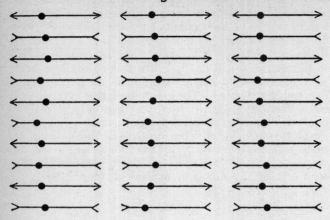

RHYTHM EXERCISE B—PLUS COMPREHENSION

You will need a pad of paper and a pencil for this exercise. The symbols o and x will be used in designs representing number patterns. You focus on the first stop (symbol or number pattern), slide rapidly to the next, and then to the last. As you do so, your mind must try to determine the total number of o's or x's in each pattern.

Example: o   xx x xxx   o

> You would write 6 on your pad. There are 6 crosses in the pattern.

Keep writing the numbers *as your eyes sweep to the next line*. Don't break the rhythm, and don't do more than about 10 of these at one sitting. AND NO REGRESSIONS!

This device combines eye-movement training with comprehension. Let me caution you to register the entire number pattern in your recognition span at once. Do not try to count one by one. This will defeat our purpose. You can check your results with the answers at the bottom of the exercise.

A

X	OOO O OO	X
XX XX XX	O	O
X	X	OO O O
XXX XXX XXX	O	O
X	O O OOO	X
O	O	XX XXX XXX
X	O O O	X
O	XXX X XXX	O
X	X	OO OOO O
O	O	XXX XXX XX

B

X	OOO O O	X
XX X XX	O	O
OOO OOO OOO	X	X
O	X X X	O
X	X	O OOO OOO
O	O	XXX XXX XXX
X	OO OO OO	X
XX XX XXX	O	O
OOO OOO OO	X	X
O	O	XXX X XX

C

x	ooo oo ooo	x
o	xxx xx xx	o
x	x	oo ooo o
xxx xxx xxx	o	o
x	x	oo ooo ooo
o	xxx	o
x	ooo ooo ooo	x
xx xx x	o	o
x	x	o o oo
o	x xx x	o

D

x	oo ooo ooo	x
xxx x xx	o	o
x	x	o oo oo
o	xxx xxx x	o
o o o	x	x
xx x x	o	o
x	x	ooo ooo ooo
o	xx xxx x	o
x	x	ooo o o
x x x	o	o

ANSWERS: a. 6, 6, 4, 9, 5; 8, 3, 7, 6, 8.
        b. 5, 5, 9, 3, 7; 9, 6, 7, 8, 6.
        c. 8, 7, 6, 9, 7; 3, 9, 5, 4, 4.
        d. 8, 6, 5, 7, 3; 4, 9, 6, 5, 3.

RHYTHM EXERCISE C—PLUS COMPREHENSION

Now we'll try a similar exercise, this time with number patterns written out rather than in o's and x's. Again your eyes stop on symbol or number patterns as they pause three times per line. *Do not skip the symbols! Write the number on your pad (in figures) while your eyes are executing the return sweep.*

Example: o   two fifteen   o

Your eyes move from the o to the number and then to the final o. As they sweep to the left, you write 215 on your pad.

A

x	one twenty-five	x
three twenty	o	o
x	x	four nineteen
o	five thirty	o
x	nine twenty	x
o	o	two forty-three
x	eight sixty-seven	x
one nineteen	o	o
seven fifty	x	x
o	two thirty-seven	o

B

x	x	three fifty-six
nine eighteen	o	o
ten fifty	x	x
o	four eighty-two	o
x	x	two seventeen
o	seven twenty-eight	o
x	x	five thirty-nine
o	eight forty	o
six fifty-one	x	x
six sixty-two	o	o

C

x	twenty twenty	x
one twenty-two	o	o
x	x	four forty-four
o	o	seven sixty-six
x	nine eighty-eight	x
two hundred two	o	o
five hundred six	x	x
o	o	eight eighty-four
x	three sixty-eight	x
six forty-three	o	o

D

x	three forty-five	x
six eighty	o	o
x	x	nine twenty-five
o	two sixty-eight	o
five hundred six	x	x
o	o	eight forty-four
four eighty-three	x	x
o	seven twenty-nine	o
six sixty-two	x	x
o	o	one hundred one

E

one ninety-nine	x	x
o	two eighteen	o
x	x	nine eighty-three
o	eight twenty-four	o
three sixty-two	x	x
o	o	four thirty-five
x	six seventy-seven	x
o	o	seven forty-six
five twenty-one	x	x
o	two fifty-two	o

Here are the number sequences:

A	B	C	D	E
125	356	2020	345	199
320	918	122	680	218
419	1050	444	925	983
530	482	766	268	824
920	217	988	506	362
243	728	202	844	435
867	539	506	483	677
119	840	884	729	746
750	651	368	662	521
237	662	643	101	252

RHYTHM EXERCISE D—PLUS COMPREHENSION

This is an extremely difficult exercise, and you should not attempt it until you are well along in your training program. Besides the rhythm and comprehension aspects, there are two other features. The drill forces your mind to do considerable actual analysis, and it challenges your will power to avoid regressions. It will be very tempting for your eyes to go back over a line, but you *must resist* the impulse.

Example:

upon (1)   on the table cloth   below (2)

We are now dealing with word phrases. You notice that each one is associated with two words. One of these two words has some relationship in meaning to the phrase. Your eyes continue their rhythmic movements across the lines. They stop on the word, or the *phrase in one piece*, in order. As your eyes go into their return sweep to the next line, you write the number of the word that has something in common with the phrase. In the example above, you would write 1.

A

there(1)	across the river	here(2)
in the middle ages	then(1)	now(2)
above (1)	below(2)	on top of a hill
forbid(1)	with your permission	allow(2)
six feet in height	tall(1)	short(2)
unfair(1)	both sides of a quarrel	fair(2)
innocent(1)	evidence against him	guilty(2)
on the Republican ticket	voter(1)	candidate(2)
costly(1)	free(2)	haven't paid a penny
shooting off his mouth	silly(1)	wise(2)

B

poor(1)	rich(2)	has about everything
stale(1)	drew out the air	fresh(2)
night before Christmas	holy(1)	evil(2)
local(1)	travel(2)	trip around the world
married(1)	fiftieth wedding anniversary	single(2)
toasted English muffin	thrown(1)	eaten(2)
buttons at the waist	style(1)	height(2)
mystery(1)	the stroke of midnight	breakfast(2)
real(1)	unreal(2)	in a dream world
easy(1)	hard(2)	a good day's work

C

lowered his glasses	down(1)	up(2)
tomorrow(1)	wasn't long ago	recently(2)
closed(1)	was given the secret	open(2)
he enjoyed it	for(1)	against(2)
and(1)	despite the setback	although(2)
wallop(1)	strikeout(2)	two-run homer
certainly(1)	perhaps(2)	if I do ride
This is the life.	bad(1)	good(2)
wonderful climate there	pleasant(1)	unpleasant(2)
celebration(1)	seven persons killed	accident(2)

D

many thousands of persons	empty(1)	crowded(2)
fell(1)	flew(2)	hurtled off a cliff
well(1)	had taken some pills	sick(2)
spoken(1)	silent(2)	upon her suggestion
faces of the young	clear(1)	wrinkled(2)
armed(1)	guards were posted	unarmed(2)
politics(1)	sports(2)	nominated a Democrat
five distinctive colors	variety(1)	monotony(2)
complicated(1)	single-knob control	simple(2)
nothing but the best	highest(1)	lowest(2)

E

small(1)	big(2)	running an empire
ran(1)	walked(2)	was in a hurry
large body of troops	many(1)	few(2)
included in the group	out(1)	in(2)
dry(1)	pail of dirty water	wet(2)
perhaps(1)	definite(2)	if you want to
unskilled(1)	fine craftsmanship	skilled(2)
beautiful spring day	cloudy(1)	sunny(2)
roughly(1)	gently(2)	with a tender look
in a hot tub	restful(1)	active(2)

ANSWERS:
a. 1, 1, 1, 2, 1;   2, 2, 2, 2, 1.
b. 2, 2, 1, 2, 1;   2, 1, 1, 2, 2.
c. 1, 2, 2, 1, 2;   1, 2, 2, 1, 2.
d. 2, 1, 2, 2, 1;   1, 1, 1, 2, 1.
e. 2, 1, 1, 2, 2;   1, 2, 2, 2, 1.

Again let me say that the drills are necessary in helping you master the mechanical aspects of stretching your recognition span and acquiring proper eye rhythm, but they cannot do the whole job for you. Your greatest progress will be made in actual reading situations. You are therefore being asked to try your new skills in the selections that follow. We will start modestly in the first two articles and ask you to try to cover each line in no more than four stops. If you think you can go faster, by all means make the effort and don't worry about the markings. To vary the procedure, we will indicate the suggested recognition spans by printing them alternately in boldface (dark) and regular (light) type. Try to absorb the entire word phrase in one stop, as it appears in boldface or regular type. Move right along; *no regressions, no roadblocks, no fears about missing something.* There will be a brief comprehension test after each selection to convince you that you have derived the main ideas despite your failure to look at one word at a time.

Review Selection 1—Four Stops Per Line

Only a Medium of Exchange

"CASH," the 2,000-year-old Chinese copper coin with square hole, has come to mean the money in our pockets.

Of the moneys of the world, cash has also meant the Yap stone disks about 30 inches in diameter, weighing over 100 pounds, valued at 10,000 coconuts or a wife. In India cash could mean the smallest coin in the world—one grain of gold the size of a pinhead.

Coming down to 1525, the silver Joachimthaler of Bohemia became a pattern for many European coins because of its convenient size. The thaler is the ancestor of our dollar. Coins about the same weight and size of the thaler were issued by Spanish colonies before our Revolution. These Spanish milled dollars were the chief circulating medium in our colonies in the latter half of the 18th century. They were also the "pieces of eight" of *Treasure Island.* Halves and quarters of these dollars, cut to make change, became known as four bits and two bits.

The Continental Congress issued notes to finance the Revolution. These notes "died in the hands of the people," and thus originated the phrase "not worth a continental." The United States issued its first coin in 1787, called the

Fugio cent. It was also called the Franklin cent because of the inscription, "Mind Your Own Business." The closed chain of 13 links on the reverse side symbolized the unity of the thirteen original colonies.

Before the Civil War, a New Orleans bank issued $10 bills with "DIX" in large type on them. Widely circulated through the South, they were called dixies—hence Dixieland.

If we run out of "cash," remember there is grain, man's first money. Or we could borrow nails, once used as commodity money in Scotland and New England, or the gum drops of Eskimos, or the soap of Mexico. Specimens of these moneys and many others are exhibited in the Chase National Bank Collection of Moneys of the World, New York City.

COMPREHENSION TEST

Write T (true) or F (false) in the spaces provided next to each statement.

_____ Coins have always been small and light.

_____ "Two bits" is derived from the Spanish pieces of eight.

_____ A continental was once official American money.

_____ Jazz musicians invented "Dixieland."

_____ Nails and gumdrops have been used as money, too.

ANSWERS: F, T, T, F, T.

Review Selection 2—Four Stops Per Line

In this exercise, the limits of a particular recognition span will be indicated by diagonal lines. You are to focus your stops somewhere between the lines, not on them, and are, of course, to use your peripheral vision to absorb the word groups. KEEP MOVING! NO REGRESSIONS! NO ROADBLOCKS! JUST GET THE STORY!

The Terror of Muse, Pa., Has a Very Busy Day

The menfolk of Muse/ are a hardened bunch,/ as tough/ as the rock/ that they dig/ for coal.

But they moved/ like scared rabbits/ when Joey/ (Two-Gun) Coleman,/ the toughest hombre/ in all the East,/ strode down Main St./ at sunset yesterday.

In one hand,/ Two-Gun held/ a .45 caliber automatic./ In the other/ he held a .25 caliber/ repeater. And/ both were blazing away.

Some of the men/ tried to plead/ with Two-Gun./ The answer they got/ was lead.

Some tripped and fell/ in the scramble/ to escape./ They had to dance/ to get away.

For two hours,/ Two-Gun kept/ most of the town's/ 1,600 behind shuttered windows./ The others/ watched from hiding places well protected/ from Two-Gun's slugs.

Two-Gun/ had emptied and reloaded/ both his pistols/ when his father, Joe,/ appeared on behalf/ of the town.

"Give yourself up,/ Joey,"/ Two-Gun's father/ begged softly. "Give yourself up."

But Two-Gun aimed/ at the telephone pole/ sheltering his father./ His father fled/ down the street.

Finally/ three men decided/ it was about time/ they did something/ about Two-Gun./ Two of them/ hid behind some hedges while a third/ ventured out in the street/ to lure Two-Gun/ his way.

Two-Gun fell/ into the trap./ He was grabbed/ from behind

104

and disarmed./ But they never/ would have got him/ if he hadn't run out of ammunition./ Then, later,/ they turned Two-Gun/ over to the cops/ and still later/ the cops turned him over/ to Juvenile Court authorities.

Because,/ after all,/ Two-Gun is only 10.

COMPREHENSION TEST

True or false, as before.

_____ The incident took place in a mining town.

_____ Both of Two-Gun's weapons were of the same caliber.

_____ Two-Gun fired at everyone except his father.

_____ Two-Gun gave up voluntarily when his ammunition ran out.

_____ He was not put into jail.

ANSWERS: T, F, F, F, T.

Exercises like the last two can readily be set up by you. Take selections from magazines or books and either underline every other word phrase or insert diagonals at various points along the lines of print. Whether you mark off the precise recognition spans you will eventually employ is not too important. The arbitrary divisions are there primarily to remind you to read in word groups. *Even you* would find it difficult to predict where your own eyes will stop on a given line. While you are preparing the articles for practice, try to avoid getting any meaning from them so that your eventual reading of the marked paragraphs will be your first effort to derive their sense.

We now increase the pace. Be certain you do some preliminary practicing with the 3-stop o and x rhythm exercises presented earlier in this chapter. Get into the swing of it first. Then try to absorb the word phrases below (in alternate boldface and regular type) in single stops, and sweep across the lines at a three-stop speed. It won't be easy, and you will need all your concentration and self-control. The usual comprehension test will follow.

Traveling with a Camera

BY JOHN RYAN

There's no question that a photographic record of a trip helps to prolong pleasure in the places visited and the people met, and also helps you share this pleasure with people back home.

I, for one, am seldom bored with home movies (if they are edited), or with color slides (if they are projected on a screen)—when the people showing them are people I like. But I must say I get pretty tired of listening to descriptions of the wonderful shots they missed because they ran out of film, left the camera in a hotel, had it stolen from a car, etc., etc., etc. . . .

Professional photographers and serious amateurs take their cameras wherever they go. But some not-too-experienced travelers seem to feel self-conscious about doing so because a camera hanging around the neck or over a shoulder has become the badge of the tourist.

What's so wrong about being a tourist? The more I travel, the more I am pleased to be identified as an American tourist; natives of foreign parts who look down their noses at tourists are not in the majority—and usually are merely the ones who are jealous because they aren't touring in some foreign (to them) spot themselves.

Getting back to the strap, slinging it over a shoulder is often inconvenient because it keeps slipping off. I've found it better to let the strap out to its fullest length and sling it **across my chest**—like the shoulder strap of a Sam Browne belt—pushing the camera around **back of my hip when** I'm walking **through crowded streets**; this leaves both hands free **and prevents damage** to the camera **that might result from** its banging into people **or posts**.

Most amateurs **know enough to keep the strap** around the neck when making pictures. (**It's pretty horrifying to watch** such an expensive **piece of equipment** get smaller and smaller **as it sinks** through the crystal clear waters **of a tropical** bay.) **But in foreign restaurants** you see many Americans who **don't seem to realize** that cameras are almost **as negotiable as** currency in some countries **and so are** a great temptation **to thieves**.

When I go into a restaurant, or into a grill car **on a train**, I never put my camera **even on a chair beside me**; I put it at my **feet and hook** the strap around an ankle so **that if I should try** to leave without it **I'd go flat on my face**. And I never trust **my camera** to porters, baggage handlers, **check room attendants**, or hotel servants. **When I have to leave it** in a room or in a ship's **cabin**, I lock it in a suitcase.

COMPREHENSION TEST

Insert the usual T or F in the spaces.

_____ Color slides should be projected on a screen.

_____ You should avoid carrying a camera because it labels you a tourist.

_____ It is best to sling the camera strap across the chest, not over a shoulder.

_____ One must be careful about a camera in foreign restaurants.

_____ On a train, one should place his camera on the seat beside him.

ANSWERS: T, F, T, T, F.

Again you will find the diagonal lines to indicate the limits of the individual recognition spans. Remember, you do not focus on the lines but somewhere between them. NO ROADBLOCKS! FULL SPEED AHEAD! THREE STOPS PER LINE!

It Doesn't Come Out in the Wash

In 1936 when Adam Yulch/ was a cop on Long Island/ in charge of the lost property bureau,/ he was ordered/ to find the shop which had cleaned/ a certain suit,/ the only clue found in a hold-up car of bank robbers./ All through the summer/ he trudged/ to several thousand cleaning shops/ in the metropolitan area./ Finally, he found the right shop/ and broke the case.

Tracing people/ through laundry marks/ was no new idea. Criminals and victims/ had been identified that way/ since 1883. But to Adam Yulch/ the individual search,/ shop by shop, was the hard way to do it./ So he suggested the idea/ of a central bureau/ of laundry and cleaning marks./ His superiors gave him permission,/ and he started out/ on his one-man search and study of cleaners' marks/ from all over the country.

Each shop or company/ has its own system—/ usually a letter or symbol followed by numbers./ No two marks are alike./ Some use ink,/ some indelible pencil;/ some print, or write or stamp their signs./ Even six-point stars/ used by so many Chinese laundries/ are different/ under the magnifying glass.

Most laundry marks, for example,/ are made up/ of a master symbol,/ a route sign and a mark or initials/ designating the customer./ For instance, to trace shirt owner H7JO19,/ he would turn to his laundry cards/ which had "H" for the master key./ If several,/ he would compare the actual mark/ with samples in his file/ until he found the right laundry./ The "7" shows the bundle was handled by Route 7 driver./ The "JO"/ gives the customer's last name,/ Jones, let us say./ The final number "19" gives Jones' street number./ There are also signs/ to tell whether the customer is a transient, say at a hotel,/ or if he is a regular customer./ Certain signs/ indicate family bundles.

Over the years,/ Mr. Yulch has collected/ 300,000 such marks and has indexed them/ in his filing cabinets./ A dirty handkerchief or trousers/ will put him on the trail./ He can identify victims or clues/ in twenty-four hours,/ and his evidence is final.

While building the Bureau,/ his early successes/ came to the attention of other states,/ the FBI/ and the Royal Canadian Mounted./ He has lectured on his system/ and has helped set up bureaus/ in other parts of the country,/ which at the same time has kept his file growing.

COMPREHENSION TEST

T or F, as usual.

_____ Adam Yulch's first case with cleaners' marks dealt with bank robbers.

_____ A central bureau had been in existence for many years before Yulch.

_____ Unfortunately, laundry marks are frequently similar.

_____ A series of letters and numbers on a shirt means nothing in particular.

_____ Mr. Yulch has gained international attention.

ANSWERS: T,   F,   F,   F,   T.

This may well be the final test of how far you can eventually stretch your recognition span for ordinary reading purposes. As was said, there are some people who miraculously are able to absorb an entire 12-word line in a single stop. This, however, is not a goal you should try to set for yourself. For one thing, it is not readily attainable. Very, very few can do it. Secondly, there remains the question whether those who can read so quickly aren't missing something of the details or the beauty and richness of the language in their haste. You should be perfectly satisfied if you can ultimately do what the following exercises are going to demand of you. I want to caution you not to try them seriously until you have made considerable progress in your practice to lift yourself to the above-average level of reading ability. Once you are ready, make the effort to read the selections exactly as I shall shortly direct you. Afterwards, you will, of course, be able to provide yourself with any number of additional similar exercises by consulting your daily newspaper.

Below is a typical newspaper column. The lines average 5 words. Focus your eyes somewhere in the center of the line *and try to absorb the entire line in one stop.* You move down the column, with no eye movements to left or right. It's difficult, and at first confusing. But it can be done! A comprehension test will follow.

Smoke Scare

Cigarettes are really "coffin nails"—that was the gist of a report presented to the American Medical Association in New York last week by Dr. Cuyler Hammond, director of the American Cancer Society's statistical research. The report, billed as "final," was based on a study of the smoking habits of 183,783 men in the 50-to-70-year age bracket, who had been traced for an average of 44 months during which 11,870 of the subjects died.

Among the scary findings:
•There was an "extremely high" association between cigarette smoking and deaths from cancer of the lung, larynx and esophagus, as well as deaths from gastric ulcers. "Very high" or "high" associations were found with other types of cancer, pneumonia, influenza, coronary heart disease, cirrhosis of the liver, and other diseases.
•Death rates from lung cancer were ten times higher for regular cigarette smokers than for non-smokers, and as much as 64 times higher for men who smoked two or more packs a day.
•Persons who gave up smoking lowered their risks of death considerably.

In a press conference that followed the presentation, Dr. Hammond and his assistant, Dr. Daniel Horn, both ex-cigarette smokers, puffed away on their pipes and gave as a "rough estimate" that cigarette smoking decreased life expectancy by seven to eight years, cigar smoking by a year and a half, and pipe smoking by only two to three months.

But one group at least did not sound too impressed. Said the Tobacco Industry Research Committee: "The causes of cancer and heart disease are not yet known to medical science. Today's Hammond-Horn statistical statement, like their previous reports, does nothing to change this fact."

COMPREHENSION TEST

T or F, as before.

_____ Only a handful of men were tested.

_____ Cigarette smokers rank as high possibilities among lung- and throat-cancer victims.

_____ The death rates from lung cancer were at least 10 times higher for cigarette smokers than for non-smokers.

_____ Giving up smoking made no difference.

_____ Cigar and pipe smoking do not decrease life expectancy.

ANSWERS: F, T, T, F, F.

Some magazines, like _Coronet,_ from which the next article has been selected, print their material in adjoining vertical columns on each page. Read _down each column_ without any left-to-right eye movements. Remember, don't attempt this exercise until you are reasonably sure that you will be able to handle _a line at a glance_. You will recognize the contents as the continuation of the interesting story about crabs that you encountered in Chapter III. DOWN THE MIDDLE! NO LATERAL EYE MOVEMENTS! NO REGRESSIONS!

Popular view pictures the crab as well-armored and with dangerous claws. Yet many of the some 1,000 different kinds are small, weak and forced to depend on their wits to keep alive.

A crafty crab which inhabits tropical waters is a master at disguise. Look right at him, but you won't see him. What you will see is just what hungry marine predators see—a sponge. For this amazing crab has neatly camouflaged himself with a sponge cut exactly to size.

One of the most humorous sights in nature is to watch this so-called sponge crab deftly seize a sponge with his claws, clap it onto his back and shift it around until he has it in what he considers the best position. One naturalist described the process as startlingly like a woman trying on a new hat.

Once the crab has placed the sponge just so, he briskly snips around the edges with his sharp pincers until not an inch of him remains uncovered, nor is there any surplus sponge extending beyond his shell. How does he have sense enough to use one or more sponges to conceal himself, and to cut same to right size? Just another example of the crab's amazing adaptability is about all naturalists can say.

The fiddler crab has his own fantastic way of discomfiting an enemy. Watch a fiddler being worried by a dog. Suddenly

112

the crab clamps his larger, pincer-like claw on the dog's nose. The dog howls with pain.

While he is fighting to loosen the pincer, something astonishing happens. The dog jerks away from the crab, but is left struggling to free himself from the tormenting pincer, which is, incredibly, no longer part of the crab.

The crab has quickly and easily lost his claw. Odder still, nature has endowed the fiddler with the capacity to grow a new claw.

By human standards, the crab's locomotion may often seem ludicrous. But there are kinds that get around with astonishing speed and agility. In some, the well-known crab walk is occasioned by a slight mix-up in leg operation. The ordinary crab, for instance, moves sideways. While his four legs on one side are pushing, those on the other side are pulling.

Some crabs do not really swim, but walk sedately along the sea floor, as though they were on land. They are equipped with gills.

Gordon Hunter, of the University of Texas' Institute of Marine Science, observed a blue crab swimming past the dock, when suddenly a fish darted at it. The fish was a sheepshead, a fast-maneuvering predator, which seemingly should have made a quick mouthful of the crab. But when the fish's jaws snapped shut, the crab wasn't there.

The fish turned, and caught sight of the crab, who had taken refuge exactly above the fish's tail fin where it would be impossible for the sheepshead's mouth to reach it. The fish seemed to spin through the water, but the crab persistently kept its position directly above the fish's tail.

The fish swam in a tight circle, then tried wild acrobatics, including quick figure eights. Still the crab swam calmly in the same safe spot. Finally the fish gave up.

COMPREHENSION TEST

If you were able to do this exercise according to instructions, you will observe, by answering the questions below, that you derived more than enough of the details to give you a good understanding of the article, despite your great speed.

Write T (true) or F (false) in the spaces next to each statement.

_____ All crabs are well armed with large claws.

_____ Some species pretend to be what they are not.

_____ A crab may lose its claw and grow another.

_____ All crabs move extremely slowly.

_____ The blue crab is capable of outmaneuvering a fast fish.

ANSWERS: F, T, T, F, T.

❋   ❋   ❋

There you have it—your training program for stretching your recognition span. Doubtless you will have no trouble devising additional exercises. Perhaps what will be most beneficial to you will be the awareness that words must be read in groups for maximum speed and comprehension. *Knowing what you should do*, at least in so far as reading is concerned, is often the first giant step toward *doing what you should!*

CHAPTER VII

STEP THREE:

Shift into High!

RECORDS ARE MADE to be broken.

Man is constantly proving this statement to be true, and sports provide us with rich evidence. Before Johnny Weissmuller became a movie Tarzan, he was recognized as the world's fastest swimmer. And yet, most of his speed records have long since been broken. In the thirties Glenn Cunningham's flashing feet helped make the mile run the most exciting event in track and field. Any time he broke the tape in less than 4 minutes and 10 seconds, it was considered remarkable. However, since Roger Bannister of England ran the "miracle mile" in 1954, more than two dozen others have run the distance in the formerly impossible time of less than 4 minutes. And so it goes. Sprinters, pole vaulters, and weight throwers are continually running faster, leaping higher, and hurling objects farther than any before them have done.

Many theories are advanced for the short life of a record. Some say our diets are better and we are healthier generally; we break records because we have more energy and stamina. Others suggest that skills and techniques become refined with the aid of science, making us perform better and more efficiently. Perhaps the best reason for our steady improvement is that we have come to believe an expression that became popular during the Second World War:

"The impossible we do today; the difficult we leave for tomorrow."

It all adds up to the breaking of psychological blocks. Numerous experiments have shown that we tend to operate at considerably less than our full capacity. We stop at a certain point not because we can't go on but because we have talked ourselves into the belief that we have reached our limit. Whether it's in sports, aviation, automobiles, or something else, the experts will periodically raise their heads and shout, "That's about as fast as it is humanly possible to go." For a while most of us accept their verdict.

Then one person tells himself that this isn't the best that can be done. Once he has overcome the mental barrier, he proceeds to push his abilities to prove that he can do better. Before long many others brush aside their own blocks and follow suit. The impossible becomes the usual!

There is a good lesson here for you and your reading problems. You are dissatisfied with your speed and comprehension, but perhaps you, too, have convinced yourself that it's the best you can do. Even as you were learning how to eliminate roadblocks and stretch your recognition span, you may have been unable to overcome the feeling that the suggestions were not going to help very much. Past experiences have not offered you much encouragement.

If this is so, you must overcome your personal psychological block. Convince yourself that you *can* read faster, break your present record of *words per minute*, and having done it once, keep on breaking it. Only then will tomorrow's record become today's normal rate.

Let's say that right now you read about 150 to 200 words per minute. This has been your rate for years. You've never seriously tried to go faster. You've told yourself that stepping up your pace will only get you confused. Or you've been satisfied to offer yourself what seemed like a reasonable excuse. You wanted to increase your rate but didn't exactly know how. Well, now you do. The only thing that can hold you back hereafter is your own failure to exert the extra effort required to break an old habit and establish a new one. You must start doing the impossible every day and stop thinking about the difficult. YOU MUST PUSH YOURSELF!

It's possible that you have already given yourself a sample of what you can do under pressure. In one of the diagnostic tests you took in Chapter III, you were asked to force yourself to read faster than you normally do. You probably were able to increase your rate at least a little bit simply by concentrating on speed. Our objective in this chapter is to show you how to set up the third phase of your daily program. You will spend a few minutes each day pushing yourself to read a trifle faster than you did the day before. Once you have established in your mind that you *can* do it, you will have gotten over the mental barrier. Doubling your present reading rate, at the very least, will then be a matter of a relatively short time.

Lest you get the impression that I am suggesting that you train yourself to read under a constant strain, let's look into the problem a bit further. As was said, most people use only a fraction of their maximum abilities. Thus our purpose in asking you to push yourself is to get you to the point in your reading skill where you are working at 100 per cent of your capacity. During your early practice sessions it will be quite a challenge to you to keep hustling along beyond what was formerly a comfortable, easy pace. But in the long run you will not be trying to do more than you can. You will be encouraging your "reading muscles" to function at their best. Once they have become accustomed to full output, they will fall into a pattern of operation that will be just as comfortable for you as your present one now is. The strain will disappear. What will remain is a remarkably accelerated normal reading rate.

I can almost hear you asking this question:

"You mean that I will eventually be able to read anything at all at a speed of 350 words per minute or better?"

No, I certainly do not mean this. Sheer speed in itself, without increased comprehension, is worthless. We decidedly do not want you to race across a page and then wonder what the author was talking about. It is still true that faster reading is usually accompanied by better understanding. But this fact does not imply that you will be able or will want to read all material at the same rate. You will have to learn to operate pretty much like a car equipped with standard shifting gears. Sometimes, in rough going, you will proceed in first; at other times, in second; and when you are out for a pleasure drive, you will use third gear, or even overdrive!

The student, scientist, engineer, or doctor who is reading highly technical material must place comprehension first. He should read only as fast as he can while readily absorbing the ideas or data. If 200 words per minute seems just right, that should be it. There should be no pushing under these circumstances. But as your normal reading speed improves, you will be surprised later on, however, when you find yourself confronted with complicated reading matter, to find that even then you will make slight increases in the rate at which you read.

A second kind of material that you should read at whatever rate is consistent with complete understanding is a book, article, or report that presents controversial ideas or seriously examines a topic in a scholarly or analytical way. You won't want to hurry past the author's conclusions. Moreover, he may write in so concentrated
118

a style that every sentence gives much food for thought. Take your time. Get his point. You can go faster than with technical material, but not at your maximum rate. Here is a good example of an article, which you might find in a newspaper, that you should read carefully if you are interested at all. About 300 words per minute would be fast enough.

How Much for a Home?

BY WALTER H. STERN

How much of its income can a family afford to spend on a home?

Experts in the field say there is no single answer to the question. But there are several guiding principles that enable a prospective buyer to stay within his means and at the same time obtain the maximum his income entitles him to enjoy.

Generally speaking, a family's means can be determined from its annual income. Real estate brokers, mortgage lending institutions and Government housing agencies calculate that, under normal circumstances, a family can buy a home that costs about two and one-half times its annual income.

This figure, however, may be deceptive unless it is considered in the light of individual cases. For some families, three times the annual income is not an unreasonable obligation to be assumed. In other instances, how-ever, even the lower figure represents a serious risk. This arises when other large expenditures loom, such as known medical outlays that will continue for a long time, or a plan by the head of the family to enter a new business that may not earn a profit at the start.

The second consideration is that of the mortgage financing. This is tied directly to the question of a down payment, a figure that many prospective buyers seem to determine from the amount of ready cash they have at their disposal. This, however, should not be the sole guide. It is considered unwise for a family to strip its savings completely to make a large down payment.

Observers in the housing field feel that the mortgage should not exceed twice the family's annual income.

A family with an income of $8,000 a year, according to this

rule of thumb, can spend about $20,000 for its house and may, under favorable conditions, go to $22,000 or $24,000. The maximum mortgage it should obtain is one of $16,000. This is exactly what a conservative lending institution would extend anyway, unless, of course, the loan were backed by the Government, through the Veterans Administration or Federal Housing Administration. A V.A. or F.H.A. mortgage can be a larger percentage of the total price, but only because a portion of it is backed by the Government.

It is difficult to pinpoint the relationship of a family's income to the purchase price because in some cases the price may be different from the ultimate value. There are many extras, not represented in the price tag of a dwelling, which must be paid for by the buyer sooner or later if he is to own a completely usable residence.

If it is a new home bought from a developer, there usually follows the acquisition of storm windows, screens and appliances, additional landscaping and other items.

On the other hand, while a second-hand home may be fully equipped with screens, storm windows, appliances and landscaping, other incidentals may arise in the immediate future. Foremost among these are repairs to heating and plumbing installations and the roof. To ignore these items when calculating the purchase price is considered unrealistic, because they are essentials to normal enjoyment of the property.

With regard to monthly carrying charges, it must be remembered by prospective purchasers of suburban homes that commuting costs, where they are necessary, are part of the regular house budget. If a family head bases his ability to buy a house in the suburbs on the income he makes in the city, he must realize that, were he to discontinue paying for transportation, he would lose his income as surely as he would lose the house if he failed to pay his taxes.

On the whole, various formulas are applied by lenders and Government agencies alone or in combination. While none of them appears to be entirely foolproof, they have considerable value as guideposts. This is borne out by the fact that the rate of mortgage delinquency at the end of 1956 was only 2.27 per cent, according to a survey by the Mortgage Bankers Association of America.

Editorials, professional-advice articles, and most non-fiction books should also be given a little more reading time so that important ideas are not overlooked. About 350 words per minute should do nicely, after your top speed has gone beyond this point. Mind you, the suggested numbers of words per minute are very rough estimates. They serve mainly to indicate relative speed. In any of the categories just discussed, if you find that you must go more slowly or can go faster than recommended, let your *degree of understanding* be your guide. The following two selections are examples of articles that can be handled at a speed of slightly less than a page a minute, assuming that the average page has 350 to 400 words. This applies to a book of usual size and set in standard type. Magazine and newspaper articles, such as those below, offer variations in length, but can be measured in terms of words per minute.

Our Children

BY ANGELO PATRI

Schools will close and vacation days will be upon us before we are ready for them if we are not thinking and planning for them beforehand. For ten months the children have been following a routine five days a week. All at once the routine is broken. It does not matter if a child sleeps late. He has no duty pressing upon him. He is free.

For a long time he has been looking forward to this freedom, and here it is and here he is with nothing to do and nowhere to go. He does not feel well. His body resents the new order. So does his mind. He begins to worry his mother with "What can I do? Where can I go? Can I go?" until she is wishing that school kept going the year round.

Yet children need this break from the routine of lessons. But they also need the support of a planned day, and this is what the mother and father of the vacationing children must consider now, well ahead of time. What are they to do? Where are they to go? How can they be kept busy and happy?

121

Of course, there are as many ways as there are homes and children. Summer school is the first thought of busy mothers, yet it is not always the best one for the individual child. If he elects to go to summer school, well and good. But if he has had poor marks, say in arithmetic, and the idea is that he attend summer school to "make up," I vote against it. Imagine how you would feel if you were told you had to work day after day at the one job you did not do well.

My experience has indicated that when the child is a healthy, normal one, he failed a subject usually because he was not ready for it; and drilling him only made a bad matter worse. Given a rest, time to prepare himself by growth and development processes, he will go ahead all right. I never have found persistent drill helped a failing pupil.

When summer school is not the answer, what then? Plan a home chore for the first thing in the morning—one for each child—and make sure they do it. Arrange, in consultation with them, a plan for work and play so that they can look forward to a busy and enjoyable vacation time. Organize a group, a club, accent the Scout and Campfire groups, plan a play for a benefit, a trip, a visit, maybe a light job for one of the eager-to-earn children. Look into what the church offers. What about museums and places of interest in your area? Books to be read? Painting? Modeling a building project, like a fireplace for outdoors, a boat, a birdhouse? The things daily living offers? Maybe a job suited to the adolescent's needs?

Vacation time must not be an empty time. It is a fine time for growth.

New Weapons Against Heart Disease

BY FRANCIS AND KATHARINE DRAKE

An energetic 64-year-old executive arose one autumn morning in 1955 with a sense of exceptional well-being. He tackled breakfast with the gusto of a man who has a first-rate medical report just behind him and days of vacation unfolding ahead. A picture of health as he strode out to join his companions, nobody would have predicted that the next day would find him fighting for life inside an oxygen tent, while a stunned nation united in prayer for his recovery. Nor would anyone have predicted that, because our Number One killer, heart disease, had felled our Number One citizen, the grim experience would eventually emerge as a blessing, not only for him, but for millions of his countrymen. Yet such has been the case, for three outstanding reasons:

First, the warning did more than save President Eisenhower's life. It demonstrated that a coronary victim need not be doomed to invalidism. The dean of American heart specialists, Dr. Paul Dudley White, cleared the President for the rigors of an election campaign and four more years of the world's most demanding job.

Second, it focused attention on the awful toll taken by heart disease. The day the President was stricken, some 1000 of his fellow Americans died as a result of coronary attacks. This happens every day of the year.

Third, it sparked a tremendous increase in research which in turn exploded a whole series of public fallacies: that coronaries are unavoidable; that they victimize only older people; that they are brought on only by exertion; and most fallacious, that they always strike unpredictably, like bolts from the blue.

Latest research findings show that coronary disease, far from being sudden, builds up through the years and explodes in youth as well as in age, in bed as well as on the golf course or the snow-piled sidewalk. It may take decades to develop to the danger point—decades during which doctors and patients alike now have an improved chance to arrest it. This improved chance does not depend on miracle drugs, trick surgery, impossible food fads or treatments available only to the rich. It depends on methods of detection and treatment available to doctors and hospitals everywhere.

First of all, medical science has now put into the hands of doctors a new tool which can be helpful in many cases: the analysis of bloodfat. It was long known that fat in general had a damaging effect, but until recently the damage was thought to come mainly from the strain imposed on the heart by overweight. This, it transpires, is only a part of the story. The large amounts of fat which accumulate on the *outside* of the circulatory system—on stomachs, shoulders, hips—are less critical than the tiny amounts deposited on the *inside* of arteries.

Now, what about the reading that you do for fun, for relaxation—those pleasure trips you take through the sports, fashions, entertainment, or general-news sections of a newspaper; the light-fiction or novelty articles of magazines; or the detective stories that are so popular? If you are like most of us, these are the materials that get your day-to-day interest. And it is here that you must begin to push yourself. Almost at once you can increase your rate in recreational reading by 20 per cent. Eventually you should be able to cruise along at 400 to 500 words per minute. With the skill and confidence you will gradually acquire, you should then go on to those novels, short stories, plays, and other literary products you have been promising yourself you will one day read. "If I only had the time!" you've said again and again. Well, if you can train yourself to cover twice as many words per minute as you once did, *you won't even need extra time* to read more.

In order to maintain a consistent program of practice in pushing yourself, you will need a notebook. Set up a chart thus:

Date	Name of article, book, etc.	*W/P/M-Normal	W/P/M-Pushing

*Words Per Minute

Before I outline how you are to make the entries and what your daily practice sessions should consist of, I want you to be able to estimate your reading rate at any time, regardless of the nature of the material. We will use the article below to illustrate how to do the necessary arithmetic. Get a watch so that you can time yourself. When the second hand is approaching the "12" on the face of the watch, begin reading. Proceed at your normal rate. Don't try to push. When you have finished the piece, jot down the total number of seconds it took.

Jai Alai . . .

THERE are very few jai alai players in the world. You can understand why, when you witness this lethal game—when you learn that in one month of play at one court in New York 23 players were injured—some requiring major surgery.

There are thousands of fanatic followers of this flamboyant sport, which may have originated with the Aztecs six centuries ago—but which, in its modern form, is generally credited to origin in the Basque mountains where, the old pros claim, the best equipment is still made.

Like the flavor of Basque olives, jai alai is difficult to capture in words—it's a subtle blend of anything but subtle action sports. It's played in a stadium known as a *fronton*, which has a court about half the size of a football gridiron. It's a ball game—and the ball's as hard as a bullet. This goatskin-covered missile is hurled and retrieved with a reed basket, in a game that's a combination of lacrosse, tennis and handball. The ball travels so fast you can barely see it—and the players contort themselves into bizarre attitudes in lunges that bring them

125

crashing down on the concrete floor, for an immediate recoil to return the jet-propelled rock. This is the fantastic game of jai alai.

Like tennis, it is played in singles or doubles competition, in a court or *concha;* like handball, it is played with a hard rubber ball or *pelota;* like lacrosse, the ball is propelled with a reinforced scoop-shaped racquet, or *cesta.*

Jai alai was introduced to the United States in 1904 at the St. Louis World's Fair. Since then it has been publicly played in New York, New Orleans, Chicago and Miami. It's in Florida, where betting is legal, that turnstiles hum today. Between the first of the year and April 10, the season at three new frontons is at the high peak of excitement.

If your travels take you to Florida—you must see jai alai. It's an unforgettable experience.

*　　　　*　　　　*

Now for the arithmetic:

1. Return to the article and count the total number of words in the first 3 lines. Your total is 31.

2. Divide 31 by 3 (number of lines), and you get approximately 10 (average number of words per line).

3. Now count the lines in the article. You get 37.

4. 37 (number of lines) multiplied by 10 (words per line) equals 370 (total number of words in the article).

5. Let's say it took you 70 seconds to complete your reading. 370 divided by 70 would give you an average of 5.3 words read per second.

6. 5.3 multiplied by 60 (number of seconds in a minute) comes out to 318 words per minute.

Don't allow the number of steps in the arithmetic process to persuade you it is complicated. The whole thing amounts to little more than finding out how many words there are in the selection, dividing by the total seconds it took you to read it, and then multiplying by 60 to determine the words-per-minute rate.

Now that you know how to work out your reading speed, we can get back to the chart. The date entry is to help you determine how long it took you to make a significant advance. The name of the article or selection will gradually give you a cross-section of the kind of material you prefer to read. This knowledge may suggest to you that you ought to try something different as a change of pace and interest.

The entries in the last two columns will not be valid unless, when you set up your practice sessions in pushing, you make certain that you use material of similar difficulty and appeal on each occasion. The best way to avoid the possibility that you may read one piece faster than another because it is easier or more interesting and not because you are pushing is to take a selection that contains at least 1,000 words. Divide it into two equal parts. Then you can read the first half at your normal rate and the second half under the speed pressure. And you will know that the material was of equal quality.

To illustrate the general technique, we'll turn to two paragraphs from the opening chapter of *A Tale of Two Cities*, by Charles Dickens. There is, incidentally, a general point that can be made here and that should apply to all your reading in fiction. When you come across descriptive passages that are designed to give you the background of the story or a certain atmosphere, there is no reason to drag along the lines. The color and setting will come through much more clearly if you read briskly than if you insist on studying every last detail.

We'll get back to this problem when we talk about skimming.

Both paragraphs are of equal length. Read the first one at your normal rate. No pushing—no straining. Don't forget to time yourself! When you have finished, make the entries in your notebook: the date, the name of the book, and your rate in words per minute.

NORMAL RATE

France, less favored on the whole as to matters spiritual than her sister of the shield and trident, rolled with exceeding smoothness downhill, making paper money and spending it. She entertained herself, besides, with such humane achievements as sentencing a youth to have his hands cut off, his tongue torn out with pincers, and his body burned alive, because he had not kneeled down in the rain to do honor to a dirty procession of monks which passed within his view, at a distance of some fifty or sixty yards. It is likely enough that, rooted in the woods of France and Norway, there were growing trees, when that sufferer was put to death, already marked by the Woodman, Fate, to come down and be sawn into boards, to make a certain movable framework with a sack and a knife in it, terrible in history. It is likely enough that in the rough outhouses of some tillers of the heavy lands adjacent to Paris, there were sheltered from the weather that very day, rude carts, bespattered with rustic mire, snuffed about by pigs, and roosted in by poultry, which the Farmer, Death, had already set apart to be his tumbrils of the Revolution. But that Woodman and that Farmer, though they work unceasingly, work silently, and no one heard them as they went about with muffled tread: the rather, forasmuch as to entertain any suspicion that they were awake, was to be atheistical and traitorous.

You count the words in the first 3 lines and divide by 3 to get your average words per line. Multiply this result by the number of lines in the passage. Do it now, before you read the next sentence in this paragraph. Your result should be approximately 220 words in all. Finally, work out the words per second and then multiply by 60 to get the words per minute. Make the notebook entry.

Now we're ready for the pushing exercise. Forget about eliminating roadblocks or stretching your recognition span when you do the forced-speed drill. We don't want anything to interfere with your concentration on reading as fast as you can. Besides, if you do make the conscious effort to move right along, you won't have time for roadblocks and you will be indirectly giving yourself the finest possible training in increasing your recognition span. Get ready to time yourself. If it took you almost a minute to read the first paragraph, make up your mind to do this one in less than 50 seconds. There will be a brief comprehension test at the end to enable you to prove to yourself that you got the important ideas in both selections, even though you were straining for speed in the second.

REMEMBER:

You don't have to look at every word!

You don't have to study every detail!

All you want to know is what England was like in those days!

SPEED!   SPEED!   SPEED!

PUSH YOURSELF!

In England, there was scarcely an amount of order and protection to justify much national boasting. Daring burglaries by armed men, and highway robberies, took place in the capital itself every night; families were publicly cautioned not to go out of town without removing their furniture to upholsterers' warehouses of security; the highwayman in the dark was a City tradesman in the light, and, being recognized and challenged by his fellow-tradesman whom he stopped in his character of 'the Captain,' gallantly shot him through the head and rode away; the mail was waylaid by seven robbers, and the guard shot three dead, and then got shot dead himself by the other four, 'in consequence of the failure of his ammunition'; after which the mail was robbed in peace; that magnificent potentate, the Lord Mayor of London, was made to stand and deliver on Turnham Green, by one highwayman, who despoiled the illustrious creature in sight of all his retinue; prisoners in London gaols fought battles with their turnkeys, and the majesty of the law fired blunderbusses in among them, loaded with rounds of shot and ball; thieves snipped off diamond crosses from the necks of noble lords at Court drawing-rooms; musketeers went into St. Giles's, to search for contraband goods, and the mob fired on the musketeers, and the musketeers fired on the mob, and nobody thought any of these occurrences much out of the common way.

*　　　*　　　*

Do your words-per-minute calculations now and make the entries in your notebook. If you really pushed all the way, there should have been a significant increase. And to check your comprehension, here is the test.

COMPREHENSION TEST

From the five statements below, select the two that most accurately cover the *main ideas* in each paragraph.

_____ 1. A man in France had his tongue cut out.

_____ 2. There was much lawlessness in England.

_____ 3. The Mayor of London was robbed.

_____ 4. Abuses in France were already sowing the seeds of rebellion.

_____ 5. Tradesmen were frequently thieves at night.

ANSWERS: The correct ones are *not* one, three, and five.

I shall now give you three more sets of exercises so that you can become thoroughly familiar with the techniques you are to use in setting up your daily practice sessions in pushing your reading rate. For a while, when you force yourself to read faster, you will continue to feel uncomfortable and will have doubts about your comprehension. If you are persistent, however, you will weather this trial period and will gradually become more and more confident. When *both* of the last two columns in your chart show steady increases, you will know that you are making real progress.

With each of the sets below:

1. Read the first part at your regular rate.
2. Work out your words-per-minute speed.
3. Make the notebook entries.
4. Read the second part at your pushing rate.
5. Again make your entries for words per minute.
6. Check your comprehension with the test that follows the second part in each set.

Slow, Slow—Quick, Quick

BY GEORGE DUKE

[*Normal Speed*]

"When we get to Florida, we don't want to make fools of ourselves . . . so we've hired a private dancing instructor!" This female proclamation unraveled to mean that our group would be a bunch of clods if we couldn't cha-cha-cha, fandango, tarantella and rock 'n' roll like seasoned Murrays. To remedy this fate, a Mr. Peter Patter would bring his practice records and powdered floor wax to one of our homes twice weekly until we left for our vacation, a slickly trained troupe of dancing fools.

The first lesson began with Mr. Patter observing, while we self-consciously dipped and circled about him. I was sure he was deciding he might as well pack up his sapphire needle and patent leather pumps and leave after seeing our polished 1939 junior prom style, when he said: "I can see it will be some time before we get to those cha-cha-chas you talked about. Tonight we'll concentrate on the basic box step." Someone courageously explained that we knew all about those simple basics, having all attended Miss Simpkin's Fortnightly Dancing School years ago . . . "so let's go on, unless we're too advanced for Mr. Patter?"

The third lesson—after we had learned that dancers should glide from the hips, lead with the upper body, do the box step in right angles—we were introduced to the rhumba. "Now we're getting somewhere," I said, with my usual gift for turning a brilliant and apt phrase.

Where I got, unfortunately, was on the basement stairs. This may not seem odd to you, until I tell why I was there. The rhumba, Mr. Patter explained, has a charming hip rhythm, accomplished by throwing one's hips opposite to the natural way they move when one places one's weight on one's legs. For example, rhumba hips go the way hips go when one walks up stairs.

The women caught on, and were jiggling around the floor with South American abandon in no time. One of the husbands (a salesman who takes a lot of out-of-town business trips) smugly whipped his derrière around with gelatinous authority. The rest of us burned—then all were relieved, except me.

"Mr. Duke," Mr. Patter said, as he undulated my way, "you just don't seem to be applying yourself. Here, try it with me." Clenching my teeth, I shifted my sacrum with determined vigor. "No, no, no, Mr. Duke . . . you're placing the weight on the wrong foot!" He didn't mean his, although at the moment I wished he did; he meant that my hips refused to behave abnormally, as required by his Cugat record. So—I was assigned the basement stairs, where I soon learned to rhumba with proper grace. In fact, Mr. Patter had the class gather around and admire my rhythmic motion, as I plunged up and down the steps.

Our last class was tonight. We've all packed our cars, so we can get an early start for Florida in the morning. Although we never got to the cha-cha-cha, we've mastered the rhumba. I'm looking forward to discovering an authentic Latin-American nightspot, where I can show off my rhumba motion—provided, of course,

there is a stairway near the bongos, and I can find a
partner who can follow my escalator style.

COMPREHENSION TEST

Select the two statements that most accurately cover the
main ideas in each part.

_____ 1. According to Mr. Patter, the couples didn't
dance correctly.

_____ 2. Some vacationing couples hired a very strict
instructor to teach them the latest steps.

_____ 3. Mr. Patter wore patent leather pumps.

_____ 4. The author found he could dance best on the
basement stairs.

_____ 5. Mr. Duke didn't make very much progress
with his lessons.

ANSWERS: One, three, and four are *not* correct.

SET II

Sticker Styles

BY OSCAR GODBOUT

[*Normal Speed*]

It is becoming increasingly apparent that more and
more of the nation's automobiles are being used as
mobile bulletin boards for humorous, opinionative communications. In Los Angeles, where the car is regarded
with the same fondness accorded Mom, apple pie and the
Flag, neatly printed little proclamations are blooming
like crocuses in spring. The fashion seems to date from
134

a few years back when autos assembled somewhere in the Southwest were exported with stickers reading, "Made in Texas by Texans." Here are some variations on the theme:

The German-made Volkswagen, which seems to multiply with astonishing rapidity, is a favorite vehicle for messages. Frequently adorning the little cars is a sticker reading, "Made in the Black Forest by Elves." Then another comes along declaring: "Made in Pasadena by Little Old Ladies."

The television commercials that conclude with "It's a Ford" were the obvious basis for this statement printed in fine old Gothic lettering across the back of a diminutive Volkswagen bus: "Ist Ein Fooooooord!"

Regarding the Volkswagen, the ultimate seems to have been reached by a mechanically inclined owner with a sense of humor. From the rear of his tiny auto protrudes a meticulously fashioned windup key built in scale with the rest of the machine. Scooting down the Hollywood Freeway it looks for all the world like an outsized toy that got loose to go until its motor runs down.

[*Pushing Speed*]

The not completely subtle comment on a stifling local phenomenon, air pollution, was documented when a large domestic vehicle replete with fins roared by bearing the legend, "Made in the Smog by the Blind." A second variation: "I'm Doing My Bit to Make Smog. How About You?"

A thoroughly disreputable "bucket of bolts" that looked as though it had survived bomb tests at Yucca Flats was seen flaunting this neatly printed inscription: "Made in Africa by Apes."

135

While Los Angeles is the hottest sports-car town in the country there are some who regard the trend with misgivings. A stately new Cadillac was recently spotted humming through Beverly Hills, its rear window adorned with a sticker reading, "Help Stamp Out Sports Cars." And politics, naturally, intrude. During the last elections when the town—and its cars—were plastered with a wide variety of exhortations to vote "Yes" on this local proposition and "No" on that, one driver must have become weary of all the political importuning. The brightly colored sign on his car read, "Vote Yes on No!"

Of course, the situation threatens to get completely out of control. This observer, who thought himself hardened to almost everything, suffered a slight case of shock when he spied a prim, white-haired old lady of 80 or so popping down Sunset Boulevard in a well-kept Model A Ford. The sticker on the windshield read, "I M 4 L V S 2" —or, translated, "I'm for Elvis, Too."

COMPREHENSION TEST

This time write T (true) or F (false) next to each statement below.

_____ 1. Pasting stickers on cars is very popular in California.

_____ 2. Not many people on the West Coast like the Volkswagen.

_____ 3. Even dignified cars and people seem to go in for stickers.

_____ 4. Politics are rarely the subject for stickers.

_____ 5. Some car owners have a sense of humor.

ANSWERS: All but two and four are true.

120—And Like It!

BY JACK MABLEY

[Normal Speed]

Anybody can have a good time out on the golf course when he shoots 75 or 80. It takes a golfer of character, a person with nerves of steel and the determination of a lion to shoot 120 and walk off the 18th green with a smile.

120—and like it? Well, we don't like the 120, but we do like golf. The trick is to be serious about the game—but not too serious. You never stop trying to better your score, but you don't live and die with every shot.

YOUR EQUIPMENT: Your game is only as good as your clubs. My equipment helps explain my score. It is Alex Gilchrist unmatched with Thistle putter—two woods, and irons number 2, 4, 6, and 8, or maybe it's 9. The number is worn off. Most of these clubs are survivors of a set I bought in 1927 for $5.98 with bag and a box of sand for teeing up the ball. I shot a 47 for nine holes with these clubs in 1934, and if I could do it then I can do it again with the same tools. Or can I?

WATER HOLES: Always use ten-cent repainted balls at water holes. Only new and expensive balls go into the water. (A water hole is no place for character, nerves of steel, or the determination of a lion. Let's be practical about this thing.)

YOUR SLICE: There are two approaches to curing a slice. The Pros' way—push your right thumb around to the left side of your driver. For this lesson they charge you five bucks. The Lousy Golf way—face the cows over in the field to your left, hit the ball at an angle 45 degrees to the left of the hole, and if your slice is properly trained it will come to rest right in line with the hole.

Left-handed golfers reverse everything. When you're facing south, and the ball curves west, do you call it a hook or a slice?

[*Pushing Speed*]

CADDY CARS: If you like swimming in your overshoes you'll love these little electric carts that haul you around the golf course. They have some advantages over boy caddies—they don't snicker when you drive and they can't count your strokes when you're trying to pick up a little lost ground. They don't complain, either. But they eliminate the exercise, and if a 120-golfer isn't out there for the exercise I don't know what he IS seeking.

FRINGE BENEFITS: The Lousy Golfer has advantages in golfing that the expert never dreams of. In what other sport can you get the equivalent of a college education? The 120-golfer gets laboratory sessions in higher mathematics, nature study, physical culture, psychology, and debating.

CHEAT? Never. Obey every rule, every regulation, every local variation down to the last letter and comma and period. Avoid such dodges as "winter rules." Never concede a putt to yourself. Shoot from the meanest gopher hole even if you have to dig your way in with a 9-iron. Cheating—or shall we charitably call it a casual approach to the rules—is for the 70 and 80 shooters. Also we lose part of our alibi if we don't adhere strictly to the rule book.

THE FUTURE: Here is the most glorious part of Lousy Golf. What has the expert got to look forward to?

Where is the 68 shooter going? 67? Ha. The low-handicap player shoots a 74 or 72 and he's had it, he's shot his wad. He has nothing to look forward to but memories.

If he shoots 90 or 100, he's ready for the knife. If WE shoot 100 it calls for a celebration.

The experts have nowhere to go but down. We can only go up. Aren't we the smart ones?

COMPREHENSION TEST

Select one out of each of the sets of three statements that refers to the main idea in each part.

PART I

_____ 1. Repainted balls should be used at water holes.

_____ 2. Left-handed golfers should reverse everything.

_____ 3. Inferior golfers can have fun even with poor equipment and skill.

PART II

_____ 1. A caddy car is very useful.

_____ 2. The poor golfer has the advantage of a good incentive always before him, so he can disdain mechanical equipment and cheating.

_____ 3. A poor golfer can get the equivalent of a college education.

ANSWERS: The correct choices are number two in the second part and number three in the first part.

Although we are coming to the end of this chapter, you understand, of course, that your pushing practice has only just begun. You now know how to force yourself to lift your normal reading rate to your maximum reading capacities. Success will not come in a matter of days or a few weeks. You are in the process of breaking a lifelong habit and you must be patient. But steady, dogged practice will bring noticeable results almost every day. And in 3 or 4 months you won't have to push any more. You will have broken through your speed barrier.

So spend the suggested 3 minutes daily on a selection you take from a newspaper, magazine, or book. Divide the piece into approximately equal parts and proceed with your normal-rate and pushing-rate drills. In each instance, a good way to check your comprehension is to set up a test similar to the ones you have been taking. Preparing an examination is practically as good a review as taking one. And don't forget your notebook!

One final caution: don't expect to continue to increase your rate indefinitely. How far you will go depends upon your basic capacities. Experiments have shown that, with proper practice, almost everyone can make a 20 to 50 per cent improvement in reading speed. However, for some people this will mean a jump from 150–200 words per minute to 180–300 words per minute. And for them it will represent fine progress indeed. Others may eventually manage 400 to 500 words per minute without straining.

You will know when you have reached your top level by the amount of rate increase continued practice brings. Your best indication will be the results of the last two columns in your daily speed chart. If over a period of weeks, the normal and pushing rates show little difference, you will be able to assume that you are approaching your full capacity. At this time you should take a vacation of a week or so from your speed training. Then resume your exercises. Watch the column results again. Check to see whether you haven't gone back to some old bad habit that you thought you had eliminated. If after all this there is still no progress, you can rest on your laurels. An occasional practice session will enable you to maintain your newly developed reading rate.

CHAPTER VIII

STEP FOUR:

Look for the Keys!

ALL RIGHT.
  Let's take stock again.
  What have you learned so far?

About Reading Improvement Generally

1. By practicing faithfully, you can *help yourself* improve your reading ability.
2. You get best results from short practice sessions on a daily basis.
3. To retain your new skills, you should apply them frequently to normal reading situations.

About Reading Rate

1. You must eliminate all self-imposed obstacles to rapid reading.
2. You should aim to read 100 per cent as fast as you can.
3. By forcing yourself for a while, you can substantially increase your normal reading rate.

About Rate and Comprehension

1. When you read faster, you usually understand better.
2. You need not look at every letter of every word in order to absorb the sense of a group of words.

3. Reading words in groups is essential to improving your rate and comprehension.

4. The difficulty of a selection should determine your rate. You should not read all material at the same rate.

Our summary reveals that the emphasis up to this point has been on speed. However, following most practice selections you were given a test in comprehension. There was good reason for this, as you were repeatedly told. Unless faster reading is accompanied by better understanding, you derive little benefit from your training program. Progress in rate and comprehension cannot be separated. Each is very much dependent on the other. Admittedly we treat these two abilities in separate chapters. But we do so because we are attempting to break down the basic reading skills and fit them into our 5-Step Plan.

Now, as we shift the emphasis to comprehension, you must not assume that we are finished with rate. In reality, we are approaching it from another direction. Improvement in comprehension will inevitably lead to a faster rate.

A reading authority recently said:

"A special fire is kindled when the reader and writer meet."

This is a beautiful description of the remarkable thing that happens after one person puts words on paper and another is thus enabled to obtain an intimate glimpse into the operation of a human mind. Of course, no one can expect to uncover the complete picture of the mental processes and emotional reactions that went into the writing. But the "special fire" surely burns brighter when the writer has found the best possible words and the reader brings to them his maximum appreciation and understanding.

There are many sides to the problem of comprehension. One of the difficulties is that your degree of understanding of a given passage cannot be measured as exactly as can your speed of reading it. Your rate can be timed and we can express your results in terms of words per minute. But even if we ask a few content questions after you have read a selection and you answer them all correctly, have we really proved that you and the writer had a mutual exchange? Besides knowing *what* he said, have you understood *why* he wrote what he did? Were you able to draw conclusions from *what he left out* as well as from *what he put in?* Did you note whether he had a sense of humor? Did he seem to be looking down his nose at you, or was he warm and friendly? Did you believe what he said because he proved it, because he is a well-known expert—or did you wonder whether he had a special ax to grind and was distorting the facts to suit his purpose? In short, did you try to match your own experience, background, and information with the author's; did the words mean the same to you when you read them as they did to him when he wrote them?

In connection with the last remark, I am reminded of the time T. S. Eliot's *The Cocktail Party* opened in New York and was greeted with great respect by all the critics. Each one quarreled with the others about the theme of the play. The audience, too, was split into two camps— those who were sure they had read the dramatist's message correctly and those who walked out utterly confused. Finally, the author himself was invited to comment on the storm of interpretations that had been stirred up here. His reply went something like this: *I am delighted to find so many things in my play that I didn't realize I had put in.*

I offer the story to suggest that it is possible to disagree on what a writer is trying to say. Usually, however, the meaning is perfectly plain and readily ascertained *if you know what to look for.* An author uses key words and sentences to project his ideas, attitudes, and beliefs. Your job is to find these keys so that you will be able not only to understand what he said but also to answer some of the questions that go beyond the bare facts. It would be easy to give you a set of exercises and ask you to get the main ideas, remember a few of the details, and make an effort to evaluate some of the other features that can be found in any piece of writing. But you already know that this is the way you should be reading. Your problem is mainly *how* this is done.

Something else that may be disturbing you is whether you *can* learn to read with full comprehension. Let's settle that point immediately. It has been demonstrated to you that you have not been reading as fast as you can. In all likelihood you have also not been using your total abilities to understand what you read. *How* you go about this is going to be our concern in this chapter and the next. We'll show you *how* to get at those key words and sentences so that you *can* function at your very best when you try to absorb the context and flavor of reading materials.

If you wanted to become an expert appraiser of fine furniture, you would not go to a completed cabinet for your training. You would very likely start with a study of wood grains and textures; proceed to learn how various joints are made and fastened with nails, screws, and glue; and finally become familiar with finishes. It is always a good idea to study construction before attempting to evaluate the finished product.

So it is with reading. Improving your comprehension must start with a study of how a piece of writing begins and how it develops. In this way you can learn to recognize the structural elements of reading matter and thus can easily find the keys inserted by the author to assist your understanding.

The tool of all writing is the sentence. It is the basic

means of expressing a single thought or, in combination, developing an idea. Even the poet, who takes great liberties with the language, doesn't ignore this fundamental law of communication. Observe the following:

a) I never saw a moor, I never saw the sea; yet know I how the heather looks, and what a wave must be.

b) I never saw a moor,
   I never saw the sea;
   Yet know I how the heather looks,
   And what a wave must be.

One way (prose) or the other (the way the poet, Emily Dickinson, actually wrote it), the writer must tell us what he is talking about and then say something about it.

A young child uses a sentence to express practically everything that is on his mind. He says, "I want a toy." There is nothing more to be said. He has identified an object, has expressed a desire for it, and that's that. There would be no purpose in trying to look behind or ahead of the statement. The child isn't old enough to have developed shades of meaning, subtlety, or cleverly concealed emotions.

An adult rarely confines himself to single sentences. He uses them in combination because his greater maturity prompts him to be more specific, give more details, explain the *whys* and *hows* of his remarks. In fact, we become suspicious when a grownup stops at one sentence. If a guest in your house got up suddenly, grumbled, "I'm going home," and left without another word, you would be sure that something had been said or done to offend him. In his case the sentence would not have revealed everything that was on his mind when he expressed himself. His emotions, his state of health, even the quality

145

of his judgment, might all have become subjects of discussion after he left.

When we have progressed, therefore, from the primary levels of language use, we tend to speak and write in what are called paragraphs. And yet, if we examine one of these, we must conclude that it is nothing more than a blown-up sentence. Note:

a) Our subways are old, noisy, and dirty.
   What are we talking about?
     Our subways
   What have we said about them?
     are old, noisy, and dirty.

b) Our subways are old, noisy, and dirty. Much of the equipment being used was bought more than twenty-five years ago. The worn seats, creaking doors and old-fashioned interiors make a sorry appearance. On the overcrowded platforms, one is shocked by the constant roar of incoming trains, the grinding and screeching of brakes, the shouts of guards and passengers. To complete this dismal picture, we have the dusty, foul air, the unwashed windows in the cars, and the litter scattered all about. Indeed, our transportation system reminds us of a tottering beggar barely able to stand up.

What is the main idea of the paragraph?
  Our subways are old, noisy, and dirty.
What else have we said about them?
  Nothing!

Of course, we did add details, color, and sound. But the reader came away with no important information besides that supplied by the single sentence. The latter became the *topic sentence* of the paragraph. It announced what would be discussed. Several *supporting sentences* enriched the picture suggested by the initial thought, and a *concluding sentence* gave both a summary and a lead into other ideas the writer might want to pursue.

Certainly not all paragraphs have a set length, nor do they invariably begin with a topic sentence and end with a concluding one. There is great flexibility in their construction, but every paragraph is designed to center attention on a *single idea*, just as every sentence expresses a single thought. There are more words in one than in the other, but the end result is the same.

And this isn't all. If an author wishes to write more than a paragraph, he simply expands once more. A diagram of the process would look like this:

Paragraph	Article or Short Story	Book
Topic sentence	Introductory paragraph	Introductory chapter
Supporting sentences	Body paragraph(s)	Body chapters
Concluding sentence	Concluding paragraph	Concluding chapter

All writing, therefore, regardless of its length, points in a single direction. A book has a single major theme that is the conclusion of everything that has been said. Each chapter treats a single phase of the larger subject. Every paragraph in a chapter presents a single idea to support the main point. And the sentences in a paragraph produce the single thoughts that add up to the main idea.

Students in my writing classes, who understand this feature of the writing process, have little difficulty expanding a sentence into a sensible discourse. For instance, here is what one of them did with a sentence I gave her (the first one in the article that follows):

Collecting things certainly is a hobby of mine. I acquired the habit during childhood and have continued it to this day. It's delightful, I think, to have mementos of pleasant times. When I feel myself sinking into despondency, I can pull myself out of the depths by glancing through my treasure chest.

I can truthfully say I developed my acquisitive taste at an early age. Before I went to school, I collected box tops, bottle caps, pretty pins which usually were broken, empty spools from the sewing basket, and birthday cards. All these things I saved in a small carton which I kept in the drawer of a chest. They were not toys to be played with but special possessions to be looked at only. They were stuff from which dreams are made.

It seems I have changed little in this respect during the years. Today I save programs from outstanding movies, match covers which advertise famous eating places (and I need not have eaten there to save the cover), and pictures that strike my fancy. Once while I was visiting a friend, I was taken on a tour of her apartment. As I walked into one of the rooms I was struck by the beauty and simplicity of a picture of the Christ Child which was on a calendar. I asked my escort whether I might have it when the year had come to an end. Eventually I had the portrait framed and it now hangs in my living room. Each time I look at it I get the same feeling I used to have when, as a little girl, I peeped into my treasure chest and relived the wondrous moments of days gone by—and fashioned bright fancies of days yet to come. How gently can sagging spirits be lifted by a touch of yesterday!

Although I collect things that do not have any great value, they express a part of me. Sometimes I wonder whether I will wind up like the famous Collyer brothers who died shortly before they would have had to abandon their home because there was hardly room enough left for both them and their odd collection of old newspapers, magazines, and what not. Naturally, I tell myself that I am not irrational, but on objective reflection I see that the strange gentlemen and I had much in common. Obviously, I am different in at least one respect. The items they saved were so worthless! Still I can understand their need for doing so. On second thought, haven't I already confessed that my treasures are quite worthless, too?

Notice what happened to the original sentence. It grew into a paragraph, which in turn was developed into a short essay. The introductory paragraph, body, and conclusion are all clearly there. It is certainly more interesting to read the longer piece of writing. There are emotion, color, and even a bit of humor. But it still adds up to one thing—an entertaining account of a person's hobby.

*　　　*　　　*

I hope you have come along patiently with me to this point. The technical explanation of the writing process was necessary to reinforce my recommendation that knowing how an author writes helps you understand him better when you read. Why is this information valuable? Well, you now know that an author begins with the germ of an idea, works on it until he has decided the length and direction it will take, and then breaks it down into paragraphs or chapters to express his thoughts on the subject.

When you read, you literally reverse the process! If it is a single paragraph you are reading, you know that you can get into it and out of it quickly because you are looking for one idea. You will notice the details as you go along, but if you can't add them up to a main point, you have missed it. This gives you the *how* of reading. Look for the topic sentence, which announces what the paragraph will be about, note rapidly how it is developed, and then go on to the next one. No matter how much additional time you spend on a paragraph, you will still come out with one main idea, if it has been properly written.

If it is an article or book, you know *in advance of your reading* that there is going to be a main point the author is driving at, that his supporting ideas or plot manipulations (as in a novel) will be found *one by one* in the paragraphs or chapters, and that the quality of his work will be judged by the nature of his presentation of the details in the individual sentences. This knowledge of how to direct your mind can be of tremendous help to you. It supplies you with the tool that makes it possible for you to cut through masses of words, locate the important ideas, and move on with full speed and comprehension.

Here is another point about comprehension that should be clearer to you now. If a paragraph is an expanded sentence, certainly word-by-word reading can contribute little sense. If it were possible to read whole sentences within single recognition spans, that would be the best way to arrive at the single idea a paragraph develops. But most sentences are much too long for anyone to attempt to develop such a skill. In view of this fact, there should be no question about the advisability of at least handling *groups of words* if you are not to get lost in your quest of main ideas. The author's details, comparisons, contrasts, examples, anecdotes are inserted to enable the reader to see the point of each paragraph clearly and thus move step by step in the direction of the basic theme or story of the selection as a whole.

And what about the other aspects of comprehension we mentioned before—the emotional tone of the material, its authoritative quality, the point of view, the charm and wit? Here, too, failure to concentrate on the whole, rather than its parts, prevents you from escaping the "tyranny of words." To test the quality of a suit, you wouldn't count the threads. All you need to remember a funny story is the punch line. The details come of themselves. If a speaker outlines a plan and you center your attention on his resonant voice and rich choice of words, you may not realize until it is too late that you are in no position to judge either the quality of the speech or its contents.

You must train your mind to attack every paragraph purposefully. It must try to get at the main idea as quickly as it can, form its reactions along the way, and keep going steadily—all the while building up toward the general objective or theme the writer set out to develop. Rarely does missing a small detail or word here and there seriously interfere with your understanding of the important features of the material. You shouldn't clutter up your mind with the little things. Let it be free to concentrate on the big ideas.

Now let's try to apply some of the techniques we have been discussing to the opening three paragraphs of Washington Irving's "The Legend of Sleepy Hollow." I have selected this author because, although he wrote more than a hundred years ago, he can well serve as a model for any writer who wishes to present clear, correct, and interesting material. As you read, LOOK FOR THE KEYS! Decide what the paragraph is going to talk about, race through the details, and go on to the next. After you have finished your reading, there will be a test, the results of which will indicate to you what you should have been looking for. If you do well, you will know that you have uncovered the trade secret of rapid comprehension.

About two miles from the village of Tarrytown on the Hudson there is a little valley which is one of the quietest places in the whole world. It is known as Sleepy Hollow because a drowsy, dreamy influence seems to hang over the land and to pervade the very atmosphere. Its people are descendants of the original Dutch settlers, and are given to all kinds of marvelous beliefs. Strange tales are told of trances and visions and ghostly visitors. The apparition most frequently seen is that of a headless figure on horseback which is said by some to be the ghost of a Hessian trooper who rides forth nightly in quest of his head. The Headless Horseman of Sleepy Hollow is known far and wide in the Hudson Valley and is even said to have been seen by visitors as well as by the inhabitants of the dreamy village.

In this by-place of nature there abode, in a remote period of American history, that is to say some thirty years since, a worthy wight by the name of Ichabod Crane, who sojourned, or, as he expressed it, "tarried," in Sleepy Hollow, for the purpose of instructing the children of the vicinity. He was a native of Connecticut, a state which supplies the Union with pioneers of the mind as well as for the forest, and sends forth yearly its legions of frontier woodsmen and country schoolmasters. The cognomen of Crane was not inapplicable to his person. He was tall, and exceedingly lank, with narrow shoulders, long arms and legs, hands that dangled a mile out of his sleeves, feet that might have served for shovels, and his whole frame most loosely hung to-

152

gether. His head was small, and flat at top, with huge ears, large green glassy eyes, and a long snipe nose, so that it looked like a weathercock perched upon his spindle neck to tell which way the wind blew. To see him striding along the profile of a hill on a windy day, with his clothes bagging and fluttering about him, one might have mistaken him for the genius of famine descending upon the earth, or some scarecrow eloped from a cornfield.

His schoolhouse was a low building of one large room, rudely constructed of logs; the windows partly glazed, and partly patched with leaves of old copybooks. It was most ingeniously secured at vacant hours, by a withe [twig] twisted in the handle of the door, and stakes set against the window shutters: so that though a thief might get in with perfect ease, he would find embarrassment in getting out—an idea most probably borrowed by the architect, Yost Van Houten, from the mystery of the eelpot. The schoolhouse stood in a rather lonely but pleasant situation, just at the foot of a woody hill, with a brook running close by, and a formidable birch tree growing at one end of it. From hence the low murmur of his pupils' voices, conning over their lessons, might be heard in a drowsy summer's day, like the hum of a beehive; interrupted now and then by the authoritative voice of the master, in the tone of menace or command; or, peradventure, by the appalling sound of the birch, as he urged some tardy loiterer along the flowery path of knowledge. Truth to say, he was a conscientious man, and ever bore in mind the golden maxim, "Spare the rod and spoil the child." Ichabod Crane's scholars certainly were not spoiled.

COMPREHENSION TEST

I. Main Ideas and Details

A. The over-all purpose of the author in the first three paragraphs was

_____ 1. to tell how cruel Crane was

_____ 2. to introduce the main character and setting of the story

_____ 3. to tell what school was like in the olden days

B. A title that could express the main idea of the first paragraph would be

_____ 1. A superstitious old town

_____ 2. A headless horseman

_____ 3. A Hessian trooper

C. A title for the second paragraph would be

_____ 1. A native of Connecticut

_____ 2. An eloped scarecrow

_____ 3. A funny-looking schoolteacher

D. A title for the third paragraph would be

_____ 1. Activities in an old schoolhouse

_____ 2. A stern teacher

_____ 3. A strange doorlatch

E. In the first paragraph the author seems to suggest that the descendants of the Dutch settlers were

_____ 1. a hard-working lot

_____ 2. believers in ghosts

_____ 3. gay and cheerful

F. In the second paragraph we get the impression that Ichabod Crane is

_____ 1. tall and gaunt

_____ 2. short and fat

_____ 3. not different from most people

G. In the third paragraph we learn that

_____ 1. corporal punishment was not permitted

_____ 2. Ichabod Crane was easygoing

_____ 3. the birch rod was used frequently

II. *Other Features of the Writing*

A. The author's point of view is

_____ 1. serious

_____ 2. factual

_____ 3. humorous

B. You sense early by the author's attitude that he

_____ 1. wants you to believe him

_____ 2. believes the story himself

_____ 3. just wants you to enjoy a fanciful tale

C. If we go beyond his words, we can conclude that the author is suggesting that

_____ 1. children should not be hit with birch rods

_____ 2. all Dutch people are highly superstitious

_____ 3. you should join him in having some fun

D. From the way he writes, we can judge that the author

_____ 1. can't take a joke

_____ 2. seems warm and friendly

_____ 3. talks like a stuffed shirt

ANSWERS: I. A. 2, B. 1, C. 3, D. 1, E. 2, F. 1, G. 3.
II. A. 3, B. 3, C. 3, D. 2.

We will now examine the paragraphs one by one, with the aim of suggesting what you should have been looking for as you read. First, you want to prove to yourself that all good writing follows the pattern we have recommended. Secondly, since facts alone are not enough to enable you to meet the writer on equal terms, you want to be shown wherein the factors leading to appreciation and evaluation can be found. Finally, you will be getting your first demonstration of what it means to make a full-scale attack upon the contents of a selection.

First Paragraph

The job here is to tell something about the town where the story takes place. So you learn of its *drowsy* nature, the *marvelous beliefs* of its people, and one superstition in particular, the *Headless Horseman*. The topic, supporting, and concluding sentences have been used and have achieved their purpose. You don't concern yourself with a scientific analysis of the author's facts because he has already told you that you are going to read a story involving local superstitions. Therefore, you try to lose yourself in the fanciful tale about to unfold. You aren't ready yet to draw conclusions about Washington Irving's personality, but the mere suggestion of a rider without a head tells you that this writer has imagination, to say the least.

This is a lot to say about and see in a short paragraph, isn't it? Does it mean that when you read you must consciously look for topic, supporting, and concluding sentences? At first, yes. After you have practiced sufficiently, you will find these keys to understanding automatically. Should you be taking the other points mentioned into consideration simultaneously as you read? Again, yes. Are you thinking now that you are lucky enough when you get the main idea out of a paragraph, let alone additional things? That's reasonable, too. However, you have embarked upon this training program to *improve* your skills. You wouldn't want to be shortchanged. Through exercises supplied in this chapter and with additional practice on your own, you will gradually get into the habit of *looking for all the keys* to be found in a piece of writing. What it amounts to is your being able eventually to "size up" *what* is being said and *how* it is being said.

Second Paragraph

Once more the topic sentence introduces the subject that will be talked about—Ichabod Crane. There follow the supporting sentences, which give you an accurate picture of what he does for a living and what he looks like. By now also you have probably been amused by the references to *a mile out of his sleeves, served for shovels,* and *nose . . . like a weathercock.* You know, therefore, that you can expect further expressions of the author's sense of humor, and perhaps you have already begun to enjoy his easy, informal style. We have here an almost perfect blending of the structural elements that can be found in every skillfully written paragraph.

Third Paragraph

Again an almost perfect paragraph: the single important idea—a description of the schoolhouse and the activities of its occupants—the details, the flashes of humor, are all here. You can now, since your reading has ceased, step a bit farther back and ask yourself what Irving's over-all purpose was in the first three paragraphs of his story. Obviously he wanted to introduce the main character and give us the setting of the story.

What if you had read the paragraphs without having alerted yourself to look for the keys to understanding and appreciation? Your rate might have suffered because you would have been unable to slide past words like *Hessian, wight, cognomen, eelpot,* without getting the uneasy feeling that you were missing something. As it is, you could concentrate on the total view of the selection and leave the vocabulary for some other time. Furthermore, you might have become confused by the long sentences, or you might have paid so much attention to the details that you would have missed the wit and charm of the story. But knowing what to look for makes it possible for you to plunge into a paragraph, take out of it what is necessary, and go on to the next without allowing yourself to be upset over small matters. You concern yourself with thoughts and ideas, not single words.

Knowing what you now do about writing techniques, you can begin to train yourself to keep in mind a set of guide questions that will help you find the keys to total comprehension of any material you read:

1. What is the author's purpose?
2. What is the main idea of each paragraph?
3. What details are significant?
4. What is the writer's point of view?
5. Can I believe him? Why?
6. Does he suggest anything beyond what he says?
7. Does his writing have some special quality?

Although we were able to get answers to all the guide questions in the selection from "Sleepy Hollow," it is not possible to do so with everything you read. You must first determine the *author's purpose*. Then you can decide what other questions are pertinent to the particular material. Let's see how this works with some typical selections.

GUIDE QUESTIONS—EXERCISE 1

Clever Young Man from Old Chatham

In old Chatham, so they say, there was a very clever young man. Among other things, he invented a new way to catch fish.

First, he dipped his hook into blackstrap molasses. (Or "long-tail sugar," as they used to say.) Then he cast his hook high into the air. This drew the bees. The bees stuck to the hook.

Next move, the clever young man heaved his bee-covered drail into the water. Up swam the fish, thinking the bees were big flies. But being in the water had made the bees very angry. They stung the fish to death.

Was not this young man from Chatham about as clever as they come?

Fables and Foibles

A retired sea captain in a certain Cape Cod town was taking a walk along the beach one day. He was about to turn for the homeward stretch, when he saw two men a little farther ahead engaged in a rather heated discussion.

Quickening his pace, he neared them, and called out, "What's the trouble, men?"

"Well," said one of the men, "we were walking here together, when I saw this oyster that he has in his hand, and we both want it. I say it is mine because I saw it first."

"Not so!" hotly contended the other man. "He saw it first, that's true. But I was the one who ran and picked it up. So I say it is mine."

"Hmm!" said the old captain. "Would you like me to settle the argument?" To this proposal they agreed, and he said, "Let me have the oyster."

Taking the oyster, the captain pried it open, ate the oyster, and gave each contender half of the shell.

In the two tales above, the author's purpose is clear very early. When he says *so they say* in the first, and *in a certain Cape Cod town* in the other, you know at once that he is out to tell a fanciful or tall tale. This knowledge automatically eliminates from consideration all the other guide questions. No important ideas or details are going to be presented, and since the writer is spoofing, you need not concern yourself about his attitude or reliability. He has as much as warned you not to trust him. What he wants you to do is have a laugh. Certainly this kind of material can be read at your very fastest rate because there is little challenge to your comprehension. The same is true of all articles, stories, and books whose

160

basic purpose is to amuse and entertain. You can rip right through them!

GUIDE QUESTIONS—EXERCISE 2

Here is an excerpt from a news article concerned with juvenile crime:

Commissioner Kennedy said he "deplored" the use of the problem as a potential issue by Republican opponents of Mayor Wagner.

"This is a matter of life and public safety," he said. "It should not be exploited for political purposes."

Although he deplored the injection of politics into the juvenile crime problem, Mr. Kennedy took occasion to point out that the last Mayor of New York to run with Republican backing had reduced the size of the police force.

Since this is a news article, you would know the purpose of the writer before you got to it because presumably the job of a reporter is to present an objective summary of the facts. Accordingly, you would certainly want to absorb the main idea and important details of what he said. However, you would miss something if you didn't go beyond the facts.

The comment by the reporter, "Although he deplored the injection of politics into the juvenile crime problem," indicates a considerable shortage of sympathy for the commissioner's statement. Whether the attitude is justified is not the question. What is significant to you as a reader is that your mind should be alert to a writer's point of view, when he presents facts, so that you are not unconsciously influenced in your own opinion. Therefore, the only question you would not use as a guide in material of this type would be Number 7. Newspaper writing, except in features and editorials, usually follows a fairly regular pattern and you need not look for individuality.

In fact, it is only when the reporter breaks the pattern that you can get the answers to guide questions 4, 5, and 6. It is in the side remarks that slip out, so to speak, that you can look for point of view, reliability, and "anything beyond what he says." What party do you think this paper might support?

Suppose, as another example, you were reading a summary of a day's legislative activities and the statements of a particular speaker were called "arrogant," or he was described as "chubby and rumpled." Certainly the terms referring to manner of speech and personal appearance do not conceal the reporter's point of view. To someone on the other side of the fence, the same speaker might have seemed "determined" and "delightfully informal."

You can therefore read news articles rather quickly, too, since the main ideas are suggested by the headlines, strongly stated in the opening sentence or two, and merely repeated in detail in the paragraphs that follow. But be on the lookout for the little asides that give away the attitude of the writer.

GUIDE QUESTIONS—EXERCISE 3

Misguided Missiles

The modern automobile is a triumph of engineering, quick to respond to the will of the driver. Unfortunately, the design of the driver has not kept pace.

The Travelers Insurance Company reports that 35,500 people died in traffic accidents in 1954 with almost two million injured. Excessive speed contributed to about

50% of the accidents, with recklessness and driving on the wrong side of the road closely following.

It's not the new driver who causes most harm; 97% of drivers in accidents have been driving over a year. Drivers under 25 were involved in more than their proportionate share of accidents. And for the age-old controversy: male drivers accounted for 91% of fatal accidents.

Cars were in good mechanical condition as a whole. If the care of the driver matched the care of his car, we would have 91% fewer accidents.

It is sad that for 13,980 drivers Saturday and Sunday became days of permanent rest. The middle of the week is much safer. By far most accidents per cars on the road occurred in the dark, between 1:00 A.M. and 6:00 A.M. Dry roads, fair weather and careless driving seem to go together.

Auto deaths have decreased slightly below 1941's record 39,969. But there are now roughly double the cars on the road, and deaths per 100,000 vehicles declined about 50%.

Statistics reveal that the decrease came about, not because of our drivers, but in spite of them. The 1954 report shows that the ratios of causes of accidents do not substantially differ from figures of previous years. The conclusion is unmistakable that the decrease in deaths is due far more to mechanical and medical progress than to a fundamental change in driver attitude.

*   *   *

Since the purpose of the writer, as revealed in the very first paragraph, is to express an opinion about the causes of accidents, you immediately set yourself to

163

use all the guide questions, except possibly the last. If there is something distinctive about the style it will be incidental, since the subject does not lend itself readily to creative expression. You want to get the main ideas, of course, but your attention to the details should be limited to getting an impression rather than attempting the almost impossible task of memorizing the figures. You want to check the reliability of the writer so that you can determine whether the conclusions are justified. Here's how that is done.

If the author were an acknowledged authority in the subject area, you might be inclined to accept at face value much of what is said. However, since this is not a signed article, you must look to other sources. What other evidence is there to support the writer's position? The statistics quoted from a reliable company indicate that there was research on the topic and ordinarily should influence you favorably regarding point of view and reliability.

Even under the latter circumstances, you must be careful. "The Devil can cite the Scriptures to suit his own ends." I neither want to call the writer a devil nor get into a controversy over male and female drivers, but let's examine one of the statistics from the point of view of whether numbers always tell the whole truth. You read that male drivers account for 91 per cent of fatal accidents. Has the writer told you what percentage of *all* drivers are male? Has he indicated whether some of the male drivers got into accidents because they were trying to avoid female drivers (Heaven help me)? Has he taken into consideration the hazardous occupations of men that might account for their greater incidence of fatalities—auto-racing, bus and truck driving, venturing forth on icy roads, ambulance and other emergency-vehicle driving that requires speed to get to a destination?

Later on in the article, is the author's conclusion that the decrease in deaths is due to mechanical and medical progress an acceptable one? Surely modern cars on new parkways go faster than ever, and doctors can use their new techniques to heal the victims but cannot prevent the accidents. Again, let me repeat, I am not quarreling with the writer or the ladies (could the author have been one?), but I am pointing out to you that you must look for statistics and proof, and you do not accept what you read unless all sides of the problem have been covered. In material of this kind, your guide questions are very valuable. They force you to *think with the writer* and prevent you from accepting the main ideas and details without argument.

GUIDE QUESTIONS—EXERCISE 4

AN EDITORIAL

Chance for Gas Bill

President Eisenhower, according to one congressman's interpretation, has cut two amendment hobbles off a bill to free natural gas producers from undue federal regulation and has boosted chances of passage for the needed legislation.

The congressman, Rep. Harris (D-Ark.), is author of the bill which eases government controls of prices charged at the wellhead by independent natural gas producers. The administration-proposed amendments, which Rep. Harris believes would kill the proposal, tighten federal power commission regulatory authority over prices beyond what is provided in the bill itself. The President now has indicated he would sign the bill without the controversial amendments.

President Eisenhower also favored the more liberal gas bill passed by Congress last year but vetoed it because of the "arrogance" lobbyists allegedly used in trying to influence support of the measure. This current Harris bill stops short of completely freeing the nation's approximately 3,000 gas producers from incentive-killing regulation which was never intended by Congress. (The Supreme Court handed a surprised FPC an order to take charge of far-flung gas producers in a 1954 interpretation of a 1938 law.) The new bill takes off the strait-jacket but leaves gas at the well subject to certain commodity-type price restrictions, thereby allaying consumers' fears of "unreasonable" rate hikes.

Congress now has no excuse for failing to emancipate natural gas producers, to pull back at least one tentacle of unwarranted federal regulation.

＊ ＊ ＊

It is very likely that you don't read editorials, or that, if you do, this subject would be of little interest to you. But you should make it a practice to read such articles because they reveal how your newspaper thinks. Since this is an editorial, the purpose is definitely to express opinion, and once more your guide questions are of service in helping you evaluate the conclusions drawn. Main idea? The paper leaves no doubt of its point, its attitude. How about the details? Are any offered to support the opinion other than what happened last year and the need to "emancipate" the gas producers? Is there something "beyond what the writer says"? Is it possible that some of the gas producers are in the neighborhood of New Orleans? You can see the desirability of reading editorials somewhat more slowly than other material, and being careful to go further than just the main idea.

Whether you like it or not, someone is trying to influence you. You should be ready for him with your full comprehension. Propaganda, for example, can be effective only when readers believe anything in print, when they absorb ideas without analyzing them.

GUIDE QUESTIONS—EXERCISE 5

So far we have been concentrating on articles that stress the importance of going beyond the facts or ignoring them altogether. We haven't done much with the last guide question, which refers to the author's style or personality. In the following passage you will have the opportunity to see how the latter is of particular importance.

Topics of The Times

BY LEWIS NICHOLS

The summer is moving along. It is going by at a rate calling to mind the speed of light. The Fourth of July is over now, as well as two pleasant trips to Jones Beach and half a dozen tasty picnics. The picturesque road which was found last year has been traveled again, although over the winter it has become a superhighway feeder. However, there must be other picturesque roads, and perhaps one of them will be discovered before the summer is over. The discovery had best be soon, though, for the days of the summer are numbered. They are flying by, and the comparison which at once comes to mind is the speed of light. They are vanishing as though it were nobody's business, whereas the reverse of that clearly is the truth. They must be stopped somehow. As they say in the automotive trades, their speed of passage must be decelerated. For, to be honest, unless the flying summer is slowed abruptly, this summer's planned project will not be completed. At the moment, it is not nearly as finished as is the summer. This is deplorable, and eventually will be causing loose talk.

That project was a product of the winter. Back in February there was a particularly nasty day. The wind blew, there was snow, the furnace failed to function and the radiator of the car cracked from freezing. Late in the afternoon the mind had enough of contemplating such a day, and so it looked forward to the summer. Since the mind is an active one, it did not just scheme to lie about in the sun, dozing the hours away. Instead of this lazy approach, it made plans for improvements about the place. It considered painting the outside of the house; it considered painting the trim alone. It considered widening the vegetable garden and lengthening the flower garden, and building a stone wall along the back of the property and building an outdoor fireplace near the wall. At the end of that February day all of these things were jotted down in the Diary under the heading Summer Projects. Unfortunately, the Projects also were announced publicly, at dinner. That was bad.

Spring came, and then came the summer. What with one thing and another, it was deemed best not to use the scattershot system of dealing with the Summer Projects. One by one, those deemed of lesser importance were dropped. Painting the house was the first to be abandoned, and after that, painting the trim. Although there was some rude talk about it at the evening dinner table, it should have been obvious that the trim and the house belonged together, and should be painted together, some other summer. Widening the vegetable garden then was abandoned, and not altogether because the Yankees were having a spirited double-header on the afternoon work was supposed to begin. Lengthening the flower garden happened to coincide with a dandy single game, which was a raw coincidence, leaving the garden the size it was before. Building the stone wall looked—well, the specifications for the Great Wall of China may have called for more stone, but probably not. That left, as Project—in the singular—the fireplace.

Now the summer is flying by. It is moving along at a rate akin to the speed of light. The Fourth of July has gone, as well as a couple of Jones Beach excursions and some tasty picnics. About these picnics, it must be said at once that cold foods were involved, not grilled ones. The fireplace still is in the construction stage; indeed there are those of small courtesy who say that it merely is in the planning stage. Obviously this is unfair, for are the stones not piled ready in a little mound, and are not the ingredients of concrete stored in the garage? All that is lacking to make the fireplace a finished Project is another summer. One perhaps slightly longer than this one. And one which doesn't travel so rapidly through space.

* * *

This author was interested mainly in having a pleasant chat with his reader. You can almost picture him dressed in a pair of old trousers and an open-collared shirt; sitting comfortably, drink in hand, on his outdoor patio, if he has made it yet; and amiably talking about those domestic shortcomings that are common to all of us. To enjoy this kind of article, you must set your mind to comparing your own experiences with those of the writer. You want to see whether his words express colorfully the very things you have often thought of. You aren't interested in his main ideas, details, reliability, or hidden meanings so much as you are in the personality that comes through in his style of writing.

You observe his technique of ending a paragraph with a very short sentence that nonetheless conveys a world of meaning: "This is deplorable, and eventually will be causing loose talk," "That was bad," and "That left, as Project—in the singular—the fireplace." You visualize the pictures he continually creates: "Half a dozen tasty picnics," "The wind blew, there was snow, the furnace failed to function," "lie about in the sun, dozing the hours away," and "specifications for the Great Wall of China may have called for more stone." His references to a "spirited double-header" and a "dandy single game" give you an inkling of his many-sided interests. He deliberately repeats so that you can be sure that this is not the first time the summer projects have fallen by the wayside.

Style is the trade-mark of good writers. If a writer has developed a distinctive style, it is as revealing of his personality as is his manner of talking, eating, dressing, or dancing. You decide that an individual is rather formal because you never hear him use slang or colloquialisms and his attitude toward even trivial things is too intense. Another will strike you as being informal and friendly because of his willingness to use any expression so long as it is the best for a particular thought and because he regards all matters within their proper proportions. Much of your delight from reading can come in meeting interesting people through their articles and stories. And of course, your appreciation of their material is so much the greater when you know what to look for. Isn't this concept equally true when you look at a painting, listen to some fine music, or watch a baseball game?

The selections we have just reviewed were designed to show you how to set your mind to thinking about values in your reading that go beyond just the main ideas and details. I readily grant that we have just about scratched the surface of developing judgment of a writer's attitude, motives, and style, as well as his content. However, you can use this as a start. As you read more, you will see more, and your reactions will become sharper and deeper.

Will this search for full comprehension slow you up? On the contrary! When you know in advance what you should get out of an article, story, or book, you are in a position to dictate your own speed. This is the best way to learn when to vary your reading rate. The author's purpose and the pertinent guide questions will enable you to judge intelligently the proper amount of time to spend upon a given selection. You will get into the material and stay there just long enough to get out of it what is of value. If, for instance, you start a novel that you have wanted to read, but find that the author is spending a lot of time establishing his background for the story, you may be tempted to set the book aside because you haven't the desire to wade through the dull introductory chapters. With your ability to recognize the purpose of a writer and thus gauge how and where to center your attention, you can knife through the dead spots and even skip a page or two without losing much.

Make it a practice to reread, from time to time, our analyses of the "Sleepy Hollow" excerpt and the selections just concluded. You will be helping your mind gradually acquire what the psychologists call the proper "mental set." It will LOOK FOR THE KEYS, and find them!

We are now ready for the exercises that will help you use full comprehension. The selections will be graded in difficulty, getting harder as you proceed. Don't try to push your rate just yet. You may even find it slowing up a bit. Don't worry about that. As you become more expert in picking out the essential ideas and characteristics of the practice paragraphs, your speed will automatically increase. In the long run, as we've said, because of your improved comprehension, it will be easier than ever to push yourself.

We will start modestly. Our first few exercises will require that you find only the main ideas and important details. Once you have developed the technique of LOOKING FOR THE KEYS through the topic, supporting, and concluding sentences in the paragraphs, you will be able to go on to the kind of *full-comprehension* test you took in connection with "The Legend of Sleepy Hollow." As usual, do not attempt to do all the exercises in one session. Wait for the complete instructions about your Daily Plan in Chapter **X**.

COMPREHENSION EXERCISE 1

Read each paragraph carefully, LOOK FOR THE KEYS, and then answer the questions that follow. The material in this set is similar to that of the diagnostic test in comprehension you took in Chapter III—state examinations for high-school students.

a. Almost without exception boat owners are rabid camera fans. Unfortunately, however, many of the boating enthusiasts who like to click an occasional shutter find that the results they achieve leave something to be desired. They forget that the camera's eye works on principles similar to their own, and that a bright sunlit day on the water that causes them to squint and reach for colored glasses also has an adverse effect on the film in the camera unless certain precautions are taken. Light on the water acquires an almost unbelievable intensity. A technic that would produce satisfactory results ashore is entirely unsuited to boating pictures.

The title below that best expresses the ideas of this paragraph is

_____ 1. Water colors

_____ 2. Photography on the water

_____ 3. Intensity of light on the water

_____ 4. How the camera's eye works

_____ 5. Camera technic

The writer emphasizes that pictures taken on boats are often spoiled by the

_____ 1. overenthusiasm of the photographer

_____ 2. motion of the boat

_____ 3. lack of a color filter

_____ 4. too bright light

_____ 5. use of the wrong film

b. The Eighth Army, in defeat or victory, lived exclusively on the ground. Mobile warfare provided no time to pitch tents, and the towns were uninhabitable. Shells and bombs were minor discomforts in comparison with the flies, fleas, scorpions, black spiders, and sand vipers that demanded a major share of the Tommies' living space in the Egyptian and Libyan deserts. Throughout the green belt around Benghazi there were malarial mosquitoes and typhus-bearing lice. Tripoli was a synonym for hungry red ants.

The title below that best expresses the ideas of this paragraph is

_____ 1. The endurance of the British Tommies

_____ 2. Desert pests as hazards of warfare

_____ 3. Importance of towns in warfare

_____ 4. Synonyms for starvation

_____ 5. The Eighth Army

The Eighth Army's greatest hardship in this campaign was

_____ 1. mobile warfare

_____ 2. lack of tents

_____ 3. exploding shells and bombs

_____ 4. unpleasant towns

_____ 5. insects

One condition that confronted the Eighth Army was

_____ 1. lack of supplies

_____ 2. the result of a series of defeats

_____ 3. lack of proper communications

_____ 4. a health hazard

_____ 5. not present on other battlefields

c. (*Warning: This is one of those paragraphs in which the topic sentence does not appear at the beginning.*) The electric generators in America's automobiles can produce nearly twice as much electricity in a day as all the powerful equipment at Hoover Dam. Yet electric power is only a by-product of the energy developed by the gasoline engine. Millions of horsepower to drive automobiles, airplanes, locomotives and ocean liners; billions of B.T.U.'s to heat homes and provide power and process heat in manufacturing plants—all come from petroleum. Truly man has released to his service a giant who has lain buried, unknown, many ages in the earth.

The title below that best expresses the ideas of this paragraph is

_____ 1. By-products of automobile generators

_____ 2. Heating homes with oil

_____ 3. The tremendous power of electricity

_____ 4. Sources of heat and power

_____ 5. Energy obtained from petroleum

The "giant who has lain buried" is

_____ 1. oil

_____ 2. water

_____ 3. gasoline

_____ 4. electricity

_____ 5. coal

d. In no field of history has the search for logical explanation been so diligent as in the study of the decline

175

and fall of the Roman Empire. The only known instance of the decay of a more or less universal civilization, it might serve as something of an object lesson to our own; accordingly it has been very thoroughly studied, and the attempt to explain it has engaged some of the ablest historians who ever wrote. Almost any orator or politician can tell you why Rome fell, but the men who know most about it are not so ready with glib explanations. Even they must admit at critical moments the decisive interposition of Chance.

The title that best expresses the ideas of this paragraph is

_____ 1. The Roman Empire

_____ 2. Studying reasons for the decline and fall of the Roman Empire

_____ 3. Causes for the decline

_____ 4. Chance is decisive

_____ 5. Able historians know why Rome fell

The fall of the Roman Empire has been thoroughly studied because

_____ 1. it may serve as a lesson to us

_____ 2. it affected the lives of so many people

_____ 3. it was so unusual

_____ 4. Rome was the greatest empire the world has known

_____ 5. detailed records are readily available

People who know most about the fall of the Roman Empire

_____ 1. think politicians were its chief cause

_____ 2. are uncertain as to its cause

_____ 3. prepare object lessons from it

_____ 4. give ready explanations of it

_____ 5. have been able to learn little about it

e. The artist of the Renaissance was an all-round man. From his studio one could order a painting for the church altar, a carved wedding chest, a silver ewer, or a crucifix. The master of the workshop might be sculpturing a Venus for the Duke's garden while his apprentices were roughing-out a reredos for the new chapel. Many of the well-known painters of that golden period were goldsmiths, armorers, workers in glass, enamel or iron. The engineer was artist and the artist was engineer. The great Leonardo, famous today as the painter of "The Last Supper" and "Mona Lisa," was perhaps equally well known in the sixteenth century for his engineering projects and his scientific experiments. Our own Thomas A. Edison pronounced him the greatest inventive genius of his time.

The title below that best expresses the ideas of this paragraph is

_____ 1. The great Leonardo

_____ 2. Edison and sixteenth-century scientists

_____ 3. The golden period

_____ 4. Masters and apprentices

_____ 5. Renaissance artists

177

Leonardo was famed as

_____ 1. a scientist

_____ 2. an electrician

_____ 3. a worker in glass

_____ 4. a railroad engineer

_____ 5. an apprentice

f. Just why some individuals choose one way of adjusting to their difficulties and others choose other ways is not known. Yet what an individual does when he is thwarted remains a reasonably good key to the understanding of his personality. If his responses to thwartings are emotional explosions and irrational excuses, he is tending to live in an unreal world. He may need help to regain the world of reality, the cause-and-effect world recognized by generations of thinkers and scientists. Perhaps he needs encouragement to redouble his efforts. Perhaps, on the other hand, he is striving for the impossible and needs to substitute a worth-while activity within the range of his abilities. It is the part of wisdom to learn the nature of the world and of oneself in relation to it and to meet each situation as intelligently and as adequately as one can.

The title that best expresses the ideas of this paragraph is

_____ 1. Adjusting to life

_____ 2. Escape from reality

_____ 3. The importance of personality

_____ 4. Emotional control

_____ 5. The real nature of the world

The writer argues that all should

_____ 1. substitute new activities for old

_____ 2. redouble their efforts

_____ 3. analyze their relation to the world

_____ 4. seek encouragement from others

_____ 5. avoid thwartings

ANSWERS (Score 2 points for each title question and 1 for the details. Your grand total is 20 points. See page 34 for your standing in relation to your score.): a. 2, 4; b. 2, 5, 4; c. 5, 1; d. 2, 1, 2; e. 5, 1; f. 1, 3.

COMPREHENSION EXERCISE 2

This exercise will test your ability to see the relationship between the details of a paragraph and the main idea, as expressed by the topic sentence. It will also train you to detect where the author has gone off his subject. This knowledge is important as it prevents you from becoming confused by poor paragraph construction on the part of the writer.

Below the topic sentence you will find additional sentences. Place a check next to the sentences that do not belong because they have no specific connection with the main idea of the paragraph.

Topic sentence: No one can expect to have a good lawn without proper maintenance.

Supporting sentences:

_____ 1. There is the semi-annual feeding, which strengthens roots and promotes vigorous growth.

_____ 2. One should not wear new shoes because the fertilizer will make them dirty.

_____ 3. Another necessary procedure is the application of lime when the soil tests show acidity.

_____ 4. Every three or four years a liquid spraying or dry spreading of a chlordane compound will control insect larvae and prevent root damage.

_____ 5. Insects represent a powerful threat to man's health and comfort.

_____ 6. Such other chores as weeding, rolling, aerating the soil, and reseeding bare spots must be undertaken during the season.

Concluding sentence:

_____ 7. Only by following a regular schedule can the home owner grow grass that will be a joy to his eye and an improvement of his property value.

_____ 8. The English are noted for their fine lawns.

ANSWERS: The following numbers should have been checked as being undesirable in the paragraph—2, 5, 8.

COMPREHENSION EXERCISE 3

This exercise is similar to the one before. Place a check next to the numbered sentences that do not belong in the paragraph:

Topic sentence: Three English officers and a group of natives were hunting for two lions that had made a raid upon a village the night before.

Supporting sentences:

_____ 1. In the course of the day one of the pair was killed, but the other escaped to the jungle.

_____ 2. Proceeding cautiously, after a few steps the lieutenant saw the lion and instantly fired, thus enraging the beast so that it rushed toward him at full speed.

_____ 3. The officer was wearing a regular khaki hunting outfit.

_____ 4. Captain Woodhouse saw the movement and knew if he tried to get into a better position for firing, he would put himself directly in the way of the charge; so he decided to stand still, trusting that the lion would pass close by, unaware of him, and that he could then perhaps shoot to advantage.

_____ 5. But he was deceived.

_____ 6. The furious animal saw him, and flew at him with a dreadful roar.

_____ 7. The lion is considered to be the king of the beasts of Africa.

Concluding sentence:

_____ 8. In an instant, the rifle was broken and thrown out of the captain's hand, his left arm at the same moment being seized by the claws and his right by the teeth of his antagonist.

_____ 9. Rifles can be broken by one swipe of a lion's paw.

COMPREHENSION EXERCISE 4

In the following article, the paragraphs have been numbered. After you have finished your reading, number the subtitles below the selection to match the numbers of the paragraphs. For example, if you think the first subtitle fits the first paragraph, write 1 in the space provided. This gives you further training in selecting main ideas. Since your purpose here is to get to the main idea, you will want to read rather quickly so that the details do not interfere. The title has deliberately been omitted, and you will be asked to supply one later.

*   *   *

[1.] Many people believe the glare from snow causes snowblindness. Yet, dark glasses or not, they find themselves suffering from headaches and watering eyes, and even snowblindness, when exposed to several hours of "snow" light.

[2.] The United States Army has now determined that glare from snow does not cause snowblindness in troops operating in a snow-covered country. Rather, a man's eyes frequently find nothing to focus on in a broad expanse of barren snow-covered terrain. So his gaze continually shifts and jumps back and forth over the entire landscape in search of something to look at. Finding nothing, hour after hour, the eyes never stop searching and the eyeballs become sore and the eye muscles ache. Nature offsets this irritation by producing more and more fluid which covers the eyeball. The fluid covers the eyeball in increasing quantity until vision blurs, then is obscured, and the result is total, even though temporary, snowblindness.

[3.] Experiments led the Army to a simple method of overcoming this problem. Scouts ahead of a main body of troops are trained to shake snow from evergreen bushes, creating a dotted line as they cross completely snow-covered landscape. Even the scouts throw lightweight, dark colored objects ahead on which they too can focus. The men following can then see something. Their gaze is arrested. Their eyes focus on a bush and having found something to see, stop scouring the snow-blanketed landscape. By focusing their attention on one object, one at a time, the men can cross the snow without becoming hopelessly snowblind or lost. The problem of crossing a solid white terrain is helped.

Now number the subtitles so that they match the numbers of the paragraphs.

_____ Causes of snowblindness

_____ Traveling the Arctic waste

_____ A common wrong idea

_____ The need for dark glasses

_____ The solution to snowblindness

A good title for the entire selection would be

_____ 1. The United States Army

_____ 2. Winter problems

_____ 3. People's misconceptions

_____ 4. Causes and cures of snowblindness

_____ 5. The duties of scouts

ANSWERS: 2 Causes of snowblindness
            1 A common wrong idea
            3 The solution to snowblindness
        The best title is 4.

COMPREHENSION EXERCISE 5

We'll try the numbered-paragraph exercise again. Match the subtitles following the selection with the numbers of the paragraphs. A general title will also be requested. Remember, don't bog down in the details.

Unloading a Box Car

[1.] If a box car could talk, what a fascinating story it could tell! It is a professional nomad, forever wandering, forever visiting strange places, never knowing what sort of adventure the immediate future has in store. Like the weather-beaten stone cutter in the quarry, who, upon being asked what he was doing, beamingly replied that he was "helping to build a cathedral," the box car, if it could speak, might say with equal pride that it is helping to feed and clothe and house a nation, that it is helping to make people healthy and comfortable and happy.

[2.] Many years ago, each railroad kept its freight cars on its own rails, and each shipment of freight destined to off-line points was unloaded at the junction point and loaded into a car owned by the connecting railroad, and so on to destination. Sometimes several transfers were necessary, and freight shipments were exceedingly slow. Then, soon after the railroads had adopted a uniform standard gauge, they worked out a plan whereby they interchanged cars. Since the adoption of interchange, freight cars are loaded and shipped to all parts of the United States, and even to Canada, Mexico, and Cuba, without transferring the contents en route.

[3.] That is why the freight car is such a wanderer today, and that is why it is a common sight to see a freight train made up of cars of many railroads—some located hundreds or thousands of miles away. When a freight car has been unloaded off the line of the owning road, railroad employees and shippers, under a code known as "Car Service Rules," endeavor to find loading for the car which will take it back to or in the direction of the owning railroad, in order that the car may be returned economically to its home road.

[4.] A journey for an active box car might be about as follows: *packaged freight,* Atlanta to New York; *printing machinery,* New York to Bangor, Maine; *empty,* Bangor to Millinocket, Maine; *newsprint paper,* Millinocket to Boston; *empty,* Boston to Haverhill, Massachusetts; *shoes,* Haverhill to Dayton; *electric refrigerators,* Dayton to St. Louis. But this would be only a start. Here's what its waybills might show us about the rest of its work: *empty,* Houston to Galveston; *chemicals,* Galveston to Chicago; *telephones and parts,* Chicago to Los Angeles; *ship machinery,* Los Angeles to Portland, Oregon; *canned salmon,* Portland to Minneapolis; *flour,* Minneapolis to Baltimore; *empty,* Baltimore to Lancaster, Pennsylvania; *linoleum,* Lancaster to Green Bay; *empty,* Green Bay to Appleton, Wisconsin; *paper,* Appleton to Hamilton, Ohio; *empty,* Hamilton to Cincinnati; *soap,* Cincinnati to Detroit; *automobile parts,* Detroit to New Orleans; *coffee,* New Orleans to Nashville. By this time the car might need some major repairs. If so, it would be sent home to Atlanta.

Put the numbers in the spaces.

_____ Development of box-car interchanges

_____ A typical box-car journey

_____ Why box cars are repaired

_____ The purpose of box cars

_____ Why cars are wanderers

_____ How cars are manufactured

Select the title below that would be possibly better than the original for the entire selection.

_____ 1. An unusual vehicle

_____ 2. The history of railroads

_____ 3. The story of box cars

_____ 4. Products from many lands

_____ 5. A trip across the country

ANSWERS:

2	Development of box-car interchanges
4	A typical box-car journey
1	The purpose of box cars
3	Why cars are wanderers

The best title is 3.

COMPREHENSION EXERCISE 6

This exercise and the ones that follow bring you to the training for full comprehension. They will give you practice in recognizing all the features suggested by our guide questions that should be observed by the reader in addition to main ideas and details. As you read the selection, keep in mind the need for ascertaining not only *what* the writer says but *how* he says it.

Kids, Goats, and Bees

There's a family in Falmouth whose lively types of animal and insect life keep things hopping. The master of the situation (?) got some goats last year to spare him from having to mow his lawn, or so his family declares. Now, he confesses, he still has to mow the lawn; in addition he has to milk the goats.

He also asserts a fondness for goats' milk, and his mother and sister agree enthusiastically with him on this point, but remark, "We simply prefer our tea and coffee black."

He insists that his goats are gentle creatures, but his wife was the butt of a misunderstanding about this last summer, when one of the goats proved the point—without doing any serious harm.

When this summer, five puppies entered the scene, they equaled the number of cats in the family. Since then, a hive of bees has joined the ranks. One of the cats, Rusty, tried to strike up a speaking acquaintance with the hive, and from the fact that she is still running in an opposite direction, has proved that there is no rust in her joints.

The family insist, without kidding, that the goats are the most intelligent of all their livestock, and have never eaten shirts off the clothesline, but admit that one did once sample the coat an innocent bystander was wearing.

I. Main ideas and details

A. Another good title for this selection would be

_____ 1. Goats' milk

_____ 2. A family that likes pets

_____ 3. A home-grown lawn mower

_____ 4. A silly group of people

_____ 5. Pets offer many problems

B. The wife

_____ 1. likes goats

_____ 2. was once butted by a goat

_____ 3. prefers her coffee black

_____ 4. was stung by a bee

_____ 5. wants to get rid of the pets

C. The family's attitude toward the pets is

_____ 1. indifferent

_____ 2. hostile

_____ 3. favorable

_____ 4. worried

_____ 5. puzzled

II. Other features

A. The writer's primary purpose is to

_____ 1. inform

_____ 2. ridicule

_____ 3. amuse

_____ 4. condemn

_____ 5. praise

B. The writer's point of view is that of

_____ 1. scientific accuracy

_____ 2. serious analysis

_____ 3. crusading zeal

_____ 4. amiable good humor

_____ 5. violent antagonism

C. The writer achieves a light touch in his style by

_____ 1. cracking jokes

_____ 2. poking cruel fun

_____ 3. pretending to be matter-of-fact

_____ 4. stressing human weakness

_____ 5. using ordinary language

D. The two guide questions that are least important in analyzing this piece are

_____ 1. purpose

_____ 2. main ideas

_____ 3. details

_____ 4. point of view

_____ 5. reliability

_____ 6. hidden meanings

_____ 7. style

ANSWERS: I. A. 2, B. 2, C. 3.
         II. A. 3, B. 4, C. 3, D. 5, 6.

Notes on the answers

II. C. The technique employed by the writer is similar
to that of the straight-faced comedians of stage and screeen.
They don't "pull" a laugh, but they arrange their remarks so
that the humor comes out of an almost serious description of
an absurd situation. They also do not scorn the lowly pun
—a play on words like "his wife was the *butt* of a misunderstanding."

II. D. In an article written for pure entertainment, the
reader should not be concerned with looking deeply into
the meaning, nor should he wonder whether the writer is
telling the truth.

COMPREHENSION EXERCISE 7

Here again you ascertain the writer's purpose as soon
as you can and then LOOK FOR THE KEYS that you
consider important in this selection.

Sea Farmers

You have only two chances in a million to find a pearl
in the 10 million bushels of oysters eaten each year in this
country.

This large quantity of oysters, you may not know, is
not the result of just fishing, but farming. Early in the
spring an oyster farmer prepares his beds, then cul-
tivates and harvests his crops. After buying or renting
bay bottoms from cities, which by law own one to three
miles out, the oysterman prepares the ground. He clears
the bottom of all debris and spreads it with old opened
oyster shells. This "clutch," which is spread where
natural or planted beds of adult oysters are located, pro-

vides a hard surface for baby oysters to cling to. May to September is the spawning season and oysters are not as palatable then, though just as good. That is one reason fewer are eaten in the months without "R." The other reason is it gives a chance to conserve the industry for future seasons.

Baby oysters come from fertilized eggs dropped at the rate of 50 million a year by the female oyster. So small are the eggs that a quart could hold all the eggs needed to supply the nation's annual crop.

The eggs grow bivalved shells in 24 hours and begin swimming. Soon they cement themselves to the shells. By the time the new oysters grow to the size of your thumbnail, in about six months, they're crowding each other. Then the oyster farmer has to separate and replant them or their growth is retarded. So he transplants them to growing grounds, often miles away. Growing ground is chosen for availability of food particles and its immunity from storm damage, often 15 to 50 feet below the surface. A combination of fresh and salt water is best.

In the growing beds oysters are left undisturbed except for periodic inspection to look out for starfish and snails, oysters' mortal enemies.

In their third year oysters are large enough to harvest. Boats head out for the beds marked with long poles sticking out above the water. Huge dredges with steel teeth, lowered over the sides, drag along the bottom gathering up the oysters into nets.

Oyster beds are found along the Atlantic, Gulf and Pacific shores. The largest crop comes from Chesapeake Bay; the best growing ground is now considered to be the Connecticut shore.

I. Main ideas and details

A. Another title for the selection could be

_____ 1. Growing cultivated oysters

_____ 2. An oyster's mortal enemy

_____ 3. Dredging for oysters

_____ 4. Where the best oyster beds are

_____ 5. Baby oysters

B. The main idea of the second paragraph is

_____ 1. spreading "clutches"

_____ 2. months without an "R"

_____ 3. bay bottoms

_____ 4. oyster farming

_____ 5. adult and baby oysters

C. We are told that oysters

_____ 1. grow very rapidly in size

_____ 2. grow best on the surface

_____ 3. drop single eggs

_____ 4. require several years to grow large

_____ 5. are harvested by hand

D. A *clutch* is

_____ 1. part of an automobile

192

_____ 2. a bed of old oyster shells

_____ 3. a transplanting

_____ 4. a hard grip

_____ 5. a kind of dredge

II. Other features

A. The author's purpose was to

_____ 1. prove he likes oysters

_____ 2. criticize oyster farming

_____ 3. entertain the reader

_____ 4. prove he is a scientist

_____ 5. describe oysters' habits

B. The author's style shows an effort to be

_____ 1. personal

_____ 2. formal

_____ 3. superior

_____ 4. cold

_____ 5. vulgar

C. The details in the selection should be

_____ 1. ignored completely

_____ 2. memorized

_____ 3. checked with references

_____ 4. read quickly

_____ 5. studied very carefully

D. The three guide questions that are least important here are

_____ 1. purpose

_____ 2. main ideas

_____ 3. details

_____ 4. point of view

_____ 5. reliability

_____ 6. hidden meanings

_____ 7. style

ANSWERS: I.   A. 1, B. 4, C. 4, D. 2.
          II. A. 3, B. 1, C. 4, D. 4, 5, 6.

Notes on the answers

II. A. The writer is not attempting to present a text-book study but is offering the material purely for appreciation and interest.

II. B. The use of "you may not know" and "size of your thumbnail" indicates the desire of the writer to make the style personal.

II. C. Since you are reading this kind of article solely for entertainment, you observe the details but do not linger over them.

II. D. There can be no hidden meanings in such a discussion of oysters, and it can be safely assumed that the writer checked his facts.

Up to this point we have been considering the *writer's* purpose, asking you to ascertain it early and then decide how you are going to read his material and which of the guide questions you will need to apply. However, it is important to point out that there will be occasions when *your* purpose will differ from the writer's. For instance, let us suppose that some evening, having nothing else to read, you select a volume of an encyclopedia and glance through it casually, picking up bits here and there. Now, the writers of such articles undoubtedly had in mind that their material was to be used primarily in scholarly research. In this case, your purpose and the writer's would be completely different. Similarly, you might read an article like the one on oysters with the express purpose of preparing for some examination. The details then would be of great importance to you.

What you do, of course, when there is this difference between your purpose and the author's, is to let yours be the determining factor in so far as speed and the guide questions are concerned. However, you should not make the mistake of going to the wrong material to suit your need. In general, when you are reading for information or serious study, you should select articles and books that have been written carefully and authoritatively. And when you are reading for relaxation and enjoyment, you will want to turn to lighter materials. For the average reader, a good guide to whether he has selected appropriate reading matter is the closeness with which his purpose and the writer's agree.

COMPREHENSION EXERCISE 8

Continue to use the guide questions with this selection for full comprehension.

'Town Meeting' of the Stockholders

BY A. H. RASKIN

Three "capitalists" sat on camp chairs in a Schenectady armory one day recently, munching cold fried chicken and commenting contentedly on the progress of their $4,000,000,000-a-year business. One was a butcher in a Manhattan chain store, the second an Albany bus driver and the third a retired carpenter from Boston.

Together with 3,726 other share owners of the General Electric Company, they had just had their annual opportunity to let the president they hire at $259,988 a year and the other company officials know what the "bosses" think of the way things are run.

It was not the kind of meeting to give the hired hands ulcers. The stockholders applauded a report that their enterprise, already the country's biggest electrical manufacturer, was getting bigger; they voted down two insurgent proposals by margins of 50 to 1; and they yelled, "Throw him out" at the lone shareholder in-delicate enough to say he did not care much for the G. E. management.

Not so many years ago the number of share owners at the average meeting was small enough to fit in a broom closet. And many company executives made it plain that was exactly where they would like to put them. The presidents or board chairmen of flourishing corporations saw little reason to mask their feeling that the whole affair was at once a bore and an affront to their right to manage the business in accordance with their own sovereign judgment.

Now a growing list of "blue-chip" companies take their annual meetings "on the road." Instead of asking their stockholders to travel to the same city every year, they schedule the meeting in a different city each year so people remote from the company headquarters can feel they are first-class citizens in an enterprise that has owners all over. Others use closed-circuit television to let stockholders in two or more big cities share in the proceedings. Ingenuity comparable to that applied to the sale of the company products is often focused on special films, exhibits and plant tours designed to make participants feel their visit was worth while.

A Judy Holliday can lead a revolutionary upsurge of rank-and-file stockholders on the movie screen, but a similar coup outside the theatre requires a long-nurtured effort by financial interests with ties to the banks, insurance companies, pension trusts and other institutional investors that exert a dominant influence over the securities of most big companies.

This year's General Electric session, among the biggest held by any company, afforded a good insight into what goes on at a typical meeting when the business is prospering and no one is making any serious attempt to push out the top brass. A holiday spirit hung over the huge armory as the meeting began. Hundreds of the share owners were retired G. E. employees who had spent the earlier hours of the morning wandering through the company's big Schenectady works in the manner of old grads returning to their alma mater.

There were dozens of babies in the crowd, all with badges. Here and there sat an Army or Navy enlisted man. A few bobby-soxers listened listlessly. But there were fifty oldsters for every teen-ager—tired-eyed men and women waiting for word on the security of their investment in the electronic age.

A special blue-draped podium and microphone had been set up facing the dais so the stockholders would have no difficulty making themselves heard. This quickly proved a delusive expectation, to the exasperation of Philip D. Reed, chairman of the board, a normally urbane man, and a battery of G. E. sound engineers.

When Louis A. Brusati of Chicago, an old foe of the company management, took the mike to outline two resolutions he had submitted to strip the top officers of some extra pay privileges, much of what he said sounded like a Donald Duck sound track run backward.

Reed, who had been annoyed by his initial inability to make out what Brusati was saying, appeared no happier when Brusati's words finally became intelligible. The chairman snapped that some of the questions were "too utterly ridiculous" to warrant reply.

He expressed certainty that the company had benefited from setting up the incentive pay plans, and that the establishment of the stock option program had proved a "very wise thing." Most of Brusati's fellow share owners indicated by their applause that they agreed with the Reed view.

Unabashed by his apparent isolation, the Chicagoan said there was no unanimity on the plan's worth. He added that when he invested in a company, he wanted a management in which he could have confidence.

"I agree with you completely," Reed rejoined. "If you don't feel that with respect to this management, you know what you can do with your shares."

This brought a fresh burst of applause and approving laughter from the crowd. When Brusati reacted with an irate demand that Reed explain what he meant by his suggestion, some female voices hooted, "Throw him out" in notes as icy as any directed at an offending umpire by a Ladies' Day throng in Ebbets Field.

He was followed by a parade of stockholders with nice things to say about the management. One suggested that if there were a way to keep Brusati from getting the floor at future meetings it should be pursued. The chain of compliments and a continuing improvement in the acoustics visibly brightened the chairman's mood.

He was radiating good will by the time Mrs. M. Dewar Winne, the widow of a surgeon from the Adirondacks, made her ninth annual trip to the microphone. Mrs. Winne, a tiny old lady with an indelible smile and an Ike pin on the lapel of her dark gray jacket, had the whole house in high good humor with a disconnected tribute to the G. E. management, Herbert Hoover, her hat and her teeth.

The Brusati proposals to deprive the executives of incentives were voted down by votes of roughly 70,500,-000 to 1,400,000. By that time everyone was ready for lunch. A big truck backed up to the armory door as an organist broke into "I Could Write a Book," from "Pal Joey." Young men and women in white uniforms began setting up a rail down which they slid giant cartons loaded with box lunches.

A cafeteria official announced that the lunches would be carried to the stockholders but that did not stop hundreds from swarming down the aisles to get theirs in a hurry. Each box contained a half chicken, a roll, a container of milk, potato salad, fruit gelatin, a chocolate cake bar and two napkins. Some took the boxes back to their seats. Others wandered across the street to a little park and sat down on the grass, picnic style.

I. Main ideas and details

A. The main point of this article is to

_____ 1. describe a typical stockholders' meeting

_____ 2. suggest that corporations be abolished

_____ 3. compliment one particular company

_____ 4. tell an amusing story of a little, old lady

_____ 5. suggest that old-time meetings were better

B. The objecting stockholder displayed his

_____ 1. ignorance

_____ 2. blind anger

_____ 3. independence

_____ 4. uncooperative spirit

_____ 5. desire for the limelight

C. Most of the people present were

_____ 1. very rich

_____ 2. foreigners

_____ 3. ordinary Americans

_____ 4. very young

_____ 5. dissatisfied

D. To overthrow management is

_____ 1. easy

_____ 2. impossible

_____ 3. done frequently

_____ 4. rarely possible for the rank and file

_____ 5. never a problem

II. *Other features*

A. The writer's purpose was to

_____ 1. criticize

_____ 2. defend

_____ 3. support

_____ 4. inform and entertain

_____ 5. suggest a change

B. The writer's point of view is

_____ 1. unclear

_____ 2. impartial

_____ 3. biased

_____ 4. in favor of the stockholders

_____ 5. in favor of management

C. We can believe the writer because he

_____ 1. writes for a newspaper

_____ 2. uses good English

_____ 3. presents facts as he saw them

_____ 4. owns stock in G. E.

_____ 5. was sympathetic to an old lady

D. The writer's style suggests that he

_____ 1. is very formal

_____ 2. likes to argue

_____ 3. seems unsure of himself

_____ 4. considers himself superior

_____ 5. has a sense of humor

E. The guide question that figures least prominently is

_____ 1. purpose

_____ 2. main ideas

_____ 3. details

_____ 4. point of view

_____ 5. reliability

_____ 6. hidden meanings

_____ 7. style

ANSWERS: I. A. 1, B. 3, C. 3, D. 4.
           II. A. 4, B. 2, C. 3, D. 5, E. 6.

Notes on answers

II. E. As soon as you have decided that a writer is making every effort to be impartial, you can assume that there will be little, if any, hidden meaning in his material, except as it applies to his own personality. (See discussion on the poet in the next exercise.)

COMPREHENSION EXERCISES 9 AND 10

The next two selections should prove to be quite interesting for you. The first is a poem written by a sixteen-year-old boy, who won a national contest with his effort, and the second is a letter written by his twenty-one-year-old brother after the latter had read the poetry while he was on Army duty in Europe. Not only will these pieces be a change from the literary forms we have been using, but they will give you the opportunity to make certain comparisons between the writers. You will probably want to read the poem somewhat more slowly than the letter.

Death

BY STEPHEN M. SELTZER

Praise Death!
Death is not to be feared,
Death is the end of fear.
Life—fearful and unpredictable flows into Death.
Death, absolute Death!

As the short lived spray of the ocean melts finally
   into the sea,
People once more become part of the whole
In Death.
In the long, dreamless sleep, the many "I's" fall into
   nothingness.
Death, the equalizer!
Neither reward nor revenge in Death—
Just peaceful non-existence.
Death, triumphant Death!

The Letter

BY HOWARD N. SELTZER

Hi Steve,

Well, you seem to have grown quite perceptive in your usual quiet way. I'm referring to your poem, of course. It's good, if the praise of a sparsely educated layman means anything. My experience in the field of poesy is rather limited; almost non-existent except for what Mother Casey forced through my iron-bound head.

You seem to be quite knowledgeable on the subject, and while I don't understand how you got that way, I envy your philosophy.

I can't accept death as an "equalizer," a time of peace eternal or an ending of mortal care and terror. For me it is a thing to be feared, avoided, cheated at any price. It is a final and eternal ending, a finish to laughter and a farewell to sound and color and texture, and all the small pleasures that make life worth the living.

It's a selfish attitude at best, but it's mine, and I'm stuck with it. The simple little pleasures that are nothing more than the candy-coating on the pill, the spice on the cake, emotional deodorants, so to speak, are well worth the grub-like, terrible routine that most of us live our lives in.

As a case in point, I'm going to an extreme but it's a good example. After a long, queasy flight in a plane, when the order comes to "stand"—that's a partial death, a relaxation of senses, a numbing to what is ahead. One is very calm, looking around with the detached air of a slightly-intoxicated idiot, but conscious only of the man ahead and the door. It's a sort of self-induced hypnosis, an extreme concentration wherein all action, though newly-learned, is instinctive. As you leave the door, the fear comes back and the question—will it happen this time? Then you know. In four seconds you know. Subjectively though it is longer. It can be your lifetime. You're on the ground now. Completely and utterly relaxed. You roll your 'chute and carry it to the truck, meeting friends on the way, a man among men. You sit down and maybe light a cigarette, listening to the "jump" stories, funny and not so funny. The sun is on your back and little flying things are playing in a field in front of you. The consciousness, the sensuality, the extreme pleasure of simple movement are seldom so sharply defined as now. Any simple little thing, such as gazing at your dirty fingernails, is luxury.

You have avoided the finality once more. Perhaps you won't next time, but this feeling, this primitive vice is well worth it.

This is the old Cornball signing off. Take it cool.

Howard

I. *Main ideas and details*

A. The poet sees death as

_____ 1. democratic in some ways

_____ 2. an enemy

_____ 3. something to be feared

_____ 4. welcome

_____ 5. tragic

B. The letter writer regards death with

_____ 1. indifference

_____ 2. fear

_____ 3. anticipation

_____ 4. cowardice

_____ 5. contempt

C. The letter writer is

_____ 1. an aviator

_____ 2. a bombardier

_____ 3. a paratrooper

_____ 4. a diver

_____ 5. a navigator

D. The letter writer

_____ 1. agrees with his brother

_____ 2. differs sharply

_____ 3. doesn't care one way or the other

_____ 4. considers him silly

_____ 5. agrees only in part

II. *Other features*

A. The poet's purpose is to

_____ 1. amuse

_____ 2. depress

_____ 3. uplift the hopeless

_____ 4. express his feelings

_____ 5. encourage suicide

B. The letter writer's purpose is to

_____ 1. explain his reactions to the subject

_____ 2. teach his brother a lesson

_____ 3. show how wrong his brother is

_____ 4. glorify his own occupation

_____ 5. scold his brother

C. If we read deeply into the poem we find feelings of

_____ 1. puzzlement

_____ 2. insecurity

_____ 3. insincerity

_____ 4. pride

_____ 5. superiority

D. If we read deeply into the letter we find that the author

_____ 1. likes his fingernails

_____ 2. is afraid of life

_____ 3. wants to be a hero

_____ 4. enjoys his work

_____ 5. wishes he were home

E. The poet's style is

_____ 1. gay

_____ 2. youthful

_____ 3. shallow

_____ 4. serious

_____ 5. ordinary

F. The letter writer's style is

_____ 1. dull

_____ 2. imaginative

_____ 3. flowery

_____ 4. unclear

_____ 5. immature

G. The guide question that obviously need not be asked about either piece is

_____ 1. purpose

_____ 2. main ideas

_____ 3. details

_____ 4. point of view

_____ 5. reliability

_____ 6. hidden meanings

_____ 7. style

ANSWERS: I. A. 1, B. 2, C. 3, D. 2.
II. A. 4, B. 1, C. 2, D. 5, E. 4, F. 2, G. 5.

Notes on the answers

II. A. The poet is not trying to influence the reader, but just tell how a young boy feels when he begins to give serious thought to a subject that troubles us all.

II. C. A sixteen-year-old boy who has not yet achieved station in life may be concerned about the "I's," and their relationship to his own identity. Will he amount to something? Will he be successful? There is almost a sense of security in the facelessness of death. This is a normal problem of adolescence.

II. F. The highly imaginative quality of the letter comes through in the writer's attention to detail about nature, his emotions, the small things about his existence.

II. G. Certainly since each is writing about his innermost feelings, we can assume sincerity and truth.

Which of the brothers is the better writer? I'm not going to answer this for you, but you might find it stimulating to discuss your choice with another person. You would, of course, have to point to specific qualities of the writing technique of either to support your position. This sort of discussion would give you valuable training. The more you study the tools of writing the better you are able to recognize a good piece of work and the deeper becomes your appreciation of the things you read.

COMPREHENSION EXERCISE 11

Here is an editorial from a Southern newspaper. It is a splendid example of how attention only to ideas and details would make it difficult for the reader to enjoy the piece for its other features, which are far more important.

Peck of Trouble Looms in Abandoning Bushel

There's mischief afoot. They're tampering with the

measuring system, trying to replace the bushel with the hundredweight.

It's all a part of a foreign plot to eventually substitute the metric system, common in Europe and over the rest of the world, for our American standard of weights and measures. It is all being attempted in the name of simplicity, but what is more complicated than the meter, the basic unit of measurement under the system? The meter is defined as approximately "one ten-millionth part of the distance measured on a meridian from the equator to the pole. . . ." Anybody got a slide rule?

The hundredweight, they tell us, is being chosen to give us uniformity of measurement, because the weight of a bushel varies from state to state. That's well and good, but who says everybody agrees on the weight of a hundredweight? In England a hundredweight comes to 112 avoirdupois pounds, while in this country it tips the scale at a 100 pounds. Now what's to keep this difference of opinion of the size of a hundredweight from cropping up in this country?

That's not all the difficulty involved, either. There's the loss to the language. Suppose hundredweight replaces bushel. Can you imagine anyone saying, "I love you a hundredweight and a peck," or a youngster deriding a "butter-fingered" ball player with, "Why you couldn't catch a ball with a hundredweight basket." And what about the Biblical passage? Shall it become, "Neither do men light a candle and put it under a hundredweight"?

Be it known anybody who tries to remove the bushel from the channels of commerce, and consequently from our language, is in for a peck of trouble.

I. Main ideas and details

A. The main point of the writer is that

   _____ 1. foreigners are mischievous

   _____ 2. the new system of measurement will be good

   _____ 3. the old system has serious defects

   _____ 4. the change will result in no improvement

   _____ 5. there is no agreement on how heavy a hundredweight is

B. The reason the change is advocated in this country is that there is

   _____ 1. improper understanding of a bushel

   _____ 2. lack of uniformity in bushel weights

   _____ 3. better sense to the hundredweight

   _____ 4. the need for a change

   _____ 5. legislation pending

C. The change, according to the writer, will also introduce problems of

   _____ 1. language

   _____ 2. interstate commerce

   _____ 3. international law

   _____ 4. import duties

   _____ 5. rural finance

II. Other features

A. The writer's purpose is to

_____ 1. offer savage criticism

_____ 2. support the movement for change

_____ 3. disapprove the change on patriotic grounds

_____ 4. furnish half-serious, half-comic opposition

_____ 5. show he doesn't care

B. The writer apparently is different from those people who favor products and ideas just because they are

_____ 1. local

_____ 2. scientific

_____ 3. imported

_____ 4. new

_____ 5. old

C. The writer's point of view shows his ability not to make

_____ 1. enemies

_____ 2. friends

_____ 3. trouble

_____ 4. mountains out of molehills

_____ 5. fun

D. The writer's use of the pun (play on words) in the title and text of the article gives his style

_____ 1. an ungrammatical construction

_____ 2. a humorous quality

_____ 3. a loose quality

_____ 4. a lack of clarity

_____ 5. a solemn touch

E. The guide question that is least important in analyzing this selection is

_____ 1. purpose

_____ 2. main ideas

_____ 3. details

_____ 4. point of view

_____ 5. reliability

_____ 6. hidden meanings

_____ 7. style

ANSWERS: I. A. 4, B. 2, C. 1.
          II. A. 4, B. 3, C. 4, D. 2, E. 5.

Notes on the answers

II. A. Although the article is obviously written in a humorous vein, the author is definitely opposed to the idea of a measurement change. His technique of objecting is used frequently by skilled writers. They reduce a suggestion to laughter and thus destroy its serious influence on the reader.

II. B. The answer here requires a little digging. One can detect a strong rejection of the idea that things abroad are done better.

II. E. You don't worry about the writer's reliability since he presents easily checked facts and his purpose is not scientific accuracy.

COMPREHENSION EXERCISE 12

This is the last of the series of exercises designed to help you develop full comprehension. You should now be well on your way to knowing how to LOOK FOR THE KEYS so that your reading is characterized by not only increased understanding but deeper appreciation as well.

Editorials are written so that the newspaper will have an opportunity to comment on the events of the day. During an election campaign particularly, one expects strong opinions to be expressed and definite sides taken. But the selection you are about to read is remarkable for a certain quality that I shall ask you about later.

The Day of Decision

The long days and nights of campaigning are over. Eight hundred and fifty-eight candidates competing for two hundred and sixty-three seats in the Canadian House of Commons have sounded their appeals and now stand waiting for the verdict of the people. One other seat already has been filled by acclamation and for another the voting has been deferred because of the death of a candidate.

Today is the day when men and women from the Avalon Peninsula of Newfoundland to the Queen Charlotte Islands of British Columbia, from the forty-ninth parallel to the Arctic outposts, parade into booths to mark their secret ballots. They will select the candidates who will serve as their law makers and their policy makers in the nation's capital, who will defend their rights and redress their wrongs, for the next four to five years. And they will be choosing by their collective votes the political party from whose elective ranks will be named the federal cabinet that will exercise such a tremendous influence over their lives in the period ahead.

More than nine million Canadians are entitled to make these choices. If the trend in the past continues in this election, only six million will take advantage of their opportunity, will respond to what is an important duty of all who hold the franchise.

Why have one third of the eligible voters stayed home in the past? Is it because the cacophony of the appeals has confused them? Is it because in this age of an expanding welfare state, there is little difference between the basic philosophies of the parties?

Whatever it is, three million people refraining from voting are three million too many. The right to an unfettered vote is a sacred heritage won for the peoples of democracies today with the blood and sweat of generations that have gone before. And it is a right which, through our apathy, could easily be lost again as history of very recent years in other lands has shown so well.

The franchise is too valuable to be disregarded. The type of government that is to preside over the destiny of our nation and the lives of its individual citizens and the calibre of men and women who are to make our wishes known in Parliament, whether in the front seats or the back benches, and who, equally as important, work for us behind the scenes is something that we cannot afford to take lightly.

Today is a day that calls for the greatest wisdom each and every one of us can muster. We must judge carefully and act conscientiously.

I. Main ideas and details

A. Another title for the selection could be

_____ 1. Candidates and voters

_____ 2. The obligation to vote

_____ 3. Nine million voters

_____ 4. Canadian provinces at election time

_____ 5. Election eve

B. Of the eligible voters, those who didn't vote last year represented

_____ 1. a half

_____ 2. a third

_____ 3. a fifth

_____ 4. a mere handful

_____ 5. an undetermined number

C. Most of the officials elected will serve at least

_____ 1. two

_____ 2. three

_____ 3. four

_____ 4. eight

_____ 5. ten years

II. Other features

A. The purpose of the writer is to

_____ 1. defeat one party

_____ 2. bring out the vote

_____ 3. praise Canada

_____ 4. analyze the system of elections

_____ 5. express opposition

B. The interesting point we referred to in the introduction to this editorial is found in the point of view of the writer. It is

_____ 1. prejudiced

_____ 2. indifferent

_____ 3. humorous

_____ 4. impartial

_____ 5. unclear

C. A hidden meaning that may be found in the selection is that

_____ 1. elections are fraudulent

_____ 2. the various parties have selfish interests

_____ 3. Canada should change its system of elections

_____ 4. people are lazy

_____ 5. the progress made in behalf of people's interests must be maintained

D. The writer gets close to the reader by

_____ 1. appealing to his duty

_____ 2. urging him to vote

_____ 3. citing past statistics

_____ 4. identifying himself with the voters

_____ 5. recommending wisdom

E. The guide question whose answer is obvious is

_____ 1. purpose

_____ 2. main ideas

_____ 3. details

_____ 4. point of view

_____ 5. reliability

_____ 6. hidden meanings

_____ 7. style

ANSWERS: I. A. 2, B. 2, C. 3.
         II. A. 2, B. 4, C. 5, D. 4, E. 5.

Notes on the answers

II. C. The use of historical example by the editor to warn the reader of the possible loss of liberties shows his concern for and approval of the reforms.

II. D. The use of phrases like "*our* apathy," "*our* nation," and "*we* cannot" indicates that the writer is aligning himself with the reader.

❋   ❋   ❋

You will recall that at the beginning of this chapter you were told that improved comprehension can have a favorable effect on your reading rate. It should be clear to you now that the use of the guide questions to help you FIND THE KEYS contributes greatly to your deciding how fast you should read a particular selection. Thus by training yourself to allow what you are looking for to determine how you will handle an article, story, or book, you are, in a sense, killing two reading problems with one approach.

CHAPTER IX

STEP FIVE:

Build Your Vocabulary!

WE'RE GOING to begin this chapter by conducting an experiment.

Read the following selection with every effort aimed at full comprehension. If you have difficulty with some of the words, don't let it stop you. Keep going at a good speed, and then take the usual test that follows the paragraphs. There will be one set of questions, however, that you haven't tried before!

***

BY ROBERT BIRD

Last fall an ingenious young man, perched high up in a typical New York skyscraper on Madison Avenue, was confronted with a rather perplexing problem. His employers, members of a prominent advertising agency, had none too subtly implied recently that his work had been a bit shallow of late, and unless he rapidly crystallized on the Piel's Beer account they would certainly miss his congenial company. The young man pondered his somewhat precarious situation and embarked upon a voyage into the realm of fancy in a desperate effort to rescue the ad that threatened such ominous consequences for him. He really wanted to stay a while longer in that company.

Only a few months later, people found themselves following the antics of a tall, thin, soft-spoken man and his short, stocky, wind-baggish brother with as much interest as they did their daily comic strips. Wonder of wonders, instead of abandoning their television sets when the commercial came on and scurrying into the kitchen for a quick snack, viewers were reported to be looking forward to each new animated cartoon episode of Burt and Harry. The quiet advice and modest efforts at bird-calling of one of the team brought audible chuckles, while the brow-beating and threats of the other were hilarious in the eyes of a completely captivated audience. A beer account had suddenly come to life and a job had been saved.

The young man is probably sojourning in French Morocco by now, or some other equally exotic resort, with lots of flowers, expensive cigars, and quite possibly a couple of enchanting local denizens draped attractively on his arm. He could also be contemplating accepting the vice-presidency those "wonderful chaps" at the agency have been thrusting under his nose or perhaps he is deciding to continue to soak up some more of that transoceanic culture.

The point is, his is one of those enviable success stories that are based on a facile imagination, incisive action, and an acute awareness of what the public (a very ambiguous term) enjoys these days in the way of ads. John Doe's opinions change as erratically and as often as the products that beckon to him. As many bitter ad men are realizing, it is as necessary to keep abreast of new advertising methods as it is of technical progress in industry. Both are equally vital in sales appeal.

Our bright young man knew the sacred trinity of achieving his mission. First, and most fundamental, he employed the idea of avoiding mundane imitation and, instead, used an entirely new and refreshing approach. Secondly, he kept the contents of the ad within the confines of a simple layout and devoid of prodigious copy. Third, and to my mind the genius of good advertising, he threw in copious quantities of good old American humor. These three concepts are basic in the creation of appealing advertisements.

I. Main ideas and details

A. A good title for the selection would have been

_____ 1. A harsh employer

_____ 2. Madison Avenue problems

_____ 3. How to write successful ads

_____ 4. Traveling abroad

_____ 5. Two amusing characters

B. Burt and Harry are

_____ 1. real people

_____ 2. cartoon creations

_____ 3. vice-presidents of the firm

_____ 4. radio announcers

_____ 5. beer drinkers

C. The young man

_____ 1. lost his job

_____ 2. resigned

_____ 3. was offered a promotion

_____ 4. left to live abroad

_____ 5. was lost in French Morocco

II. *Other features*

A. The writer's purpose was to

_____ 1. praise a beer company

_____ 2. defend a young man

_____ 3. solicit advertising customers

_____ 4. suggest changes in advertising policy

_____ 5. describe successful advertising methods in an interesting way

B. The writer's point of view was

_____ 1. pleasantly informative

_____ 2. very serious

_____ 3. prejudiced

_____ 4. highly belligerent

_____ 5. not too clear

C. The writer's reliability

_____ 1. should be questioned

_____ 2. is established by his evidence

_____ 3. cannot be determined

D. The writer's style indicates that he uses unusual words in order to

_____ 1. befuddle the reader

_____ 2. show off his learning

_____ 3. force the reader to use a dictionary

_____ 4. create sharp and clear meaning

_____ 5. hide his ignorance

E. The hidden meaning here is that in advertising you

_____ 1. either produce or get out

_____ 2. can see the world

_____ 3. can enjoy good company

_____ 4. have a lot of fun

_____ 5. must always do things in threes

ANSWERS: I. A. 3, B. 2, C. 3.
          II. A. 5, B. 1, C. 2, D. 4, E. 1.

Now, using the phrases in the column at the left as definitions, find the words in the column at the right that match. Write the number of the proper word in the space before its definition. For example, in the first space you write _15_ because _ingenious_ means _very clever_. DO NOT GO BACK OVER THE SELECTION TO PICK OUT THE WORDS!

The young man

    a. __15__ was *very clever*

    b._____ and had a *puzzling* situation.

The employers

    c._____ not very *delicately*

    d._____ *told indirectly*

that he

    e._____ *prepare a plan with a definite form*

    f._____ or his *well-liked* presence would be removed.

He was

    g._____ forced to *think seriously*

    h._____ because he was in a *dangerous* spot

    i._____ and faced with *threatening* results to his job.

The ad brought forth

    j._____ *noisily laughing* reactions

    k._____ from a *fascinated* audience.

Today the young man is

    l._____ *visiting* a romantic place

    m._____ enjoying *foreign* resorts

1. acute
2. ambiguous
3. captivated
4. congenial
5. copious
6. crystallize
7. denizens
8. enviable
9. erratically
10. exotic
11. facile
12. hilarious
13. implied
14. incisive
15. ingenious
16. mundane
17. ominous
18. perplexing
19. ponder
20. precarious
21. prodigious
22. sojourning in
23. subtly
24. transoceanic
25. trinity

n._____ meeting some interesting *inhabitants*

o._____ and looking for further *across the seas* enrichment.

He

p._____ *is one who excites the desire to have or be like him*

q._____ has *ready* and *skillful* visual powers

r._____ takes *clear-cut, sharp* steps

s._____ and has a *keen* understanding of

the public which has

t._____ *uncertain* tastes

u._____ and changes *unpredictably*.

The young man

v._____ knew the *threefold* approach

w._____ tried to escape from *ordinary* copying

x._____ avoided *extraordinarily* bulky language

y._____ and used *generous* amounts of humor.

ANSWERS:

a. 15	f. 4	k. 3	p. 8	u. 9
b. 18	g. 19	l. 22	q. 11	v. 25
c. 23	h. 20	m. 10	r. 14	w. 16
d. 13	i. 17	n. 7	s. 1	x. 21
e. 6	j. 12	o. 24	t. 2	y. 5

Did you do as well in the vocabulary quiz as you did in the comprehension analysis? If you did, you need not be concerned about extensive training in building up your vocabulary because it already is above average. You will perhaps want to browse through the remainder of this chapter to see whether you can make a few valuable additions to your present stock of words.

On the other hand, if you are like most readers who are trying to improve, you had considerable difficulty with the words. And yet you probably had little trouble answering most of the comprehension questions correctly. That's what made our experiment so interesting. You were able to get the main idea of the selection and some of its other features even though you were not very familiar with the meanings of 25 or more important words. Various questions must be arising in your mind regarding this situation. Suppose we answer them.

How was it possible for me to get the main ideas and some of the other features despite the fact that I missed many words?

For one thing, you were able to grasp the central point the author made because you are undoubtedly familiar with the subject matter. It is practically impossible for anyone to escape the impact of advertising these days. Your own experience, therefore, enabled you to bring much knowledge to the article.

Secondly, you were able to do what most readers unconsciously do, or should do, when they come across unfamiliar words. They work out acceptable meanings from the context. For example, *ingenious* tied in with *young man, office building, Madison Avenue,* had to have a positive rather than negative association. Similarly, *perplexing* attached to *problem, none too subtly implied* followed by *work had been a bit shallow,* and *unless* preceding *crystallized* were all combinations that left broad hints about their probable rough definitions. In effect, then, if you read alertly and kept going, you were able to make enough good guesses to avoid confusion.

Finally, since most of the difficult words are adjectives —*ingenious* is an adjective describing the noun *man,* etc. —you could have concentrated on the nouns and come up with a reasonably good interpretation. If you look back at the phrases in the vocabulary quiz, you will see this point easily. Certainly you had no trouble with *young man, office building, problem, employers, Piel's Beer account, company,* and others like these words.

Consequently, it is not surprising that a reader can understand a passage even when 10 per cent of the words are not entirely meaningful to him. I have pointed out repeatedly that if difficult words are sufficiently scattered in a selection they need not seriously impair your ability to comprehend the main ideas, provided you keep moving along and set your sights on the broad ideas of the contents.

Since I understood the passage, what difference did it make whether I knew the words or not?

Let's look at it this way. You listen to some fine music and enjoy yourself immensely because it is tuneful and it puts you into a favorable mood. Or you examine a painting and like the scene or the way the people look, and are impressed with the richness of the colors. Or you reluctantly permit yourself to be dragged to a play, a ballet, or an interpretive-dance performance, and surprising yourself by your ability to follow the themes and stories presented, make a comment like "Not as bad as I thought." You understand a little here, appreciate a little there, but you are secretly bothered that others about you are getting so much more out of the same thing. You wonder whether you wouldn't more actively follow what the composer was trying to say if you had some knowledge of the technical phases of musical composition. You ask yourself whether the painting wouldn't have deeper meaning for you if you understood why the artist used a particular technique, what determined his choice of pigments, and why he placed certain objects or figures where he did on the canvas. And you know you would have been more comfortable at the play or dance recital if afterward you had been able to offer sensible reasons as to why it was a good or bad show. In short, you feel like a person with a heavy cold who is eating a delicious-looking dinner, can identify every dish, but cannot taste a thing!

This brings us back to our words. If your only objective in reading were to get main ideas and a few details out of the average article or book, you could probably do quite satisfactorily if you didn't encounter too many strange words. But you must be convinced by now that comprehension means much more than merely the surface interpretation. Since it does, how else are you to get to the personality and depth of a piece of writing except through the author's words? They are as necessary to him as notes are to the composer, paints and brushes to the artist, agile limbs to the dancer. You can no more fully appreciate what you read without a solid vocabulary background than you can any of the arts without some knowledge of the materials and techniques involved.

Here's another reason why it does make a difference if you miss some of the words. If a writer wishes to describe a certain expression on a person's face or a movement of his body, he doesn't accept the first adjective or verb that pops into his head. He frequently goes to great lengths just to select, or even invent, a particular word to fit a particular effect he wishes to create. A good illustration of this point can be found in the following article by a professional author:

New Words for Old

BY B. J. CHUTE

Language, like gunpowder, is an invention; and, like gunpowder, it is a very lively one. It marches on with the times out of necessity, and any new biological, medical or electronic discovery demands new words to describe it. A word like *television* is as obvious as it is indispensable, and dictionaries grow thicker every year while keeping up with the growth of a new world of scientific language.

Words of this kind are made because they are needed. But needed almost as much—and invented less often— are the words devised for pleasure, for the delight of discovering how the English language can be shaped a little or exaggerated a little to produce the exact word the writer needs. The Elizabethans, throwing a new language about, had a wonderful time of it, and in due course many of the vigorous, exciting words they had coined have found their way into dictionaries. Even the Victorians enjoyed this privilege. A pleasing example is Lewis Carroll's invaluable *chortle,* a word that was needed in the language because *chuckle* is too bland and *snort* is rude.

The magnificent range of the English language is one of the wonders of the world, but even so, a writer will occasionally find that the precise word he wants for his purpose simply does not exist. I had this experience recently when I wrote a novel called *Greenwillow* about a village of that name. The village was pure invention, along with the people in it, and in order to give a faintly antique and ballad-like quality to the writing I made free use of the words that the dictionary labeled as rare and even obsolete. Yet, in spite of this freedom to draw on the color and charm of words that have almost become heirlooms, I several times found myself at a loss for exactly the expression I felt I needed. More than once I was obliged to take advantage of the beautiful adaptability of a language that has never stopped growing and to invent my own words for my own use.

An example of this occurred when I wanted to describe an old lady, stiff in her bones but flighty in her manner, crossing a room in a hurry. *Scuttled* was possible but had a faint sound of harassment; *skimmed* came a little closer in sound but was too graceful and elegant. I solved my problem by inventing a verb, and in my final version the old lady "*skimmered* across the kitchen floor."

Another example involved the same old lady when she was half asleep and humming to herself, rather like a bee in June. A *droning* described the effect of monotony, but the rhythm of the sentence demanded an adjective as well, and none seemed quite right. *Humming* was not available; it had already been used as the verb. *Buzzing* was not right, being too energetic a word. I wanted something lazier, and I experimented and played with vowels and consonants until I came up with *mizzy*, again an invented word but one which had the sleepy *m-m-m-m* and the buzzy *z-z-z-z* and needed no definition in the sentence: "As she rocked, she hummed, a *mizzy* droning hard to tell from the sound of the brown bees."

It is not only in accommodating itself to invented words that the English language is so generous. Words are tools, and it is not absolutely necessary to use tools only for their exact, original intention. A word can be technically wrong by definition but right in context, and the one

230

absolute requirement is that the meaning must be clear. For instance, the dictionary definition of *feathered* is perfectly straightforward: "clothed, covered or provided with feathers," with a secondary meaning of "winged; swift." But when I wanted to describe someone as irresponsible and vague and short-memoried, I said she was "very feathered in her head," and I think it carried the idea I had in mind.

Another example of using a word in a manner it was not intended for occurred when I wanted to describe a litter of kittens in a haymow. The word *litter* had no softness. A *nest* of kittens sounded more appealing, but was still not quite right. There exists a rather rare word for kittens en masse, the word *kindle*, and a "kindle of kittens" had somewhat the quality I wanted but was still too sharp-edged, something kittens definitely are not. I finally found exactly what I wanted by adapting an accepted and everyday word and describing it as a "cuddle of kittens."

A dictionary within easy reach is a necessity for a writer, and I do not envy the Elizabethans who had no dictionaries—no wonderful volumes for crisp references or for delighted wandering. But I am glad that I inherit a language so rich and flexible and free that a writer need not apologize for his own invented words, knowing that it is out of this same stuff of imagination and necessity that dictionaries grow.

       ❖   ❖   ❖

What difference does it make if you miss a word or two? Think of all the effort a writer sometimes uses to select a single word. You may not miss the thought, but you certainly won't *taste* it, if I may be permitted to use a word out of its usual setting.

You can see, therefore, that the fewer words you are unfamiliar with in a selection, the fuller your comprehension is, the easier it is for you to look for the keys to understanding and appreciation. You should not be satisfied with a blurred picture of meaning. An extended vocabulary is your best device for bringing it into sharp and clear focus.

Haven't I been repeatedly told to concentrate on groups of words and not to worry about individual words, if I wish to avoid being a slow and confused word-by-word reader?

Yes, you have been told quite emphatically to STRETCH YOUR SPAN. Nor is there any intention here to change this advice. However, it is once more a matter of *how much meaning* you get out of each word phrase. Take the following sentence from our first selection:

The young man is *probably sojourning* in French Morocco by now, or some other *equally exotic resort,* with lots of flowers, expensive cigars, and quite possibly a couple of *enchanting local denizens* draped attractively on his arm.

If you read it properly, you permitted your eyes to stop no more than three or four times across a line. We will assume that you were able to get the thought of the sentence—the young man is probably in some faraway place and is having a good time. But notice the phrases in italics. Suppose you didn't know any of the three key words involved. You could still handle each of the word groups in single recognition spans without loss of speed or understanding of the central thought. However, wouldn't you wonder what one does when he "sojourns,"

232

whether an "exotic" resort is good or bad, and what kind of women "denizens" are?

No, you are not suddenly being told that you must start concentrating on one word at a time in a line of print. Indeed not! You *are* being told that an increase in your vocabulary will make what you include in your recognition spans so much more interesting and meaningful.

Further evidence that word study is not a contradiction of phrase-by-phrase reading is that almost all standardized tests that measure reading ability contain not only questions in paragraph interpretation but also in word recognition. What's more, results on such examinations usually show remarkable similarity in the areas tested. Readers who do poorly with the paragraphs perform just as poorly in the vocabulary section. A few pages back you read of the "sacred trinity" of advertising. Reading has one of its own: rate, comprehension, and vocabulary. They are so interdependent that unless progress is made in all three it is difficult to make progress in any one of them.

This is how rate fits into the picture. No matter how quickly you may try to read a selection that has many unfamiliar words, you will be slowed up considerably because of the numerous blanks that appear in the images you send to your mind. These continual frustrations you experience in your efforts at rapid comprehension necessarily affect your confidence and skill. You find yourself submitting to regressions, perhaps, because you feel compelled to take a second look at a word, or you may unconsciously try saying the word aloud to help you understand it, or, what is worst of all, you keep jumping from book to dictionary and then back again. There seems to be no end to the problems a limited vocabulary can create: more roadblocks, narrower recognition span, lower speed, and inadequate comprehension.

Is it worth all the effort to learn more words just so that I can get a little more out of my reading?

That's up to you. I have already given you many good reasons why an expanded vocabulary will help your reading:

•You will be able to understand *all* of what a writer says, not only most of it. You will readily grasp his hidden meanings as well as his expressed ones, the charm and flavor as well as the sense.

•You will be able to increase your rate more readily because you won't have to hesitate so often.

There are additional benefits that grow out of improved reading. Your own speech and writing activities can be favorably influenced. An ever-widening range of reading experiences provides you with more to say and a better way of saying it.

A better vocabulary and more efficient reading can also bring you more material success. This is not a sales plug, but a fact brought out by several studies in the field of vocabulary. We joke about people who use "long words." However, top executives in the world of industry consistently scored higher than even college professors. Successful people read a lot, know a lot of words, and have a lot of information on all kinds of subjects besides their own specialty.

Perhaps the greatest advantage you will derive from increased reading and vocabulary skill is that you will be encouraged to branch out in your reading interests. You won't hesitate to tackle "deep stuff," as you have called it heretofore. New worlds of thought and imagination will be opened for you.

For example, like most people, you probably would not deliberately buy or go to the library for a collection of poetry. If you happened to see a poem in a newspaper or magazine, you might read it, puzzle over it for a while, and then dismiss it. You would *very frankly prefer to leave your poetry rather than take it*. Yet, liking it all boils down again to a matter of words. If an increased awareness of what words mean and how they behave were to result from your vocabulary studies, you might even go out of your way to read a poem now and then, or as the writer of the passage below suggests, you might realize a secretly held lifetime ambition:

Everyone Writes (Bad) Poetry

BY JOHN CIARDI

The office mailbag bulges daily with envelopes full of bad poems that bear paper-clipped to them laborious little notes that breathe, however shyly, the most grandiose hopes. "Dear Editor," the little notes say in substance, "please tell me that I am a great poet." And between the lines they whisper: "And I will believe it!"

Bad poetry is what we all have in common—bad poetry and a secret persuasion. What man has ever awakened to his ego's passion on the planet without at some time committing a poem, and without cherishing the dream that deep in his soul a poetic talent lay asleep, awaiting only the kiss of discovering circumstance?

Ask John Doe whether or not he can play the violin and he would not dream of answering "I don't know. I've never tried." But ask him whether or not he can write a poem and it will be a rare and saintly-humble John Doe indeed to whom it occurs that the poem requires at least as much technical devotion and at least as many years of practice as does the violin. It's all done with words, isn't it? And everyone uses words.

Yes, everyone does use (or misuse) words, but not as a poet does. A buzz-saw and a rusty hinge have certain vibrations in common with those of a violin, but the violin properly played puts its vibrations to measured uses, *and it speaks its music not in the vibrations but in the inner relations of those measures.* When a poet uses a word he is using not only a label for something but a picture, a feeling, an association, a history, a sound, and a rhythmic impulse. The word "Brazil" in a geography book is a simple label. But find a lonesome Brazilian in a 14th Street bar and whisper in his ear "Braz-eel" and you will have awakened the blood of things. We are all lonesome Brazilians where we live most. Poetry is what comes up behind us and whispers the singing name of home in our ears.

The good poet lives to awaken words and phrases in this way, and the principal language of his poem is in the relation of these awakened measures to one another. And he is not only awakening his words, he is eliciting one word from another, his poem giving rise to itself, the individual words answering to their inner measure rather than to the dictionary of prose usage. Nothing is more characteristic of a good poem than the fact that the interplay of those measures *releases* more meaning than could be *stated.*

*   *   *

Not only does Mr. Ciardi give us a very valuable lesson in poetry appreciation, but he points up the value of paying attention to words as the vehicles of an author's thoughts and emotions. Surely it must be worth the effort to acquire the background that will enable one to get closer to great minds and fully comprehend their inspiring messages. When your stock of words has increased and your readiness to understand has been strengthened, you will find something of value in all the forms of literature and you will seek them out.

What is the best way to improve my vocabulary?

If you had twenty years of leisure time ahead of you and you could devote at least 3 or 4 hours a day to reading, I would be able to suggest *the best way* to increase your vocabulary. My advice would simply be—*read!* Read anything and everything. Read newspapers, magazines, books, pamphlets—poems, essays, short stories, novels, plays, biographies, textbooks. With all this reading you would be exposed to new words over and over again. The context alone would be sufficient to establish your familiarity with them. Many would rapidly become part of your recognition vocabulary, and eventually you would include the formerly strange words in your speech and writing activities.

This, by the way, is how you learned most of the words you use today. As a child, between the ages of two and six, you picked up one word at a time by listening and looking. No one gave you a list of words to study. In the lower grades of school you added many more words as the result of wider experiences and a few at the direction of the teacher. Certainly as your education proceeded, you had increasing amounts of direct word study, but most of your vocabulary improvement occurred in an indirect way. Today you couldn't put your finger on exactly how you learned more than a few hundred of the thousands of words you know now.

Had this process continued, you would be in no need of additional vocabulary training. But as you passed from adolescence to adulthood, you found that you had literally reached a standstill. You didn't do as much reading, you had more responsibilities, and your youthful zest in learning new words was conspicuous by its absence. You were like most people, who, it has been estimated, learn fewer than 25 new words a year after they have stopped going to school. They lack the opportunity, the energy, even the desire, to add to their vocabularies.

Therefore, it would be a mistake for me to tell you to read extensively and let your vocabulary take care of itself. Beyond a doubt, that would be best. But let's face it. You just can't or haven't the time to do it that way. Even if you had a great deal of leisure, you couldn't increase your reading program drastically through sheer will power alone. Human nature is against it. You resist being pushed into activities you don't do well.

When you learn to read faster and comprehend better, you will want to read more. You won't have to be urged to do so. In the long run you will get into the cycle of wider reading bringing about a better vocabulary and *vice versa*. But in the early stages of your training, you will have to settle for the second-best method of acquiring new words. That is to study them directly.

Remember, it was one of the methods used to help you learn to read in school and it's a perfectly valid device today. It will quicken your interest in words, prove to you that you *can* increase your vocabulary, and set the stage for the improvement that will come as the result of frequent and varied reading without special study.

Our aim in the rest of this chapter is to show you effective procedures whereby you can master an average of 20 words a month, *a rate that will be 10 times faster than your present one*. It is a system that has been tried with great success for more than ten years in my English classes at New York University. The students range in background from those with one or two years of high-school education to others with professional degrees.

238

Somewhere a need for language improvement has been generated in them and they have joined the class. In vocabulary we cover from 6 to 10 words a week, and at the end of the semester (5 months) the group consistently averages well over 90 per cent retention of a basic list of 150 words.

These are busy people. Most of them have full-time jobs. Many are married and have families. Yet they manage to spend the few minutes a day necessary to master their assignments. What is most gratifying is that after they have worked with the list for a while they become word-conscious. They report a thrill of recognition when they find some of their favorites in the things they read and hear. They tell interesting stories of their valiant efforts to impress their friends and associates with their newly born vocabulary skill. When they reach this point, I no longer worry about their progress. I know they'll get there!

You can get there, too. But you're going to take a somewhat different road, one more suited to your needs and abilities. You will follow the same system my classes do, with one important difference.

When one accepts the responsibility of studying by himself, he should not become dependent upon a list. This statement may surprise you since I have already said that I use one with my students. I do this out of necessity because it is more efficient to use uniform material when it is to be studied by a group of 25 to 35 adults on a university level. On an individual basis, such as yours, this procedure is not quite so advisable because there are important limitations, especially since this is direct word study.

Most vocabulary lists are prepared as follows. A careful and extended survey is made of representative newspapers, magazines, books, pamphlets, speeches, television

239

and radio programs, motion pictures, and existing vocabulary manuals. Then a table of frequency is established; that is, an actual count is taken of the number of times particular words appear in the samplings. In this way the words are graded as to difficulty and a list evolves.

My list, neither better nor worse than many others, has the same disadvantages all possess. *I* chose the reading materials from which I took the words, *not you*. I may have guessed wrong in deciding what *you* like to read. Most of my words may already be known to you if my estimates of your tastes were too low. Or I may have picked words that you would never use and see rarely.

Secondly, it is an established law of learning that best results are obtained when the materials selected for attention arise out of the needs of the students. In other words, if *you* pick the words, you are more likely to be interested in studying them because the need to do so has come out of your own experience. Your aim will be neither too high nor too low. The collector of a list may have left out many words that he concluded were too easy for you. Consequently, hundreds of words that you may need to study first are omitted and you struggle with others that are too much for you at the moment. To avoid being discouraged by what seems like an unattainable goal, you must spend your time on words that are suited to your immediate reading, social, and professional interests. Of course, in the future, when your reading ability has increased and your range has widened, you will go far beyond the confines of a list.

It is for these reasons that the vocabulary-building program about to be described will not be based upon a list, even though you will find mine reprinted at the end of the chapter. I have included it only to provide you with a means of checking your own studies. If some of the words you pick appear on my list, you can assume that yours have been found useful by others, too. Also, if in preparing your study units you find yourself short a few words, you can use mine to fill in. Lastly, if through your own efforts and selections, you reach the point where my list offers you no challenge, you will know that you have moved ahead of the average vocabulary class.

And now, you are ready to learn how to become your own list maker.

VOCABULARY PLAN

There are fours steps. Each will be explained and illustrated. Read through all the instructions first, so that you become familiar with the mechanics of the plan before you do independent work.

I. Choosing the Words

"When I read I keep a dictionary at my side. As soon as I come to a word I don't know, I look it up right away. Then I go on reading."

You've heard people say this, or perhaps you've used this method yourself because you thought it was a good way to learn words. Well, it's not—for several reasons!

Stop-and-go reading destroys the continuity you must maintain if you are to achieve full comprehension. Your primary objective is to get the author's ideas quickly and to enjoy the other features of his writing. You can't do that if you interrupt yourself every minute to look up the meaning of a word.

Secondly, it has been demonstrated to you how the context can give you enough information about strange words to enable you to continue reading without stopping. To refresh your memory, we'll review the process by taking an excerpt from a newspaper article:

If the women of Kabul had the vote, the chances are that the *chadri* would quickly vanish from Afghanistan's capital.

When your mind registered *Kabul*, it probably vaguely wondered where it was. And when it spotted *chadri*, it was definitely stopped. However, by the end of the sentence your problem about the location of the city was already solved. Observe what happened if you moved right along to the next sentence:

But as matters stand, the chadri, also known as the burka, still envelops the Moslem female population here.

By this time you can guess that *chadri* and *burka* refer to some sort of garment because of the presence of *envelops*. Let's say you continued to the next two sentences:

The hooded robes banish them from view and virtually shut out the sun. Eyeholes are provided to give the women a peek at the outside world and enable them to maneuver about.

Is there any further doubt about the meaning of *chadri* or *burka*? The same sort of thing usually happens when you read material written by skilled writers. They know it is their responsibility to make the meanings of uncommon words clear without forcing you to run to a dictionary.

There is another inescapable fact that speaks against what I call word-hopping. An unabridged dictionary of the English language contains more than 600,000 entries. Certainly no one can expect to learn more than a small fraction of this enormous quantity in one lifetime. Indeed, very few of those remarkable people who seem to know any word that comes up have a vocabulary that even approaches 10 per cent of the grand total. This fact indicates *why* it is a waste of time to try to learn every word you see and *how important it is that you choose the right ones to study.*

Before you make any choice, you must decide what use you want to make of the word. Actually, you have four vocabularies. The largest is the one you bring to your silent reading. Here you have at your disposal not only the words you feel capable of using in speech and writing, but also many more that you have learned to recognize in context. The latter group is very much part of your vocabulary, but it does not play an active role.

Somewhat smaller is your listening vocabulary. Because you must absorb the material as fast as the speaker talks, you lose the meanings of some of the words you would ordinarily recognize in printed form. Your ability to recall is less effective when you hear than when you see.

Going down the scale, we come next to your writing vocabulary. Experience has taught you that you must know a word thoroughly before you can safely include it in a sentence. A rough idea is not enough because failure to pick the right form or meaning in a given situation can prove to be very embarrassing. For instance, an individual hears and sees combinations like "*condign* punishment" or "*condign* reward." He guesses rightly that the word means "well-deserved, worthy." How distressing it must be to him, however, if someone calls his attention to the mistake he has made when he writes (as one of my students once did):

"The rascal *condigned* everything that was done to him."

The fact that the word had no verb form had never occurred to him. To avoid such situations, most people tend to leave out a good percentage of their vocabulary when they write, and so they use far fewer words than they can recognize.

Your weakest is your speaking vocabulary. Here again the time factor is significant. Your words must come out at a reasonably rapid rate to avoid giving the impression that you are fumbling. Hence, you discard a great many words that you know well enough to write with and many more that have meaning for you when you read or listen.

Your objectives in vocabulary study, then, should be threefold:

1. Not to allow it to interfere with your rate and comprehension.
2. To use the context of the materials you read to add words to your recognition vocabulary so that your reading and listening experiences become more meaningful.
3. Through study and practice, to gradually move more words into your "use" vocabulary. You have really learned a word when *by your own choice* you use it correctly and comfortably in your writing and speaking activities.

With the preceding information in mind, you can establish a regular pattern of selecting words for study. Keep a pad of paper and a pencil at your side whenever possible during reading sessions. Draw a line down the center of each page so that you have two columns. We'll come back in a moment to how you are to use the pad.

In the same notebook that you use for your Time

Charts in reading-rate development, set up a Vocabulary Chart divided thus:

Word	Pronunciation	Meanings	Forms	Original Sentence	My Sentences

You will need two pages across to allow enough space for the entries. For the time being, we'll concern ourselves with the entries in only the first column.

You are now ready with two of the tools you will need to handle the unusual words you are likely to encounter in any one reading session. You treat such words very much the same way you do people you meet.

There are some you are introduced to for the first time at large gatherings. You nod politely, undoubtedly forget their names five minutes later, and possibly never see them again. Similarly, in the average column or page you may come upon a word or two that you have never seen before, which can be classified as a chance acquaintance. A word like *chadri* would fall into this category. You do the best you can to identify its meaning from the contents, and that's all. You may or may not recognize it a second time, but you make no special effort to retain it. If it becomes part of your recognition vocabulary, good. If not, you haven't lost much.

To continue with our comparison, we mention those people whom you see two or three times at various places. In time you reach the point where you make a conscious effort to remember their names, but you haven't exchanged home visits yet. They are acquaintances, not friends. They are like the words that begin to look familiar to you after you have come across them in your reading *several times*. You are certain you will meet them again, and you decide that you should begin to know them a little better so that they will at least become part of your reading and listening vocabularies. With such words, you do this:

1. As you read, note the number of the page on which the word appeared and jot it down in the *left-hand column* on your pad. Learn to do this mechanically so that it does not cause you to remove your eyes from the material.

2. When you have finished your reading, go back to the pages noted and find the words you thought you wanted to look at again. This way you avoid interruptions, you get valuable training in skimming (see Chapter XI), and you have time to determine which of the words you have selected should constitute the group that will get a second look. Don't be too ambitious. About two or three such words are enough for one sitting. Then you:

   a. Look at the word again.

   b. Guess at the meaning again by reviewing the context and using the techniques that will shortly be described.

   c. Check the meaning and pronunciation with a dictionary.

   d. Say the word aloud.

   e. That's all! *You do not enter these words in your notebook yet.*

Finally, we come to those words you have met often enough to convince you that you ought to begin treating them like friends, like the people you know intimately and expect to see regularly in your social activities. For the sake of providing you with a definite yardstick, let's say you have come across these words at least a half dozen times in your reading and have *heard* them used by speakers whose cultural background you respect. This is the group you should study seriously:

1. As you read, jot down in the *right-hand column* of your pad the page numbers on which the words appear. You are going to move them up from your recognition to your "use" vocabulary. They will soon make their way into your speech and writing.

2. Enter the words in the first column of your Vocabulary Chart. Make certain you get the spellings correct.

3. Number the entries from 1 to 5. When you have accumulated 5 words, you have a 1-week study unit.

4. Put your notebook aside. Once you have started a program of this kind, you will always be in the midst of word-study units. You take each group of 5 in its turn. You need not study a particular word on the spot. There is no hurry. The words have been around for years. They'll still be there even if it takes you a few months to catch up with them. There is no sense deluding yourself. You won't become vocabulary-rich in a week, ten days, or a month. It is a process that takes time, but the rewards are so worth while that there can be no question about the desirability of expending the effort.

II. Studying the Words

A. HOW TO GUESS INTELLIGENTLY

Since you need not include a word in a study unit until you have seen and heard it used more than a half dozen times, you will be depending mainly upon your ability to guess at its meaning so long as it remains a part of only your recognition vocabulary. True, you will check with a dictionary now and then, but you must have found out by now that definitions have a habit of eluding you shortly after you have looked up a word. Therefore, it is sensible for you to reduce the probabilities of developing the wrong idea of a word by perfecting various techniques that can serve as your "guessing dictionary."

1. Context

You have already had several examples of how to use the context of a selection to work out the meaning of a strange word. The point to stress here is that you must not get panicky if the sentence in which the word first appears does not give you enough of a hint to enable you to guess reasonably accurately. The sentences that follow usually add more to the meaning, assuming that the material has been skillfully written. Therefore, you must keep moving right through the paragraph and try to pick up more information about the word as you read further.

There is one caution. If you begin reading something that has about four or five words per page that are entirely new to you, I would suggest that you lay the material aside. You very likely aren't ready for it. It is unwise to jump in over your head. Try again when your vocabulary is stronger.

2. Breaking words down

Like most living things that grow larger and heavier as they get older, languages gain lengthier and more complicated words as they mature. This is not to say that all short words are simple in meaning, but the bulk of your "difficult" words contain more than two syllables. In many instances, this stretching process has occurred by the addition of "pieces" before or after the original easily understood monosyllable (one syllable), thus forming a polysyllable (more than one syllable).

English is no exception to this language process and

has its full share of polysyllables, many of which seem to be difficult by virtue of their length. However, if you train yourself to become familiar with some of the more common "pieces" that are added, you will possess a second guessing device that will unravel the meanings of a surprisingly large number of words.

For example, we can start with a monosyllable like *port,* which came from the Latin *porto,* meaning *to carry.* Note how it can be built up:

*ex*port	to carry out
*im*port	to carry in
port*able*	able to be carried
port*er*	one who carries
*trans*port*ation*	that which carries or means of carrying across or from one place to another

There is no limit to the number of "pieces" that can be added at the beginning or end of a shorter word. A well-known monstrosity can be traced to the Latin *sto,* meaning *to stand.* It wasn't enough to put *en* (in) in front and *able* (able to) and *ish* (to make) at the end, thus forming the word *establish,* meaning literally *to make able to stand.* Look what happened to the word by the time some others got through with it:

*dis*establish	*to break up* the ability to stand
*anti*disestablish	*against* the above
antidisestablish*ment*	*that which* is against breaking up the ability to stand
antidisestablishment*arian*	*one who* favors that which is against breaking up the ability to stand

249

| antidisestablishmentarianism | *system or belief* of those who are against breaking up the ability to stand |

Actually, the word was formed to express the opposition of certain groups to the separation of church from state.

Fortunately, very few words get out of hand this way. Rarely are more than four or five syllables used. You can see, however, that when it is broken down, the long word is not nearly as formidable as it seemed.

These "pieces" that we have been talking about are called:

Prefixes	*Pre* (before, in front of)
	fix (to fasten)
Suffixes	*Suf* (from *sub*, under)
	fix (to fasten)
	(Since we cannot fasten *under* a word, the word has come to mean that which is attached after.)
Roots	These are the forms that function exactly as the word implies. When prefixes and suffixes are added to roots, words grow in size.

Before giving you a list of the more common "pieces," let me advise you not to try to memorize them. The object is to get into the habit of looking for them when you are guessing and to become increasingly familiar with them as you learn to break words down. You will discover that you will remember most prefixes, suffixes, and roots after you have consciously identified them for a time in your dictionary work.

Another point to bear in mind is that English words, like those in other languages, are subject to what is called *assimilation*. This comes about as the result of the normal human habit of adjusting things so that they are easier to say or do. For instance, *affix* comes from *ad* (to) and *fix* (to attach or fasten). However, people found it difficult to say *adfix,* and so gradually those who spoke the word assimilated the *d* into the *f* that followed, thus giving us *affix*. Sometimes, instead of assimilating one letter into another, speakers simply dropped the offending one, and we have a word like *amend* developing from *admend*.

The curious influence of speech upon spelling is most often found in the prefixes. Therefore, you must be alert to the effects of assimilation as you break down words:

TYPICAL EXAMPLE

Prefix AD	*ac*commodate	*am*munition
	*af*fluent	*an*nex
	*ag*gregate	*ap*ply
	*a*kin	*ar*rest
	*al*ly	*as*sist
	*a*mass	*at*tack

a. Common prefixes

ab	from	*ab*normal	*dis*	apart	*dis*miss
ad	to	*ad*mit	*en, in*	in	*en*trance
	toward				*in*sert
be	by	*be*side	*ex*	out	*ex*it
bi	two	*bi*sect	*per*	through	*per*ceive
com,		*com*pose	*pre*	before	*pre*pare
con	with	*con*nect	*pro*	in front	*pro*hibit
con	against	*con*test		for	*pro*noun
de	from	*de*tract	*re*	back	*re*mit

251

sub	under	*sub*tract
super	over, above	*super*vise
trans	across	*trans*port
un	not	*un*fit

b. Common suffixes

able, ible	able to	lik*able*, admiss*ible*
age	act or process, relationship, place of abode, fee	marri*age*, shrink*age*, orphan*age*, tow*age*
al, ial	pertaining to, like	loc*al*, best*ial*
ance, ence	act of, state or condition	assist*ance*, viol*ence*
ant, ent	one who, that which	serv*ant*, lat*ent*
ary, ery	that which, relation to, one who, place, act	station*ary*, diet*ary*, no*tary*, bak*ery*, arch*ery*
ate	characterized by or caused to	desol*ate*, fascin*ate*
ful	full of, containing	taste*ful*, beauti*ful*
ice	act, quality, condition	serv*ice*, apprent*ice*
ine, in	characterized by, name of	sal*ine*, chlor*ine*, gas-*oline*, maudl*in*
ion, sion, tion	act or result of, condition	un*ion*, eva*sion*, sta*tion*
ist	one who	violin*ist*
ive	quality of or tending to	act*ive*, conclus*ive*
ment	state, quality, condition	amaze*ment*, judg*ment*
or, er	one who, that which	act*or*, raz*or*, writ*er*
ous, ious	full of, like, having qualities of	fam*ous*, bulb*ous*, poison*ous*, delic*ious*
ure	act or process, being, result of	expos*ure*, legislat*ure*, pict*ure*

252

Suffixes usually do not cause changes of meanings in words as do prefixes. As you have gathered by now, most of the suffixes help to create people or things, describe them, or compare them. Another way of saying this is that these word endings help form the various parts of speech:

Noun	right
Verb	right
Adjectives	righteous, rightful
Adverbs	righteously, rightfully

c. Common roots

The roots are the most important "pieces" since they are the sources of the basic and extended meanings of words. Most roots come from the French and Latin importations, as well as the ancestor of our language, Anglo-Saxon, although we have also borrowed liberally from the rest of the world. Again, it would be silly to try to memorize the thousands of roots in English, but it is a good idea to become familiar with the more common ones because they help you not only in working out new words but in discovering a deeper meaning in words you thought you already knew.

mote	move	*mo*tion, pro*mote*, e*mote*, e*mo*tion, de*mote*
jur	swear	con*jur*e, *jur*y, ab*jur*e, per*jur*y
serve	guard or serve	*serv*ice, dis*serv*ice, *serv*ant, *serv*iceable, de*serv*e, con*serve*, pre*serve*
solv	loose, free	*solv*e, dis*solv*e, re*solv*e, ab*solv*e, in*solv*uble

253

vent	come	*event*, ad*vent*, con*vent*, in*vent*, pre*vent*
ject	throw	pro*ject*, pro*ject*ile, ab*ject*, ad*ject*ive, de*ject*ion, pro*ject*ion
tend	stretch	at*tend*, pre*tend*, con*tend*, dis*tend*, superin*tend*ent, in*tend*
vert	turn	con*vert*, a*vert*, di*vert*, in*vert*, re*vert*, sub*vers*ion
gen	born	*gen*ial, *gen*eration, con*gen*ial, *gen*der, *gen*erous, *gen*erate, *gen*ocide
greg	flock, group	*greg*arious, con*greg*ate, se*greg*ate, ag*greg*ate, con*greg*ation
pend	hang	*pend*ant, de*pend*, ap*pend*, ex*pend*, sus*pend*
scribe	write	de*scribe*, in*scribe*, a*scribe*, con*scrip*tion, pre*scribe*, sub*scribe*
spect	look	in*spect*, a*spect*, *spect*acle, *spect*acular, re*spect*, su*spect*
terr	earth	*terr*ace, *terr*a cotta (cooked), *terr*ain, *terr*itory

Being able to break down words into their roots plus their suffixes and prefixes is an invaluable aid in your eventual mastery of a word as well as in your early efforts to guess its meaning. If you met *introversion* for the first time and knew some of the common "pieces," you could so easily come up with an acceptable interpretation:

intro	in, inward
vers (from *vert*)	to turn
ion	act of

(act of turning inward, being withdrawn in personality)

Certainly if you decided to study the word so that you could use it, you would have established a firm foundation upon which to build a permanent addition to your vocabulary.

In general, when you are trying to break down a word, attack the root first, then go on to the prefix, and finally to the suffix. You can practice doing this by going back to the sample words offered after the list of roots and testing your skill with those words that are not very familiar to you and then checking your results with a dictionary. It can become a fascinating game, and it is a wonderful way to observe the logic that exists in language structure and the simplicity that underlies even the most difficult words. It is a never-ending thrill for me to come across a word like *arenaceous*, for example, look for and find *arena* in it, and with the help of the context, decide that the word must mean *sandy* because arenas were originally sandy areas for various activities and games. When the dictionary confirms my guess, I feel like a Sherlock Holmes among words.

You will want to review the words you become familiar with as the result of intelligent guessing made possible by your ability to break down a word into its prefix, root, and suffix. One way of doing it is to prepare exercises similar to the following. There are ten sentences, in each of which is a word in italics. Below the sentences are two columns, the one on the left (lettered) containing the literal meanings of the words in italics, and the one on the right (numbered) containing acceptable synonyms. In the space before each sentence, place the proper letter and number for the italicized word.

Example:

h	1	There was a *disingenuous* quality about his broad smile and flattering words.
___	___	The building had a look of *immobility* that seemed to defy time and the elements.
___	___	His *subservient* air made him despised by the other employees.
___	___	The use of public funds for the project was called unauthorized *subvention*.
___	___	There was a *disingenuous* quality about his broad smile and flattering words.
___	___	The act was delightful because the audience was not prepared for the *interjection* of humor in an apparently serious dance.
___	___	The car mounted the sidewalk when the driver *inadvertently* placed his foot on the accelerator instead of the brake.
___	___	Huge black clouds and a sudden stillness gave ample warning of the *impending* storm.
___	___	After the riots, a *proscription* was placed against all gatherings of more than two persons.
___	___	An excited voice on the radio was announcing the landing of wild-looking creatures who were surely not *terrestrial* beings.
___	___	So lengthy a *prospectus* indicated that much planning had gone into the formation of the company.

a. pertaining to the earth   1. artificial

b. that which is thrown between   2. ban

c. not able to be moved
d. that which looks ahead
e. hanging in or over
f. act of serving under
g. that which is not turned toward
h. quality of not being natural
i. act of writing before
j. that which comes under or supports

3. heedlessly
4. fixedness
5. earthly
6. set of proposals
7. subsidy
8. abrupt insertion
9. subordinate
10. threatening

ANSWERS:

immobility	c,	4
subservient	f,	9
subvention	j,	7
disingenuous	h,	1
interjection	b,	8
inadvertently	g,	3
impending	e,	10
proscription	i,	2
terrestrial	a,	5
prospectus	d,	6

You can easily set up additional exercises of this kind. The first time you look up a word, jot down the literal meaning, a synonym, and the original sentence in which the word appeared. After you have collected about ten such combinations, write down the sentences in order and mix up the meanings and synonyms as was done in the previous exercise. Put the work aside for a few weeks or months, and when you get back to it you will have an excellent review.

3. Word families

This third technique designed to help you guess intelligently can often solve your problem of what to do about a word whose root seems foreign to you because it is not one of those you have worked with often enough to know at a glance. Let's say you come across *apathetic.* You can guess that the root is probably *path,* but it isn't on the list of roots you have learned. Your next step is to try to think of a word you do know that contains the same root. *Sympathy* readily comes to mind. In this word, *path* rather obviously refers to feeling or emotion. Once you have come this far, you turn to the prefix *a,* which you know means *from* or *away.* The logical conclusion, then, is that *apathetic* refers to the absence of feeling.

Many words come in families, and often by identifying one word you can become acquainted with all the relatives. With the above information, for example, you could do something with:

pathos   apathy
empathy   pathetic
            antipathy

Sample sentences

There was great *pathos* in the story, and handkerchiefs were freely used by the audience.

The new play was greeted with considerable *apathy* by the critics, and it closed in a week.

Watching little children at play stirs an *empathy* in people who recall their own carefree days.

The *pathetic* look on his face brought many coins into his box.

His *antipathy* for formality accounted for his wardrobe of slacks and casual jackets.

Now try your skill in the following exercises based on word families.

1. *Chili con carne* consists of red peppers with *meat*.

   The *carnage* of battle produces

   _____ a. great glory

   _____ b. broken bodies

   Carnal pleasures are those of

   _____ a. the mind

   _____ b. the flesh

   Belief in *reincarnation* includes the expectation of a return as

   _____ a. a live person

   _____ b. a ghost

   The *carnation's* original color was

   _____ a. red

   _____ b. white

   A *carnivorous* animal eats

   _____ a. vegetables

   _____ b. other animals

2. If someone gives you *credit*, he *believes* you will pay.

   An *incredible* story is

   _____ a. very factual

   _____ b. a pack of lies

259

A *credulous* person can

_____ a. be told anything

_____ b. see through you

My *credo* is part of my

_____ a. conscience

_____ b. information

If I place *credence* in your statement, I

_____ a. want more evidence

_____ b. accept it

3. A *courier* is a *runner* or messenger, and *current* events
are *going on now*.

When he *incurred* a debt, he

_____ a. paid it

_____ b. assumed it

Recurrent attacks are those that

_____ a. keep coming back

_____ b. stop

Cursory reading is

_____ a. very slow

_____ b. very fast

When people *concur*, they

_____ a. agree

_____ b. disagree

Precursory events bring us

_____ a. confusion

_____ b. hints

An *incursion* on my rights reflects

_____ a. invasion

_____ b. cooperation

4. I *comprehend* because I actually *seize* the meaning.

The *prehensile* tail of the monkey helps him

_____ a. grab branches

_____ b. swat flies

I am *apprehensive* if I feel my heart

_____ a. jump with joy

_____ b. pound with fear

When a person is *apprehended*, he is

_____ a. caught

_____ b. released

A *reprehensible* deed is

_____ a. praiseworthy

_____ b. blameworthy

5. The *medieval* period is also called the *Middle* Ages.

Mediocre talents are

_____ a. unusual

_____ b. ordinary

An *intermediary* is a person who

_____ a. starts an argument

_____ b. settles one

A *mediator*

_____ a. takes sides

_____ b. sits between opponents

A *median* in a set of figures occurs

_____ a. at the beginning

_____ b. halfway down

A *medium* claims her mind floats

_____ a. between heaven and earth

_____ b. along the surface of the earth

If you were able to handle the exercises just concluded without too much trouble, you became familiar with a group of thirty words that are above average in difficulty. Together with the words you picked up when you practiced with the common roots and their families, you added an astonishingly large number of new words to your recognition vocabulary in a short space of time. Make it a habit when you look up a word in a dictionary to find its root. Then think of various prefixes and suffixes that might be added to it, and browse through the pages to discover whether you have come across another word family. When you have become expert at doing this, not only will you learn many new words but you will be fascinated by the interesting possibilities that exist in word study.

B. USING THE DICTIONARY

You will, of course, need a dictionary to help you in your vocabulary work. Make sure yours is a good one. Here are some features it should have:

1. Pronunciation

The symbols used to indicate vowel and consonant sounds should be easily followed and illustrated by sample words. In addition, the pronunciation key should be repeated at the top or bottom of *every page*. You should not be annoyed by being forced to refer to the front of the book when you want to figure out how to say a word.

There should also be a guide to pronunciation in the opening portions of the dictionary to explain the symbols used and to give some general rules about their application. The appendix should include special sections devoted to the pronunciation of places and names.

2. Etymology

This refers to the origin or derivation of a word in terms of its basic root, prefix, and language ancestry. Such information should be supplied with every word so that you can identify word families, gain increasing familiarity with word parts, and enjoy the fun of seeing how a language develops. Some dictionaries either leave out the etymology or insert it only now and then.

Very often a look at the etymology of a word will set its meaning in your mind permanently. You obtain a *clue*, so to speak, that doesn't easily escape you because the unusual nature of the information may help you retain it in the same manner as you tend to remember odd and silly things better than you do logical or factual ones. Suppose, for example, you look up *supercilious* and learn that it breaks down into *raised (super)* and *eyebrow* or *eyelid (cilium)*. You now have a picture in your mind of the expression on a person's face when he is attempting to act superior. Certainly knowing this forms a stronger bond for you between the word and its meaning than the definition alone.

Or you learn that *debonair* is derived from *of (de)*, *good (bon)*, and *type* or *class (aire)*. Besides now knowing that the word means *courteous* or *graceful*, you also have a strong clue to help you uncover its meaning when you meet it again. It is for such purposes that you should make sure your dictionary has ample etymological information.

3. Sample phrases or sentences

Each unusual word should be illustrated by a phrase or sentence so that you will not be studying the meaning in isolation. You can compare this usage with the way the word was used in the sentence in which you found it. Also, these examples help you develop proficiency in using the various forms of the word—noun, adjective, verb, etc.

4. Illustrations

There should be pictures, diagrams, and sketches whenever these seem necessary to support the definition. Although the expression "One picture is worth a thousand words" is not always true, it very frequently is in a dictionary, especially in connection with technical and scientific terms.

5. Synonyms

Sufficient synonyms should be provided so that you can use your dictionary not only to get a definition but also to substitute a word for the original if you should desire to avoid repetition. Moreover, a synonym, too, will sometimes help you remember the meaning of a word. For instance, *inebriate* is a more polite way of referring to a drunk. The oddity of so imposing a word meaning what it does may in itself influence you to use it more often and thus strengthen your recollection of its definition.

6. Varied meanings

Good dictionaries number the meanings of a word that is used under varying conditions. Usually, the first definition is the most common and the ones that follow are specialized in nature. A simple word like *dog*, besides its obvious meaning, also refers colloquially to "a rascally fellow," astronomically to a star cluster, mechanically to a type of fastening used in logging, and meteorologically to a "sundog, fogdog," etc. Unless all the meanings of a particular word are in your dictionary, you may not find the one that suits the sentence you are trying to comprehend. It is very important to avoid forming a completely false idea of how a word is generally used when you first meet it.

7. Spelling

Common spelling rules should be listed, generally in the introductory portions, so that you can learn how to handle large groups of words. Look up the accented-syllable rule sometime and see how it will solve for you the spellings of thousands of words that may have given you trouble before. What is just as important is that good spelling habits are extremely important to vocabulary development. You have been told that you really know a word when you use it voluntarily in your writing. If lack of confidence about the spelling of certain words prevents you from using them, you can see how long it will take you to make them part of your "use" vocabulary.

8. Abbreviations

You will want to use these occasionally when you write, and you should be able to find them in the same book you use for definitions.

9. Proper nouns

Any noun that is spelled with a capital letter is a proper noun—a name of a person, place, or thing. Such entries should be in the text of the dictionary; other proper nouns should be found in the special sections reserved for giving you the pronunciation of well-known people and places. If you can look up *Colosseum*, for example, you can find out how it is said, the fact that it was an amphitheater built in about 80 A.D., and that the name came from *colossus* (gigantic), a term also used to name one of the Seven Wonders of the World. Such information makes a dictionary a biographical, geographical, and historical treasure chest.

10. Punctuation

The rules for punctuation should be listed in a special section. This will help make your dictionary a complete writing instrument.

When you consider how much useful information can be found in a good dictionary, you can understand why it is unwise to short-change yourself. Get one that can do the job for you. Don't use an inferior tool.

We are now ready for the instructions in the use of a dictionary to help you study words. For this purpose we return to our Vocabulary Chart. A description of how to make each entry follows. Since we have already discussed in detail how to choose a word for Column 1, we continue with:

Column 2—Pronunciation

Enter the word as the dictionary has it, with the vowel symbols and accent mark. In words of four or more syllables, you may find two accent marks: a primary (heavy) and a secondary (light) stress. Note that when the pronunciation is shown the spelling is frequently altered to accommodate the sounds. Column 1, of course, is the official spelling.

Should you have trouble determining whether you are accenting the syllable indicated, try this simple device. Cut a strip of paper, about an inch wide and six or seven inches long, from a newspaper. When you are about to say a word, hold the strip vertically in front of and about an inch away from your lips. Exaggerate the force of air you expell as you accent the syllable called for in the pronunciation breakdown. If the strip jumps back at the proper syllable, you have accented the word correctly. If it moves as you hit some other syllable or doesn't jump at all, you will have to try again. Of course, you don't exaggerate the pronunciation once you have the accent well in hand.

Column 3—Meanings

Jot down the common meanings, and a few synonyms. Do not bother with the specialized definitions unless you are particularly interested or you think you will have use for them. If your study of the etymology turns up a word family or provides you with an unusual clue to the meaning, write that in, too. In the latter case, underline the entry so that it stands out when you review.

Column 4—Forms

Insert the various parts of speech into which the word can be formed. In some instances it might be necessary to enter a negative phrase as a warning; for example, *condign—not as a verb*.

Column 5—Original sentence (facing page of notebook)

Copy the sentence from the material in which you last found the word used. Underline the word.

Column 6—My sentences

Form original sentences using the word in its various forms so that you approach total familiarity with it. Try to compose the sentences so that the context will define the word. These will be of great help to you in your reviews and will also be of value when you get to the paragraph technique, which will be described next.

C. PARAGRAPH TECHNIQUE

You begin your study of a word when you fill in the columns of your Vocabulary Chart. However, you can't stop there if your objective is to learn to *use the word*. That's why you must look upon your chart work as only preliminary. There is more to be done before you can be satisfied that you have made an addition to your "use" vocabulary.

Assuming that you have numbered your entries, you are ready to begin a study unit as soon as you have a group of 5 words. Once you have organized your vocabulary work along these lines, you can make your final contribution to the basic 15-Minute-a-Day Plan, which thus far has covered the elimination of roadblocks, the training in reading words in groups, the acceleration of your rate, and the improvement of your comprehension. You know how to spend from 2 to 5 minutes daily practicing the first four skills. This is what you do about the fifth.

Monday through Friday

Take one word each day. On one side of an index card write the word; on the other, the common meaning, any clue (etymology—prefix, etc.), and the various forms. This should take about a half minute, during the evening, so that you are prepared for the next day's practice.

In the morning put the card into your pocket or purse when you leave for the day. Some time before lunch, take the card out. Don't look at it closely until you are certain the side containing only the word is facing you. Then try to recall the meaning, clue, and forms. Spend no more than 15 seconds on this procedure. If you can't remember, turn the card over and read the summary. Your next step is to compose and write out a *sentence using the word* on a scrap of paper. Read the sentence aloud. Throw the paper away.

During the afternoon repeat the whole process. However, when you get to the sentence, use a different form of the word. Again, in the evening, check your card, and then write another sentence, this time using a third form of the word (if it has more than one or two forms). Don't omit the oral reading. You want to be able to handle the word in your writing *and* speech activities.

The next day continue with your second card of the week. Check it; write a sentence; read it aloud—on three separate occasions. With training you will be able to do the practice work for any period of the day in less than a minute. You are not trying to create sentence masterpieces. Your main purpose is to look at the word, recall its meaning, write it in context, and say it.

By Friday evening you should have completed your work with 5 cards. That makes you ready for the paragraph technique, to be developed on week-ends.

Saturday and Sunday

On *each* of these days, spread out the 5 cards on a table or desk. For a minute or so just look at the words. Try to build up a relationship among them that will suggest a topic for a paragraph.

This won't come easy at first. You are attempting to pull an idea out of the air and then work with words that are relatively new to you. But again it's a matter of mental set. You are forcing your mind to think creatively. After you have done a few of the paragraphs, you will be surprised at the ease with which you will "see" any number of topics in a group of unrelated words. You will find the exercise a real challenge, interesting to do, and perfectly possible to complete within a reasonable amount of time. My students, and I am including the least skillful, manage to compose original and sensible paragraphs in less than 15 minutes, after they have had the experience for a few weeks! Here's an example of how it's done.

Your aim is to write a short, meaningful paragraph containing all 5 words you have studied during the week. Suppose we take a set from among the many words you met in this chapter and trace the writing operation:

supercilious   debonair   mediocre   cursory   credulous

Perhaps one of the sentences you composed during the week or entered in your Vocabulary Chart will suggest something to you. If not, try to think of a person, place, or thing that could be described by the words. Or it may suddenly occur to you that *supercilious* and *mediocre* are rather contradictory of each other. This train of thought may lead you to think of someone who has a higher opinion of himself than he merits. Now you have a concrete idea, so you write:

Wilson's *supercilious* smile and *debonair* manner fooled most people. In their *credulous* acceptance of the man, they were easily convinced that he had superior abilities. However, one who gave him more than a *cursory* look soon discovered that he was far from the genius he pretended to be. In fact, his talents were quite *mediocre* when put to the test.

Or perhaps you thought of a supersalesman:

A *credulous* public had long been his victims. Never allowing people more than a *cursory* inspection of his product, he wore them down with his *debonair* disregard for the facts. In the face of his *supercilious* smile, one dared not question him. This made it possible for him to sell *mediocre* products with the air of one offering jewels.

Or you might have been in a romantic mood:

Charlton approached her with the *debonair* charm of a Continental. His reward was a *supercilious* smile that seemed to say that he was not worth more than *cursory* attention. Her attitude tested his *credulity* to the limit. Charlton couldn't believe that anyone would dare treat him as if he were a *mediocrity* among men.

You will note that in the last paragraph different forms of some of the words were used. This was in accordance with our suggestion that you develop flexibility in your handling of words so that you can select any form called for by the construction of the sentence.

Are you beginning to get the idea of how to write these paragraphs? Give your mind free rein and it will usually come up with a topic suitable enough to include at least a few of the words. Then the problem of adding the remaining ones becomes relatively simple since you have an idea to attach them to; getting started is generally the hardest part of this exercise.

Let's try the paragraph technique with another set:

apprehensive   carnage   antipathy   introvert   gregarious

You see *introvert* and *gregarious* and again find contrasting meanings. *Carnage* suggests war or battle, and you should be about ready for your first idea:

Only the *gregarious* personality accepts the crowded life of an army camp uncomplainingly. To the *introvert*, the lack of privacy is a severe shock, and he approaches his barracks existence with a natural *antipathy*. Moreover, the withdrawn person cannot help feeling *apprehensive* about the *carnage* of battle he will one day have to witness.

Occasionally you may enjoy trying to fit serious-sounding words into a light subject. This gives you practice in developing further versatility with your vocabulary. For instance, with our second group we might try something like this:

The new puppy could hardly be called an *introvert*, judging from the awful *carnage* he left in his wake the first time the family went out for the evening. Shoes strewn all over the living-room floor, overturned lamps, and slipcovers wildly disarrayed attested to his *gregarious* nature. He had to play with someone—or something. Obviously he had greeted the prospect of being left alone with considerable *antipathy*. There may also have been in his mind the thought that henceforth we would be so *apprehensive* about what he might be up to that we would think twice before making a hermit out of him again.

Sometimes, if you can't think of anything special, a very ordinary daily occurrence offers interesting possibilities. Here's what can be done with bargain day at your favorite department store:

An *introvert* would not have set foot into the store that day. It required a highly *gregarious* nature to plunge oneself into the mass of shrill-voiced humanity that stormed about the counters and left the aisles littered with the *carnage* of the struggle for bargains. Even if one did not have an *antipathy* for crowds and noise, he would certainly feel *apprehensive* about his safety once caught in the surging mob.

To vary the procedure, you may want to compose oral paragraphs. Get an idea and then *talk it out*, inserting the study words at reasonable intervals. This will help you build up your speaking vocabulary, which for most people, it has been pointed out, is the weakest of all. The most important thing is not the topic or how you develop it. It's your use of the words.

You must be very persistent in developing the paragraph technique. Unless you force yourself to think with your newly acquired words and build thoughts with them, you will not be their complete master. And if you aren't, you will not experience the delight of finding them creeping into your speaking and writing activities, nor will they mean quite as much to you when you find them in material you read.

III. Reviewing the Words

If you follow the vocabulary plan faithfully, you give every word you enter in your Vocabulary Chart the complete treatment.

- You don't make a serious study of a word until you have seen or heard it at least a half dozen times.
- You intensify your memory image of the word by card practice during the week.
- You *use the word* in several original paragraphs that you compose over the week-end.

You would think that such a program is enough to set a word in your mind permanently. Usually, it is. However, no matter how strong an effort you make to retain material, there is a normal percentage of forgetting that must take place. This will be particularly true with some of the words you study but somehow don't manage to use very often. To guard against the possibility of your losing touch with too large a number of recently studied words, it is necessary to establish a systematic review that will refresh your memory from time to time. There are several ways this can be done. Each involves something old and something new, always a good idea when you are going over familiar ground.

A. THE CHART

Set up additional exercises like the one illustrated on page 256. From your Vocabulary Chart copy 10 of your original sentences from the last column. Confine yourself to words about which you are not yet completely confident. Below the sentences, list the literal meanings and synonyms in a haphazard order. Put this work aside for at least a month. Then, when you have some spare time, go through one of the sets, matching the literal meanings and synonyms with the words used in the sentences.

B. THE CARDS

Keep a file of all the cards you fill out when you do your weekly word study. By alphabetizing them you will destroy the original order in which you studied each group of 5 words. When you have accumulated about 50 cards, start with the first 5 and spend a few minutes glancing at the words and trying to recall the meanings, clues, and forms. Those you have forgotten should be removed from the file and set aside. Then when you have 5 of these doubtful ones, substitute them for a new group and go through the customary routine. However, the week-end work should be slightly different, as you shall see in the next item.

C. THE PARAGRAPHS

To give you an example of the kind of paragraphs you should write for restudied words, I shall select 5 words at random and pretend that you found it necessary to do a weekly card drill with them for the second time:

recurrent   credence   carnivorous   ominous   copious

The week-end comes along and you are ready for the paragraph. You proceed as usual, looking for a topic that will enable you to use the words. *Carnivorous* seems to be most prominent, and perhaps it makes you think of a jungle beast. Whether this idea or another occurs to you, as soon as you have an acceptable topic you begin to write. However, this time you do not include the words. Instead, as is demonstrated in the diagnostic test on page 35, you insert spaces and, next to them, synonyms, thus:

Although Clauson had consumed _____ (plentiful) quantities of his favorite brandy, it was difficult not to place _____ (belief) in his tale of the huge tiger that periodically raided the village. _____ (repeated) references to this legendary beast by others had convinced most of us that the _____ (meat-eating) monster was a real although rarely seen threat. Any doubts I might have had about the stories were dismissed when an _____ (threatening) snarl thrust itself through the darkness surrounding the camp fire. This was no time to argue.

carnivorous	ominous
credence	copious
recurrent	

Make a collection of such paragraphs and use them from time to time as a third review. After you have gone through a second card drill on a set of words, let a few weeks elapse and then take one of the "spaces" paragraphs, match the words with the synonyms next to the spaces, and put the material away for another day.

A continuous rotating plan such as outlined above—with the chart, cards, and paragraphs—will keep your growing stock of words in active use. The procedure will soon become a habit with you:

> Select a word!
> Study it!
> Use it!
> Review it, if necessary!

IV. The List

I promised to give you the list I use with my classes, and here it is. There are 300 words altogether. They were gathered, as previously explained, from a great many sources. There are hundreds of other words, just as interesting and useful, that might have been included. However, when a set number is decided upon, the list finally consists of those appearing most frequently. If you become a steady reader, you are likely to encounter every one of them at least a half dozen times in the course of a year.

You should eventually know all the words in the list. However, resist the impulse to let my selections become the sole basis of your vocabulary work. Let my list guide you, fill in for you, or serve as a check—but *don't* let it destroy your independent word study.

There are two sections. The second is somewhat more difficult than the first.

Section 1

abate
abeyance
abhor
acquiesce
admonition
aggravate
agile
alacrity
altercation
amity

antagonist
apathy
aperture
appall
apparition
apprehension
ardent
assuage
augment
austere

avarice
bigot
brusque
cache
capricious
carnage
chagrin
clairvoyant
concur
conflagration

conjecture
contrivance
copious
corpulent
culpable
cupidity
decorum
defunct
deprecate
depreciate

derelict
derision
despicable
detriment
devious
diffident
dilemma
diminutive
disconsolate
dissipate

docile
dubious
eccentric
effrontery
elation
elicit
emaciate
eminent
epitaph
exonerate

exorbitant
facetious
fallible
formidable
fortitude
frugal
furtive
guile
haggard
heresy

hilarious
hostile
impasse
impediment
impending
impervious
impetuous
implacable
impunity
inane

incessant
incongruous
indigent
indomitable
inexorable
ingenious
inscrutable
intermittent
intrepid
inundate

inveterate	pallid	reticent
irony	pandemonium	retribution
jubilant	penitence	sagacity
laconic	perceptible	sanguine
laudable	pernicious	shambles
lethargy	posterity	stentorian
lucrative	precarious	stigma
ludicrous	precocious	stringent
lurid	prevaricate	supercilious
malady	procrastinate	surreptitious
meticulous	prodigious	tenacity
mollify	propriety	trite
morose	prosaic	usurp
naïve	protuberant	vacillate
nocturnal	punctilious	vehement
nurture	querulous	venomous
obeisance	rancor	veracity
obsequious	reminiscence	vindicate
omniscient	respite	vociferous
opulence	restitution	vulnerable

S

acumen
adama

has its full share of polysyllables, many of which seem to be difficult by virtue of their length. However, if you train yourself to become familiar with some of the more common "pieces" that are added, you will possess a second guessing device that will unravel the meanings of a surprisingly large number of words.

For example, we can start with a monosyllable like *port*, which came from the Latin *porto*, meaning *to carry*. Note how it can be built up:

*ex*port	to carry out
*im*port	to carry in
port*able*	able to be carried
port*er*	one who carries
*trans*port*ation*	that which carries or means of carrying across or from one place to another

There is no limit to the number of "pieces" that can be added at the beginning or end of a shorter word. A well-known monstrosity can be traced to the Latin *sto*, meaning *to stand*. It wasn't enough to put *en* (in) in front and *able* (able to) and *ish* (to make) at the end, thus forming the word *establish*, meaning literally *to make able to stand*. Look what happened to the word by the time some others got through with it:

*dis*establish	*to break up* the ability to stand
*anti*disestablish	*against* the above
antidisestablish*ment*	*that which* is against break-ing up the ability to stan
antidisestablishment*arian*	*one who* favors that whi is against breaking up ability to stand

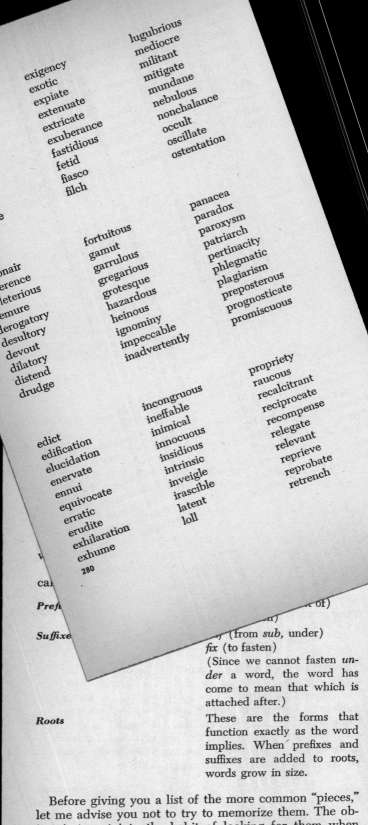

exigency
exotic
expiate
extenuate
extricate
exuberance
fastidious
fetid
fiasco
filch

lugubrious
mediocre
militant
mitigate
mundane
nebulous
nonchalance
occult
oscillate
ostentation

onair
erence
leterious
emure
lerogatory
desultory
devout
dilatory
distend
drudge

fortuitous
gamut
garrulous
gregarious
grotesque
hazardous
heinous
ignominy
impeccable
inadvertently

panacea
paradox
paroxysm
patriarch
pertinacity
phlegmatic
plagiarism
preposterous
prognosticate
promiscuous

edict
edification
elucidation
enervate
ennui
equivocate
erratic
erudite
exhilaration
exhume

incongruous
ineffable
inimical
innocuous
insidious
intrinsic
inveigle
irascible
latent
loll

propriety
raucous
recalcitrant
reciprocate
recompense
relegate
relevant
reprieve
reprobate
retrench

280

ca

Prefi

Suffixe

t of)

(from *sub*, under)
fix (to fasten)
(Since we cannot fasten *under* a word, the word has come to mean that which is attached after.)

Roots These are the forms that function exactly as the word implies. When prefixes and suffixes are added to roots, words grow in size.

Before giving you a list of the more common "pieces," let me advise you not to try to memorize them. The object is to get into the habit of looking for them when you are guessing and to become increasingly familiar with them as you learn to break words down. You will discover that you will remember most prefixes, suffixes, and roots after you have consciously identified them for a time in your dictionary work.

retrospect
ribald
scurrilous
sedentary
sedition
sinecure
sinuous
subvert
succinct
taciturn

tantamount
truculent
ubiquitous
unctuous
urbane
valiant
verdant
vicissitudes
volatile
voracious

wanton
wily
wizened
wrest
yaw
yoke
yore
zealous
zenith
zephyr

CHAPTER X

The Five-Step Plan:
15 Minutes a Day

IF YOU HAVE COME this far . . .

If you have not put the book aside with words like

Some day when I have more time . . .

If you have already made preliminary attempts to master the various techniques . . .

You can be sure of two things!

You have the patience and determination to finish what you have set out to do.

You will progress steadily, perhaps quite rapidly, toward your goal of improving your reading habits.

Chapters V through IX were the test. Had you lacked the ability to stick to a job after it was undertaken, you would have quit long ago. As you read through the previous five chapters, you had repeated evidence that only consistent, personal effort will bring results. It is not unusual, when such a realization comes to a person, for an initial enthusiasm and willingness to work to disappear quickly. Unfortunately, too many of us seek a magic formula to accomplish something instead of relying upon a little self-discipline and lots of dogged practice.

But you haven't given up. You're still willing to go on. Good. From now on the road is downhill. You've gotten over the major obstacle—proving you have the will power to see your problem through. And you are ready to be told how to organize your daily practice sessions so that you get the most out of them. Follow the various plans faithfully. You will observe your skills increasing day by day. You will become a confident, effective reader.

Daily Plan

15 MINUTES A DAY

Step 1:   **Knock Out the Roadblocks! [See Chapter V]**

Time: 2 minutes

Procedures: a. Take one bad habit at a time.

                  b. Spend at least 2 weeks on it, 10 sessions altogether (week-ends reserved for vocabulary practice).

                  c. Vary the daily practice devices as much as possible.

For instance, if you are working on the elimination of *vocalization,* select a passage and on the first day check the sounds in your throat by placing your fingers on your "voice box." Read for 2 minutes, making certain there is no vibration.

The next day try the technique of blowing air out of your mouth as you read silently. The third day, spend 2 minutes reading as you breathe forcefully through your mouth. Improvise. Mix up your attack, but keep one objective before you at a time.

Step 2:   **Stretch Your Span! [See Chapter VI]**

Time: 3 minutes

Procedures: a. Divide your practice time into two parts.

b. Spend about 1 minute each day on the card exercises described in Chapter VI.

c. Do as many cards as you can *comfortably* in the time allotted and then put the material aside.

d. After a few weeks, when you handle the phrase cards expertly, try some of the vertical-column exercises.

e. Then vary your 1-minute phrase practice from one type of exercise to the other during the week.

f. Two minutes daily should be spent on the rhythm exercises.

g. Start each day's practice at this point by going through Rhythm Exercise 1 to get into the proper groove.

h. Then, for the remainder of the time, transfer this training to some of the other rhythm exercises described in Chapter VI.

i. Keep doing this for a few weeks.

j. After you are sure you are habitually reading in word groups, go on to selections that have been marked off in advance with a certain number of stops per line.

Use the material in Chapter VI as long as you can. When it no longer brings you the value of newness, construct some additional exercises of your own.

Don't try to rush things. If you have to start with 2-word

phrase cards, do so; and don't increase them to 3-word groups until you are sure you are ready to stretch your span a little wider. Similarly, if you have to begin with five stops per line in the rhythm exercises, or the marked off passages, be patient. The four- and three-stop exercises will wait until you have developed the necessary skill. Steady progress is definitely preferable to frustration.

Step 3:	**Shift into High! [See Chapter VII]**
Time:	3 minutes
Procedures:	a. Remember to use one selection that you divide into equal parts, about 350 to 500 words each.
	b. Spend the first minute reading the first half of the selection at your nonpushing rate.
	c. Record the words-per-minute in your notebook chart.
	d. Now read the second half at a forced speed. Time your "high gear" reading effort and enter the result in the last column of your chart.
	e. The extra minute here is for the chart entries and the possibility that passages will not be of uniform length.

The second reading will not always be faster than the first. It may even be slower on occasion. But the significant results will be determined by comparing words-per-minute entries over a period of weeks or months, not days.

Keep pushing and the numbers in both of the last two columns of your chart will steadily increase.

Step 4:	**Look for the Keys!** [See Chapter VIII]
Time:	5 minutes
Procedures:	a. There is enough material in Chapter VIII to last you for the first few weeks of comprehension training.
	b. Take one exercise a day and spend your 5 minutes reading it and answering the questions.
	c. You will find additional exercises in the Appendix. Use these, too.
	d. When you run out of material in the book, prepare exercises yourself. As was pointed out before, the mere act of setting up questions on the contents of a selection gives training almost as valuable as answering someone else's test.
	e. If you wish to get more ready-made practice passages, you can write to the various state education departments or municipal and Federal civil-service bureaus. Ask them to send you typical reading questions given on examinations conducted under their supervision. Usually the material is free, or there is only a nominal charge.
	However, let me repeat. You will do very well if you look for the keys on your own. *Knowing how* to get what you should out of your reading is the main objective. Constant application of this skill must of itself bring improvement.

Step 5:	Build Your Vocabulary! [See Chapter IX]
Time:	2 minutes
Procedures:	a. Follow the daily and week-end instructions outlined in Chapter IX.
	b. Make no effort to find new words to add to the ones entered in your vocabulary chart when you do the daily 15-minute drills. Your entire attention should be centered on developing the various skills involved, and you should not allow word-consciousness to interfere. Pick your words from the materials you read at other times.
	c. As your original vocabulary paragraphs increase in number, you can use them for some of the practice exercises recommended in connection with the previous four steps.

Another important point must be repeated. The daily practice sessions can and should be completed in 15 minutes. However, you must apply your gradually improving skills to general reading as often as possible. Practice without performance will slow up your progress. Do not let a day go by without reading something besides your newspaper. Here, too, get variety. Try them all—books, magazines, pamphlets, etc.

LONG-RANGE PLAN

Every month take stock. If you find that you have eliminated all your roadblocks, make some adjustments in your schedule. Spend only a few minutes a week on Step 1 to make sure you do not slip back. Use the extra time available on what seems to be your greatest difficulty.

You will reach the point where you find yourself making a regular number of stops per line. Further experimentation may convince you that this is your best pace. You can then cut down on the time you spend on phrase practice. Let's say you eventually get to the three- or four-stop-per-line stage and you feel most comfortable in this pattern. Transfer the phrase practice time to the speed *pushing* drills.

Your over-all objective should be the elimination of most of the time devoted to the mechanical problems of reading (roadblocks and recognition span) in favor of concentration on comprehension and vocabulary, with an occasional speed drill. And beyond this point will come the time when you need practically no direct daily drills at all. You will have established good habits and these will be strengthened automatically as you continue to expand your general reading activities.

Now and then you will become bored with your daily practice. Give yourself a big lift by thinking of the not-so-distant future. Yours is not the problem faced by a person with suddenly defective vision. He must don a pair of eyeglasses and wear them permanently because they become indispensable. Improving your reading ability is not a lifelong proposition. The job can be done in months. Best of all, the skills can be maintained by participating in one of life's most worth-while activities—reading! So practice every day, and before long you won't have to practice any more.

CHAPTER XI

Skim Reading

SKIMMING is an ability you have had for a long time. From the very beginning of your experiences as an independent reader, you tended to develop this skill. The first time you voluntarily picked up a collection of stories, you didn't just turn to the first page and begin reading. More likely you browsed through the table of contents until a particular title struck your fancy. Then you turned to the story, glanced rapidly over the opening paragraphs, and decided quickly whether you had made a good choice.

You didn't have to be told to follow this procedure. It was an extension of a perfectly natural habit. Almost from infancy you have displayed a sense of discrimination. You learned early to taste a new food before committing yourself to eating it. As you grew older you followed the same impulse. It became routine for you to try on several articles of clothing before selecting one to wear, to test ocean or lake water before plunging in, to let your gaze sweep around a room to get the general impression before concentrating on individual pieces of furniture. Thus, when your reading activities passed the early stages, it wasn't necessary to explain the idea of sampling to you. It had become a part of your normal human reaction to challenging situations.

When you began to use a dictionary, you had little difficulty training your eyes to drift down a page until you spotted the word you were after. You did the same thing to locate a topic in the index of a book, a number in a telephone directory, the scheduled arrival or departure time of a train in a timetable.

Since you have done considerable skim reading before, you may be wondering why additional training in this skill wasn't included in some of the previous chapters. A good reason can be found in what a dictionary says about *skimming:* "to pass over lightly or hastily; to glide or skip along the surface; especially, to give a cursory glance or consideration."

As you can see by its definition, skimming is not the kind of reading you have been told to do to achieve full comprehension. You can hardly get everything you should get out of a selection if you pass over it lightly, skip about, or give it just a cursory glance.

The point is, of course, that when you are skimming your objectives are not the same as when you are interested in all the ideas, important details, and other features of a writer's material. Not only is the approach different, but certain adjustments must sometimes be made in the eye movements as well. So you can see that it would be very confusing to train yourself to adopt one set of procedures for regular reading and simultaneously practice another for skimming.

The last thing I want you to do is develop a helter-skelter pattern of reading. Too many people become poor readers precisely because they set up speed as their sole objective and race through material without knowing what to look for and without any real purpose. They skim-read not when the occasion warrants it but as if they knew no other way. They have never quite mastered the fundamentals, so they do not have an assortment of skills with which to meet a specific reading situation.

That's why this chapter has come at the very end. Its pages should be labeled somewhat like a Christmas gift bought in November: "Not to be opened until . . ." —in this case, until you have worked with the Five-Step Plan long enough to have shown marked improvement in your normal rate and comprehension, and your new reading habits have become firmly established.

Regard skimming as an extra, a fine point. Forget about it for at least a few months after you have started your reading-improvement program. And when you do get around to attempting to extend your skim-reading ability, remember that this is a special skill to be reserved for special occasions.

There are two broad areas in which skimming is useful and often essential. The techniques recommended for one differ to some extent from those of the other. We will examine each separately and show you how to extend the skills you already possess in this field. In the course of your training you will perhaps be able to join the group of readers who can achieve a rate of 1,000 words per minute when it suits their purpose.

I. Skimming for Specific Items of Information

Almost every day you find it necessary to check the spelling or meaning of a word; verify a name, address, or date; locate a particular fact; or glance again through something you have read before in order to refresh your memory about some detail. When this need arises, you turn to reference works—dictionaries, encyclopedias, almanacs, directories, guides of various descriptions—or to the previously read material.

In either case, you aren't interested in the entire book at the moment of your research, or even the contents of any page you consult. What you are after is generally a very brief item of no more than a line or two. You recognize it as soon as you see it because you haven't approached the information with a complete blank in your mind. You already know all or part of the item if you are merely checking, or you have decided in advance what to look for and can rapidly eliminate every detail except the one you are seeking.

The material in the reference works you have consulted in the past is ordinarily arranged in columns. Your prior experience, therefore, should have made you fairly familiar with the technique of skimming down a relatively narrow column of print. You can easily train yourself to apply this skill to other materials as well.

Let's analyze what happens when your eyes begin to slide down a column of words, names, or figures. You *don't actually read* each entry. As a matter of fact, you don't even look for the particular bit of information you want. Whether you have realized this before or not, what you do is let your eyes drift past each item and wait for the one you are seeking to hit your consciousness. As your glance moves down a page, you are vaguely aware of other word or name images, but you react positively only when the right one comes along. You don't go after it; you let it come to you. To convince yourself that this is so, try the two exercises that follow.

Words

Start counting mentally from one to fifteen. Let your eyes move down the columns of words below, and before you have counted to the last number, see whether you can locate the word *industrious*.

idea	impatient
ignorant	importance
illustrate	important
imitate	impossible
immediately	improvement
immigrant	include

increase

independence

independent

industrial

industrious

industry

influence

information

injure

injury

innocence

inquire

insane

Words and numbers

Again count the same way. This time find the Smith who lives at 1239 Tinton Avenue. Your glance should focus on a point between the names and the addresses.

Smith, Helen	2100 University Avenue
Smith, Helen	4215 Wickham Avenue
Smith, Henry	692 Claremont Drive
Smith, Henry	1160 Fulton Place
Smith, Henry	1722 Dorset Road
Smith, Henry	2288 Wallace Avenue
Smith, Henry	1640 East 50 Street
Smith, Henry	1700 West 98 Street
Smith, Henry	1239 Grant Boulevard
Smith, Henry	1888 Phelan Street
Smith, Henry	159 Bailey Court
Smith, Henry	84 East 222 Street
Smith, Henry	225 West 99 Street
Smith, Henry	1239 Tinton Avenue
Smith, Henry	1653 Brookdale Street
Smith, Herbert	1892 Eastchester Avenue
Smith, Herbert	38 Brook Drive
Smith, Herbert	922 Clinton Road
Smith, Herbert	889 Arrow Avenue
Smith, Herbert	554 Clay Avenue
Smith, Herbert	1189 Southern Place
Smith, Herman	335 Undercliff Street
Smith, Herman	8 Suffolk Avenue
Smith, Hilda	45 Holland Place
Smith, Horace	667 West 59 Street

You were able to pick out the word and the name, I'm sure, despite the fact that your mind was busy counting up to fifteen. With such interference, you could not have done so had you been concentrating fully on each of the column entries. However, you were after a preset image and you needed only part of your attention to accomplish your objective.

This is the skill you have exercised so often before. With little additional training you can learn to apply it to any line of print, whether it is the width of a word, a phrase, a newspaper-type column, or the 10-to-12-word span in a book. Use exactly the technique that has just been demonstrated whenever you are skimming for information. Focus your eyes on an imaginary line drawn down the center of the column or page you are consulting. Let your glance drift steadily downward. Allow no more than one stop per line and make no lateral movements. Take full advantage of your peripheral vision so that you cover practically the full line of print. Wait until the image you will recognize hits your consciousness. And keep going rapidly until it does! Of course when you do reach the desired point, you read all that is necessary with your normal attention to detail—and then out you go. Skim the material that is of no immediate interest to you, not the information you are seeking.

Each of the practice exercises that follow contains two training suggestions. The time limit will help you gauge the speed at which you should skim. The advance question will indicate a typical bit of information you might be looking for if you were consulting a reference work or were checking a passage you had read before in order to remind yourself of a fact.

Skimming for Specific Items of Information—Exercise 1

Maximum time: 15 seconds

Question: What is the best old-model car for
                             a beginner to choose for remodel-
                             ing?

Reminders

Focus down the center of the column.

Slide right past material that does not contribute to
answering your question.

Wait for key words to guide you to the item of information you are seeking. In this selection *old-model*
connected with *beginner* will be the signal to your mind
to stop skimming and start full concentration.

Crank Her Up Again

The fifty-year-old car seen in parades
and exhibits may have been kept on
blocks in someone's garage. More likely
the car has been reassembled with loving care by one of the many persons who
now have the old car restoration fever.

A car is an antique at 25, but enthusiasts seek even earlier models down to
the horseless carriage days. These old
cars are usually found in broken-down
condition, at a cost of a few dollars to
several hundred, depending on age,
rarity, and condition. The market for
old cars is expanding as the hobby grows,
and the going price of, say a 1914 Stutz
Bearcat, is clearly fixed. The Mercer
Raceabout is today the most sought after
and valued of antique automobiles. Oth-

295

er names to bring back the early beginnings of a wonderful industry are the American roadster, the giant Simplex, the Winton Six, the Franklin limousine or a Chadwick, the first supercharged car.

A beginner will probably choose a Model T Ford; it is easy to work on—even for an amateur, and parts are easily secured. Many hours of search, labor and mechanical work must go into bringing the car back to driving order and appearance. The first job is to find out how that particular model looked and operated—in every detail, for to have value, authenticity and interest, the old-timer must not be modernized or altered from its original state, construction, or mechanical workings.

If you were able (within the 15-second limit) to identify the Model T Ford as the best for a beginner to choose, you were skimming along at a rate of more than 800 words per minute!

Skimming for Specific Items of Information—Exercise 2

Maximum time: 20 seconds

Question: At what time of the year does the cutting of Christmas trees take place?

Down the center of the column!

No more than one stop per line!

The word *cutting* is the clue to the answer to your question. Let it be your guide.

This time pretend that you have decided to get your own Christmas tree. You are not interested in the details of the tree business. All you want to know is when to cut so that you don't ruin the tree.

The Story of 30,000,000 Christmas Trees

Have you ever felt a twinge when you looked at beautifully decorated Christmas trees? That it was a shame to cut them down? Don't feel sad. The trees that delight young and old are usually doomed trees that would have died from root or sunlight starvation if they had not been cut. The thinning of the forests actually improves them, and in any event, none of the many large companies that harvest Christmas trees—it's an annual retail $77,000,000 industry—could afford bad forest practice.

Among the largest Christmas tree sources are logging companies with acres of reforestation projects. Seedlings pop up by thousands around parent seed trees. As the young trees grow, over-crowding becomes fatal. So Christmas tree cutters are called in to thin the land.

297

Many other Christmas tree farms are found on land logged off. There Christmas tree farmers thin out the seedlings before they have a chance to spoil each other's shape, and prune off lower limbs to make slower rising, thickly limbed trees almost round (better looking Christmas trees than those of yore).

By saving seed trees and careful thinning, owners keep a crop of trees coming in the most popular market size of five to seven feet. Oddly enough, the two things that would put a farm out of business are a few years of *no* cutting or a couple of seasons of exceptionally good conditions for tree growth. A tree growing faster than a foot a year would be too spindly for a Christmas tree.

The cutting operation begins after the first freeze. If trees are cut earlier, the sap is still up and needles quickly fall off. Trucked to special yards in heavily shaded timber where it is wet underfoot and cool all day, the trees are sorted for size and quality, trimmed and finally tied in bundles for shipping.

Only a very small percentage of these 30,000,000 trees is not sold. So never think a Christmas tree grower is wasteful—for his whole livelihood depends on good forest management.

To find out (in 20 seconds) that the cutting operation

begins after the first freeze required a skimming rate
of more than 900 words per minute!

Skimming for Specific Items of Information—Exercise 3

Maximum time: 10 seconds

Question: What are the maximum salary an
                     umpire can earn and the minimum
                     age at which he can begin train-
                     ing?

Reminders

Down the middle!

The question calls for two items of information, but
this doesn't change the basic technique. Simply look for
the keys words, *maximum salary* and *minimum age*.

They Call 'Em as They're Taught to See 'Em

"Yer' out!!" This thunderous roar from
more than 140 men can be heard almost
half a mile away. These men are student
umpires enrolled in one of two five-week
courses offered every spring at the Bill
McGowan School for Umpires, at Daytona
Beach, Florida.

Most of the students at the school are
yearling umpires, but several may be veteran performers brushing up on technique.
No student can graduate from the school
unless he has learned every phase of baseball rules. Although these umpires will
probably spend their working life being
booed and hissed, they can look forward to

a minimum salary of $250 a month with a D league and a maximum of $15,000 per season with a major league.

Admission to the school requires the same standards used in organized baseball for hiring umpires—that candidates must be from 21 to 35 years of age, five feet six inches or over, and weigh at least 150 pounds. If he meets these requirements and can show good character recommendations, he's eligible for the school. Experience is not considered necessary.

You skimmed at the rate of more than 1,000 words per minute if you were able to discover (in 10 seconds or less) that the top salary is $15,000 and the lowest entrance age is 21.

Skimming for Specific Items of Information—Exercise 4

Maximum time: 15 seconds

Question: What is the name of the catalysts that help us digest our food?

Reminders

Down the middle!
No more than one stop per line!
Note that these are full-size lines.

Excerpt from The Science Book of Wonder Drugs

BY DONALD G. COOLEY

How are you able to digest roast beef with such ridiculous ease?

Imagine the difficulties of a chemist who attempts to imitate this prodigious feat. He could treat the beef with powerful acids, distill it in a vacuum, whirl it in a centrifuge, apply terrific temperatures. After many days, he might be able to show you a few substances comparable to some products of digestion.

But you digest your food quickly and easily and with no little pleasure. You do so because you have body cells that produce exceedingly minute amounts of substances that act as catalysts. They make possible the combining of molecules into new substances by inducing chemical reactions that could not take place without the catalyst. All the processes of life—digestion, growth, muscle contraction, reproduction, nerve conduction, to mention a few—proceed only because catalysts see to it that the right chemicals are present at the right time. In a way a catalyst grasps molecules that will have nothing to do with each other, bangs them together so effectively that they combine to form different molecules, and performs thousands of these forced marriages (or, contrariwise, divorces molecular partners) in a fraction of a second.

Catalysts that work these miracles for you are known as enzymes. Literally, enzyme means "in yeast." Something in yeast causes cereals and grapes to ferment, a very ancient discovery, and a far cry from present knowledge that the myriads of chemical reactions we call life take place only because enzymes make them possible.

* * *

Your rate, if you found the answer within the time limit, was again about 1,000 words per minute.

Maximum time: 10 seconds

Question: What is the oldest recorded date of
                   the sport of falconry in England?

Reminders

Down the middle!
This is the fastest speed you have yet tried. If you
succeed you will be skimming at a rate of about 1,200
words per minute!

The King's Hunter

A sound like a sudden rip of canvas. A flash of black
plummeting across the blue sky faster than the pull of
gravity. An explosive splintering of feathers. A falconer
crosses the plain to the brush where his peregrine falcon
has nailed a pheasant. He slips a hood over the falcon's
head, takes her on his heavily gauntleted fist and puts
the pheasant in his game bag.

This is the twentieth century. But the drama is identical to one practiced 5,000 years before. It is falconry,
a hunting sport as old as recorded history. In antique
China, Japan, Arabia, Iran and Syria, artifacts depict
falconry. On a bas-relief found in the ruins of Khorsabad
there is a falconer bearing a hawk on his wrist. The oldest records of falconry in Europe are in the writings of
Aristotle, Pliny and Martial. In England, from 860 to the
middle of the seventeenth century, falconry was followed
with an ardor no other sport had yet evoked. Louis XIV
spent nearly every day of his reign afield at falconry.
Today, it is still practiced ardently in Asia, not infre-

quently in European hunting preserves and sporadically in North America—where there are probably fewer than 100 practitioners.

*   *   *

The exercises you have just completed should have given you the idea of how to skim for items of information. Remember, you are not developing a new skill. You are applying an old one to new reading situations. Continue to perfect the technique involved by setting up advance questions about items of information and then finding the answers in various reference works. You already know how to figure out your words-per-minute rate. Do not forget, however, that skimming is an extra and should never become a substitute for your regular reading habits.

II. Skimming for Highlights

In the second area where you can use skimming to good advantage, your purpose is different. Now you want to get a bird's-eye view of a letter, article, story, editorial, or book. You are interested in a general impression, a main point or theme, the broad outlines of a plot, or perhaps just in finding out whether you should read the material more carefully a second time. Your objective is to pick out the highlights and to do so as quickly as possible.

Why is speed so important here? The most significant reason is that reading situations that lend themselves readily to skimming for highlights usually find the reader short of time, or desirous of getting to something else quickly, or simply not wishing to waste time on material that he has no need to examine intensively. We might consider a few typical circumstances under which these conditions are present.

Every morning a pile of correspondence must be gone over in the average office. Business or professional time is too valuable to squander on trivial pieces of mail. That's why it is so useful to be able to skim through the batch of letters, set aside the ones that can be thrown out or answered at a later date, and select those that require a careful rereading.

Here's another instance. If you are like most busy people, you have only a short time to devote to your morning newspaper. Some people solve this problem by reading a few headlines, riffling through the sports or fashion pages, and winding up with the comics. But if you wish to be an informed citizen, you can use skimming to give you the highlights of the day's news and still have time left for your favorite features.

If you are a student or technician you have to do extensive research occasionally with the aid of several books and periodicals. Rarely is there enough time to do this job in a leisurely fashion. Besides, one book may repeat in part the material found in another. There is no point in going over the same ground twice. Skimming can help you go through a dozen volumes, when necessary, in rapid style while you concentrate on only the sections that are pertinent to your research problem.

And what about the recreational reading you are supposed to get into the habit of doing on a regular basis? You will probably have to snatch an hour or so from a full day. This means that you won't be able to finish the book you choose in one sitting. Each time you get back to it you will experience difficulty in picking up the thread of the narrative or ideas unless you employ your skimming ability. If you learn to glance rapidly through the highlights of a few pages before the point at which you stopped reading, you will quickly be able to continue, with little loss of time or sequence.

Skimming is also very helpful in the selection of a book to read. In no time at all you can leaf through a few chapters, get a quick preview, and decide whether this is your kind of reading material. You can thus avoid the frustration of plodding along for fifty or a hundred pages and then giving up in disgust. The same procedure, incidentally, can be used when you have to study a part of a book. A rapid look at the text to be mastered gives you an over-all view of the subject matter and helps you decide what pages will need your closest attention.

From the foregoing examples you can understand why I said that the purpose in skimming for highlights is different from that of looking for a specific item of information. Your center of attention is on the whole of a selection, not on a small detail in it. The difference extends also to the eye movements.

When your glance is moving down a page in search of a particular bit of information, you can't permit any skipping of lines. If you do you may go right past the item you want to find. In skimming for highlights, you do not plan in advance to pick out certain facts or details. Your main concern is to get the general notion of the contents quickly. Therefore, you can skip here and there, since your failure to absorb a few details more or less in a long description, for example, will not materially affect your understanding of the story. Obviously this makes it inadvisable to focus steadily on a set point in a line. Your eyes must be free to wander about on the page.

That's why it is impossible to suggest a pattern of eye movements for highlight skimming. However, certain procedures can be recommended. You can use them separately or in combination, depending upon the material you are skimming. Each will be illustrated in the exercises that follow.

Skimming for Highlights—Exercise 1

Procedures: You can learn to skip without missing much. Use your knowledge of how a paragraph is constructed. The first sentence may give you the main point, and you can slide right past the rest of it. If an article is full of statistics that merely point up the generalizations, you can ignore many of them. You won't remember them anyway unless you study them, and this is not your purpose in skimming. Look at just enough to make the ideas clear. In the following article, for example, the word *woman* (in several forms) is used more than 27 times. This enables you to skip it whenever you see it or any reference to it. The facts will clearly be about women. You can get an idea of how this is done by reading only the words and phrases in italics. A test that will follow will prove that you got the highlights despite your skipping.

Maximum time: 40 seconds

Is Woman's Place in the Home?

For years *American males*—most of them—have been *arguing* that *woman's place* is in the *home*. But while they repeated this sentiment of their grandparents, their *wives and daughters* continued to leave the home. They *entered the professions* and got their names on the payrolls of all kinds of *industries*.

Today *women outnumber men* by about five million. This means that American females can outvote the males on election day. They certainly outspend them. Now *they are beginning to outwork them.*

Today, women earn their livings at all kinds of jobs. They have *entered nearly every occupation* held by men. The Census Bureau reports that at least some women hold jobs in every one of the more than 400 occupations listed by the bureau.

Employers have recently been told by the U. S. Labor Department that the *number of women workers* will *continue to increase.* Within the next ten years, the nation's labor force is expected to grow by at least ten million. Half of these new workers will be women.

This business of "womanpower" has been the subject of a *two-year study* by the National Manpower Council at Columbia University. The *findings* of this group were presented to President Eisenhower.

The key facts about women as the nation's "manpower" resource are:

• Some 28 million American girls and women—age 14 or older—work during the course of every year.

• *Girls* in school today will *average 25 years of outside work* (outside their homes) during their lifetimes.

• *One-fifth of the country's* total *wages and salaries*—more than 42 billion dollars—is now being received by *female workers.* Their time amounts to more than one-fourth of the total man-hours worked.

• *Sixty per cent* of all women now working are *married. Fifty per cent* are more than *40 years old.*

• *Three* out of every *ten married women* are now *working. Four* out of every *ten mothers with children of school age* work.

• The *largest single group* to come into the nation's labor force *since 1950* has been women of *middle age* and older.

The council that made the two-year study of woman-power found that the timing of *American life has changed since 1890*. In that year, some four million working women made up one-sixth of the nation's labor force.

The council found that—

• The average woman now *leaves school at age 18*. In 1890 she left at 14.

• Today's woman *marries soon after* leaving *school*. The marrying age used to be much older.

• Today's woman sees her children enter school earlier and marry earlier.

• The average woman now *lives longer* than she did in 1890.

For these reasons, today's women have more time to work. They are continuing their fight for equality with men—*equal pay for equal work*.

Some people say that the *problems* of our society can be *traced* directly to the *absence* of American women *from* their *homes*. Public opinion has not, however, yet demanded a change.

Should there be such a change?

TEST ON HIGHLIGHTS:

Mark each of the following statements T (true) or F (false).

_____ There are more women than men.

_____ Women usually do not enter the same professions as men.

_____ The number of women workers is declining.

_____ Women earn more than half the nation's salaries.

308

_____ Most women workers are married.

_____ The habits of women have changed greatly since 1890.

_____ They leave school earlier.

_____ They marry earlier.

_____ They live longer.

_____ They receive less pay than men.

ANSWERS: T, F, F, F, T;   T, F, T, T, T.

Skimming for Highlights—Exercise 2

Procedures:

Newspaper editors know that their readers are often pressed for time. It is for this reason that a standard journalistic device is to give an outline of the main point of an article in the first sentence or two. Because of this fact, it is possible to skim a news article of more than 1,000 words in less than a minute by reading the first paragraph carefully and then reading only the first line of every paragraph thereafter. Unquestionably, you won't get as much out of the article as you would if you read every word, but if it is highlights you are after and you want to skim, you will come away with a surprisingly good understanding of the contents. Try this in the next selection.

Boy in Well Rescued After 24 Hours

Seven-year-old Benjamin Kent Hooper Jr. was rescued at 7:46 o'clock tonight after being trapped almost twenty-four hours at the bottom of a well. He was weak, hungry and pale, but conscious.

The news that the boy was alive was issued from the pit near the boy's home. An oxygen cup pressed to his mouth, the boy was carried to an ambulance and rushed to the Bayview General Hospital in Mastic.

The last sure evidence that the boy was alive had come from the narrow well at 11 o'clock last night, when a jacket, which a grappling hook had pulled inside-out over the boy's head and arms, moved slightly. Since then there had been nothing but hope to sustain more than 200 workmen who labored to save him.

The fight to rescue him began minutes after the fall last night. It continued with oxygen lines, power shovels, piping and wooden shoring all through the night and all through the day. The father had first attempted to free the boy himself by digging frantically at the top of the well shaft. But firemen who arrived on the scene ordered him to stop; they feared his activity would cause earth to cave in on the boy.

Rescuers began immediately to dig a shaft a few feet from the well and parallel to it. Feeble cries from the sandy prison were heard through the first hour of the boy's entrapment. After that there were no further noises. Benjamin had fallen feet first and had apparently raised his hands above his head during the descent. The hands alone remained visible from the ground.

An oxygen hose was lowered into the well, and sufficient oxygen to sustain three men was piped to the boy continually through the hours of torment.

Hand diggers alternated with power shovels in the fevered race through the night. A power saw whined eerily through wooden beams, which were lowered into the rescue shaft and clamped against its side. A light was kept focused on Benjamin's hands until dawn.

The purpose of the rescuers was to drive the second shaft level with the base of the well and then to tunnel through. Half way down the twenty-one-foot distance, power shovels were removed and two workmen scooped sand in buckets and handed them up in a three-stage relay to the top.

The task was repeatedly complicated by sand slides at the bottom. It was necessary to construct a wooden frame 4 feet wide by 6 feet long, and this was placed at the lowest point reached. Plywood sheets were then held outside the frame and driven down into the sand with sledge hammers, making a sort of box that rescuers emptied of sand.

This done, a second frame, just large enough to fit inside the "box," was thrust down to the new base and the process was repeated. Twice again this was done until the second shaft matched the first in depth.

The problem then was to tunnel through twelve feet of fine salt sand. The rescue shaft was thirty-five feet wide at the mouth and tapered, like a cone, to four feet square at the bottom.

Through it all the boy's mother gazed impassively from the northeast windows of her home, which overlooked the well by less than twenty feet.

The tunnel walls collapsed at 6:10 A.M. today spilling sand into the cut. Workmen tried again. Again the sands descended.

Michael Stiriz, a general contractor of Patchogue, was the key man in the rescue operations. He decided midway in the morning to abandon attempts to shore up the tunnel with wood and ordered a piece of piping forty-eight inches wide into the rescue hole, which was barely big enough to contain it at the bottom.

A board was placed over one end of the pipe and heavy construction jacks, of the sort used to lift houses, were braced against the opposite wall and turned up, driving the pipe into the tube. Sand was then removed from it. The piece of pipe, four feet long, then put the workmen one-third of the distance to the boy. A forty-inch pipe, also four feet long, was then sleeved through the larger pipe and driven in again with jacks.

At 2:30 P.M. Dr. Joseph Kris, who had been on the scene almost since the start, said it was possible the boy was alive but certainly improbable.

The sun, which had risen on fading hope, began to go down on resigned hopelessness. At 3:42 P.M. the second section of pipe was lowered into the hole. At 3:50, twelve men lowered an eight-inch-wide pipe into the well where the boy was trapped.

Chimney vacuum cleaners from the Brookhaven National Laboratory were used to clear this pipe of sand. A larger pipe was then set down over the smaller pipe. The purpose of the operation was to fill the well with the larger pipe and use it to protect the boy from falling sand. The presence of the smaller pipe inside the larger one guaranteed an air shaft to the boy while the operation was carried out.

The vacuum cleaners were then used to remove the sand from between the pipes, and when this was done, the smaller pipe was hoisted out.

A searchlight, which had been trained down the well shaft through the night, was again aimed at the bottom.

Workmen said they believed the larger pipe had slipped gently over the boy's head and upraised hands. The pipe was suspended on a cable just short of his shoulders.

TEST ON HIGHLIGHTS:

Mark the following statements T or F.

_____ The boy was seven years old.

_____ Rescue operations began at night.

_____ Only hand tools were used.

_____ Fortunately there were no sand cave-ins.

_____ An oxygen hose was lowered.

_____ It took almost three hours to get the boy out.

_____ Vacuum cleaners were also used.

_____ A doctor on the scene said the boy was certainly dead.

_____ The boy's jacket at one point was grabbed with a grappling hook.

_____ He didn't have to go to a hospital.

ANSWERS: T, T, F, F, T; F, T, F, T, F.

312

Procedures:

Many articles, such as this one, make their point early and then repeat it several times. The major interest lies in the names and anecdotes that are used to introduce the human-interest angle. You can knife through the introductory material and go directly to the names and stories. In skimming here you can read the first paragraph rapidly, skip right down to *Jackie Cooper*, go through the three brief stories, and finish the 500 words in about 30 seconds. Bear in mind also that you will often come across a selection that discusses a subject about which you are quite well informed. Your attention logically belongs only on those paragraphs that present something unusual.

Academy Awards

The street of dreams come true is the long, carpeted aisle of the Pantages theater, when the world's finest motion picture talents and technicians walk to the dais to receive the awards of merit from the Academy of Motion Picture Arts and Sciences. For each selected winner there's Oscar—a gold-plated bronze statuette that has powerful influence in the celluloid world.

On a night in March, about 150 nominees will tensely wait while the master of ceremonies carefully tears

313

open the sealed balloting returns secretly tabulated by the accounting firm of Price-Waterhouse. They'll quickly run over their prepared acceptance speeches, hope their television make-up is perfect—then, when the announcement is made, they'll probably forget the speeches and smear the make-up with tears of joy or disappointment.

After twenty-eight years, the Academy Awards ceremony is still the most emotion-charged spectacle in glamorous filmland. In all the world there is no greater assemblage of beauty and talent, eager and curious, than that greeting the yearly appearance of Oscar.

From the Academy's inception in 1927, all the entertainment-conscious world has awaited the Awards with interest. Radio and television now carry the emotion-charged event to hundreds of millions of movie fans all over the democratic world. Besides the thrill and surprise of learning who the best performers are at the same time they do, each ceremony has its unplanned vignettes of human interest that make it memorable.

At the fourth year banquet, Jackie Cooper competed with Lionel Barrymore for the top male honor. There was much speculation as to how the little boy would "take it" if he lost to the veteran actor. When the time came for Barrymore to claim his statuette, tired little "Skippy" was sound asleep on the lap of Marie Dressler—herself a winner that year.

Frank Capra presided as emcee in 1939. He proceeded with caution, certainly remembering the evening four years previously when he had been nominated. Will Rogers was moved to laudatory speech-making before announcing the winner, ending his speech with, "Frank, come and get it!" Frank Capra proceeded about forty feet before he realized that Will Rogers was motioning to Frank Lloyd, who won for "Mutiny on the Bounty." Capra calls his return to the table "the longest crawl on record."

When Gary Cooper won for his portrayal of "Sergeant York," he said: "I've been in the business sixteen years and sometimes dreamed I might get one of these things. That's all I can say . . . Funny, when I was dreaming, I always made a good speech."

It's the realization and the frustration of those dreams by the movie greats that charge each Awards ceremony with suspense and emotion. It's what makes the Academy Awards a thrilling spectacle for millions of Americans.

TEST ON HIGHLIGHTS:

Mark each statement with a T or F.

_____ Oscar is the first name of a great actor.

_____ The Awards are given world-wide coverage.

_____ Jackie Cooper fell asleep at one of the affairs.

_____ Frank Capra received an award from Will Rogers.

_____ Gary Cooper found he had little to say after all.

❋   ❋   ❋

ANSWERS: F, T, T, F, T.

The major techniques for highlight skimming have been illustrated in the preceding exercises. It would be impractical, of course, to give you direct examples of procedures to be followed with entire books or batches of letters. However, one or more of the recommended devices can be applied successfully to any material. So that you can have available guides to proper skimming techniques, suppose we set down the most useful ones.

1. If the article, story, or book is written with proper attention to paragraph construction, you can get most of its ideas by reading the first sentence, perhaps one in the middle, and the last one of very long paragraphs.

2. When you come to extended scenic descriptions and you have no immediate interest in the beauty of the language, look at *only a sentence or two per page,* and then get on with the story.

3. In skimming through letters, first see who sent it. That may be enough in itself. If not, glance at the opening sentence, and if that doesn't make up your mind, read the last one. By that time you should know whether the letter is of any importance to you.

4. Don't waste time plowing through line after line of statistics that are offered in bunches to make one point. Leave the figures to readers who have serious use for them. Once you understand what the author is trying to prove, you can slide past the numbers.

5. If you wish to skim through serious material—an editorial, for example—you can do this very successfully by simply stopping at only the phrases containing the longer words and occasionally glancing at a name or date. This requires a zigzag pattern of eye movements, but you will have little trouble perfecting this technique after a few tries.

6. When you start a book, make a conscious effort to become familiar with the author's style. If he likes to stretch out his descriptions or analyses, uses dialogue to clinch a point he has already made, has a tendency to repeat, you can find valuable clues that will help you skip generously without loss of understanding.

7. In textbooks, use the illustrations, chapter headings, table of contents, and your knowledge of paragraph

structure to give you a preview of the material you will study later. It is often a good idea, if the book is yours, to underline important statements as you study. Later on, when you review, you can skim through the subject matter, concentrating almost exclusively on the underlined portions. The latter will be enough to refresh your memory.

Before this chapter comes to a close, let me caution you once more about skimming. It is an extra. It should be used only when it suits a special purpose. It is never as good as rapid reading for full comprehension.

Regard this technique as a two-edged sword. It can help you cut through material easily, but used unwisely it can cause serious injury to your normal reading habits.

Your primary objectives in your improvement program are

The fastest possible rate adjusted to purpose and material!

Full comprehension!

And ultimately

An open road to pleasure, recreation, mental enrichment—through the things you read!

Appendixes

Appendix I

How to Answer Reading Questions on Examinations

It has become standard practice to include reading questions on civil-service, professional, equivalency, College Board, scholarship, and all sorts of qualifying examinations. Many candidates, despite good reading ability, fail to do justice to themselves because they haven't learned the special techniques required to handle such questions satisfactorily.

You have already had the opportunity (Chapters III and VIII) of working with typical selections used for testing. These brief paragraphs are obviously not offered for recreational or informational reading. The examiner uses them solely to evaluate how well the candidate can interpret the printed word, especially in terms of main ideas and details. Thus questions based on the paragraphs usually take two forms.

THE TITLE

From a number of possibilities (usually five), the reader is asked to pick a title that would be appropriate for the paragraph. If he can do so accurately and consistently, it proves that he has no difficulty finding the *main idea* of a selection he reads.

DETAILS

As the word suggests, questions of this type aim to

test the candidate's ability to recognize important details that support the main idea.

The wrong way to answer either kind of question is to fish about among the possibilities until a likely looking one gains favor in your mind. This approach can become very confusing. After a while all the possibilities look right or every one looks wrong!

The proper way to handle reading questions on examinations is to use the process of elimination. You check each possibility against a set of standards and either *cross it out for good reason* or retain it as your final choice. Assuming that you have interpreted the paragraph reasonably sensibly, if you can eliminate four out of five, the remaining one must be the right answer. Let's trace the steps you should follow.

A. THE PARAGRAPH

Read it carefully, but not especially slowly. If necessary go over it a second time, particularly if you cannot arrive at a satisfactory *key word* (see below).

B. TITLE QUESTIONS

After you have read the selection, you turn to the possible titles offered. Your objective is to eliminate the unacceptable ones. You do this by applying one or more of the following standards.

1. Key word

If you have understood the main idea, you should be able to answer this question: *What is the selection talking about?* Very often you will be aided in arriving at your answer by the number of times a particular word is repeated in the paragraph, either directly or by use of a synonym. You should be able to express the answer to the question in a word, if possible; two, at most. *The title you choose must contain these words (or synonyms for them)!* Otherwise you have made an improper choice. Therefore, you cross out all possibilities that do not contain the key words. Do it this way ruthlessly. Do not be misled by an interesting-sounding title that on closer inspection has no specific connection with the main idea expressed by the paragraph.

2. Only part

Your key-word method may eliminate some choices but still leave two or three possibilities. You now examine the remaining ones in turn. If one of them refers to something mentioned briefly in the paragraph but not continued, cross it out. The title must cover the contents of the selection as a whole, and you cannot accept any possibility that refers to only part of it.

3. Not mentioned

A suggested title may sound as if it might do because it is logical and related to the subject matter. But if the author did not talk about it, cross it out.

4. Read into

You must bear in mind that the purpose of the reading question is to determine whether you can interpret *what the writer said,* not what you believe he should have said or what he might have said had he known as much as you do about the subject. Don't allow yourself or the examiner to put words into the writer's mouth. Don't allow your opinions or private information to interfere with your comprehension. Cross out any possibility that "reads into" the paragraph ideas or conclusions that exist only in the mind of the reader or the questioner. Such titles are often given as bait to the unwary.

5. Contradictory

If as much as a single word of a possible title suggests a conclusion that is the opposite of what was intended by the author, cross it out. Anything partially contradictory is as unacceptable as if entirely so.

Now we will apply these five elimination techniques to a typical paragraph.

Test Paragraph Interpretation—Example 1

THE PARAGRAPH

Shipping out food to the United States troops in all parts of the globe and supplying many foods for Great Britain has brought about dehydration. Why carry tons of water? A fresh egg is three-quarters water, many meats contain more than two-thirds water, fresh vegetables and fruits about 90 per cent. Drying foods dates back many years, but this new process makes them a lot drier and the foods keep most of their original food value and flavor. Because of dehydration these foods do not need refrigeration, nor is it necessary to package them in tin and so they require much less space in packing. Putting dehydrated foods in water is like bringing them back to life. Many foods are edible in their dehydrated state, and thus can easily be included in emergency kits for troops.

TITLE QUESTION

The title below that best expresses the ideas of this paragraph is

1. Advantages of dehydrated foods
2. Water content of food

3. Dehydrated diets
4. Saving space in supply ships
5. How foods are dehydrated

Elimination Process

Your answer to the question, *What is this paragraph talking about?* should be *dehydrated foods*. These are your key words, and you proceed to cross out every possibility that does not contain them. Therefore, you eliminate

2—because it contains only one of the key words (*food*, but not *dehydrated*)

3—for the same reason (*dehydrated*, but not *food*)

4—because it contains neither key word

This still leaves the choice between 1 and 5.

You examine 1 in terms of the additional standards:

Is it only part of the main idea?

No. The entire paragraph talks about this point.

Is it mentioned?

Definitely!

Is it "read into"?

No. It is the author's conclusion.

Is it contradictory?

No.

Therefore, 1 remains a possibility.

Now you turn to 5.

Is it only part of the main idea?

If you examine the paragraph closely, you discover that nowhere is 5 actually discussed.

Therefore, you need not bother with any further questions. You can cross out 5 at once. This leaves you with 1 as your final choice, the correct suggested title.

You can see the advantage of the process of elimination. You are forced to think with the author, arrive at *his* conclusion, and cross out possibilities because you have definite reasons for doing so. There is no wild guessing possible.

It may be that the method at first glance seems to be time consuming. Remember that you are not yet familiar with the guide questions. Continued practice will enable you to use them more rapidly and to arrive at your reason for elimination without the need for applying all of them each time you examine the possibilities. With added experience, the right questions to ask will occur to you automatically.

C. DETAIL QUESTIONS

Here, too, you use the guide questions to leave you with the correct answer.

1. Key sentences

Detail questions require that you examine only part of the paragraph to prove that you can find the details that support the main idea. Therefore, you shift your concentration to individual sentences. Your first step is to locate the sentence in which the detail asked by the question is mentioned. Then you check the possibilities with your guides against what the sentence covers.

2. Not mentioned

Again, if a possibility is not mentioned in any sentence, out it goes.

3. Read into

If a possibility suggests something that was not in the author's mind, it is eliminated, too.

4. Contradictory

Any thought opposite to the one expressed in a key sentence also cannot be accepted.

Let's try the standards with the detail question asked on the paragraph just quoted above.

Dehydration is a method of
1. preparing food for troops
2. drying food to preserve it
3. packaging foodstuffs
4. keeping food dry
5. making food palatable

Keeping the guide questions in mind, you examine each possibility in turn and try to eliminate every one but the right one. The latter will be the one you cannot cross out for any reason.

Your key sentence is the one beginning "Drying foods dates back . . ."

1—You cross it out because dehydration is not a method of preparing food for troops only. If you accept this you are *reading into* the paragraph.

2—You cannot cross this out at the moment. It *is mentioned*, it is *not read into*, and it is *not contradictory*.

3—You cross this one out because you would be *reading into* the paragraph. Dehydration is a food (not a packaging) process.

4—You eliminate this one again for the *reading into* reason. Keeping food dry (for example, in a sealed container) is quite different from drying foods to preserve them. Food that is not dehydrated can be kept dry.

5—This one is crossed out because it is *not mentioned* as the reason for dehydration. Certainly no flavor is added by the process, and the paragraph says that some is lost.

Thus your final choice is 2, the one you could not cross out for good reason.

We will try more paragraphs together so that you can become expert in using the method of elimination.

Test Paragraph Interpretation—Example 2

THE PARAGRAPH

Many observers have commented on what seems to be the fact that fear plays a much smaller part than we should think it must in the life of an animal that lives dangerously. Terror he can know, and perhaps he knows it frequently. But it seems to last only a little longer than the immediate danger it helps him to avoid, instead of lingering, as in the human being, until it becomes a burden and a threat. The frightened bird resumes his song as soon as danger has passed, and the frightened rabbit his games. It is almost as if they knew that "cowards die many times before their deaths; the valiant never taste of death but once."

TITLE QUESTION

The title below that best expresses the ideas of this paragraph is
1. A comparison of fear and terror
2. A comparison of man and the lower animals
3. Animal traits
4. Fear in animals
5. The nature of courage

Elimination Process

Key words: *animal fear*
Cross out
    1—(*fear,* but not *animal*)
    2—(*animal,* but not *fear*)
    3—(same as above)
    5—(contains neither key
       word)

Thus your title answer is 4.

Note how the key-word technique enabled you to reach the proper answer for this one without using the other guide questions at all.

DETAIL QUESTION

The writer believes that
1. terror is a permanent form of fear
2. fear is almost unknown in animals
3. fear has a permanent effect on animals
4. animals live less dangerously than men
5. animals remember fear only a short time

Elimination Process

Key sentence: When a question, such as this one, doesn't center its attention on a particular sentence you simply check out each possibility against its own key sentence.

1—Cross out. Sentence 3 makes this *contradictory*.
2—Cross out. Sentence 2 makes this *contradictory*.
3—Cross out. Sentence 3 makes this *contradictory*.
4—Cross out. The comparison mentioned here is *not mentioned* in any sentence.

Without even looking at 5, you can assume it must be the correct answer, since all the other possibilities have been eliminated. If you do wish to check it, you can see that sentence 3 supports 5.

Test Paragraph Interpretation—Example 3

THE PARAGRAPH

Honey as a core for a golf ball would have seemed a sinful waste to our ancestors; for less than two hundred years ago, honey and barley were the chief sources of sugar. Cane sugar, a rare and expensive luxury from the

New World, was sold by apothecaries in the time of Louis XIV. Because only kings and courtiers could afford it, plain people said it caused fever, chest disorders, and apoplexy—and stuck to barley sugar and honey. Those beliefs prevailed even after Napoleon Bonaparte fostered the research whereby chemists extracted sugar from beets and made it plentiful. Then there arose in France the adage "Sugar hurts only the purse."

TITLE QUESTION

The title below that best expresses the ideas of this paragraph is

1. The food of kings
2. Research under Napoleon
3. Strange facts about sugar
4. New uses for honey
5. Sugar substitutes

Elimination Process

Key word: *sugar*

Cross out 1, 2, and 4.

(Key word not present)

3—Do not cross out. It is more than part of the idea, it is mentioned, it is not "read into," and it is not contradictory.

5—Cross out. Although this is mentioned, it is *only part of the main idea* and thus not acceptable as a title.

Your answer, of course, is 3.

DETAIL QUESTIONS

Sugar was extracted from beets by

1. apothecaries
2. chemists
3. Louis XIV

4. courtiers
5. Napoleon Bonaparte

Elimination Process

Key sentence: *The fourth,* beginning "Those beliefs prevailed . . ."

1—Cross out. This is contradictory. Apothecaries *sold* sugar, did not extract it.
2—Hold as a possibility. Key sentence supports it.
3—Cross out. Contradictory.
4—Cross out. Contradictory.
5—Cross out. The sentence says Bonaparte *fostered* the research, but you would be *reading into* the thought if you assumed that he was also a chemist.

Your answer is 2.

The idea that sugar caused illness originated because sugar
1. did not taste so good as honey
2. was too expensive to buy
3. was sold by apothecaries
4. came from the New World
5. was used by the poor

Elimination Process

Key sentence: *The third,* beginning "Because only kings . . ."

1—Cross out. Not mentioned.
2—Hold as a possibility. Key sentence supports it.
3—Cross out. You would be *reading into* the thought if you accepted this bit of nonsense.
4—Cross out. The same reason as 3.
5—Cross out. Obviously contradictory.

Test Paragraph Interpretation——Example 4

THE PARAGRAPH

Every panic, or depression, has been preceded by feverish business activity, rising prices, rising profits, and a rapid extension of credit. Each depression has been accompanied by a lack of business activity, falling prices, and a very rapid increase in unemployment. In the past each has brought financial ruin to many banks and business concerns and to countless families. As long as these depressions come, we cannot have an economy of plenty for any great length of time. Progressive leaders are trying to increase the buying power of the masses of our people and to induce them to save so that they may furnish an adequate market for the products of farm and factory.

TITLE QUESTION

The title below that best expresses the ideas of this passage is
1. The causes of depressions
2. A possible cure for depressions
3. Price fluctuations
4. An analysis of buying power
5. Business activity preceding depressions

Elimination Process

Key word: *depressions*
  Cross out 3 and 4.
          (Key word not present)
  1—Cross out. Not really discussed. At best, *only part.*
  2—Hold as a possibility. The entire paragraph points toward this.
  5—Cross out. *Only part* of the main idea.
The answer is 2.

DETAIL QUESTIONS

Progressive economists feel that the best preventive of depressions rests with
1. farmers
2. factory workers
3. consumers
4. big business
5. government

Elimination Process

Key sentence: Check each possibility against its own sentence.
1—Cross out. Farmers *not mentioned;* products are.
2—Cross out. Workers *not mentioned;* products are.
3—Hold as a possibility. Last sentence supports this.
4—Cross out. This one is *not mentioned* at all.
5—Cross out. Same as 4.
The answer is 3.

Prior to depressions business has been characterized by
1. increasing profits
2. falling profits
3. the failure of banks
4. the cutting down of credit
5. balanced business activities

Elimination Process

Key sentence: *The first.*
1—Hold as a possibility. Supported by key sentence.
2—Cross out. *Contradictory.*
3—Cross out. *Not mentioned* in this connection.
4—Cross out. *Contradictory.*
5—Cross out. *Contradictory.*
The answer is 1.

Test Paragraph Interpretation—Example 5

Such homely virtues as thrift, hard work, and simplicity appear old-fashioned in these days. So probably we do well to remember the career of Benjamin Franklin, a true American. Though he had slight formal education, he became one of the best-educated men of his day, for he discovered the simple principle that one learns only what he teaches himself. Teachers can direct and organize the search for skills and information; a few can inspire. There is no substitute for the drudgery of learning. Franklin learned a trade and began reading inspirational books. He sought self-reliance and expressed thoughts that have interested more than one generation of readers. His essays and his autobiography reveal that his knowledge was useful.

TITLE QUESTION

The title below that best expresses the ideas of the passage is

1. The life of Benjamin Franklin
2. Teachers as educators
3. Formal education
4. The difficulties and satisfactions of self-education
5. The search for skill

Elimination Process

Key word: *education*

> (Note that Benjamin Franklin, although mentioned several times, is used only to serve as an example for illustrating the main idea.)

Cross out 1 and 5.
        (Key word not present)
2—Cross out. *Only part* of the main idea.
3—Cross out. Same reason as 2.
The answer can be only 4.

DETAIL QUESTION

This selection suggests that
1. old-fashioned virtues should be discarded
2. most people have the homely virtues
3. everyone can get an education
4. learning need not be drudgery
5. Franklin learned his trade by studying inspirational books.

Elimination Process

Key sentence: Each possibility must be checked against its own sentence.

1—Cross out. Sentence 5 denies this. Contradictory.
2—Cross out. Sentence 1 denies this. Contradictory.
3—Hold as a possibility. Sentence 3 supports this.
4—Cross out. Sentence 5 denies this. Contradictory.
5—Cross out. You would be *reading into* the passage if you came to this unstated conclusion.
The answer is 3.

Now you can try your skill in using the elimination process on the following sets of paragraphs taken from New York State Regents Examinations. In each set the total credits will add up to 20, the title questions being worth 2 points, and the detail questions, 1. A final score of 13 to 15 is average, 16 to 18 is good, and 19 to 20 is excellent.

a. I have heard it suggested that the "upper class" English accent has been of value in maintaining the British Empire and Commonwealth. The argument runs that all manner of folk in distant places, understanding the English language, will catch in this accent the notes of tradition, pride and authority and so will be suitably impressed. This might have been the case some five or six decades ago but it is certainly not true now. The accent is more likely to be a liability than an asset.

It is significant that the Royal Family in their speeches and broadcasts use a considerably modified form of the accent. The public English of George V was magnificently free from all affectations. His children and grandchildren have done their best to follow his example.

The title below that best expresses the ideas of this passage is:
1 The "King's English"
2 The affected language of royalty
3 The decline of the British Empire
4 Changed effects of "British accent"
5 Prevention of the spread of Cockney........( )

According to the author, the "upper class" English accent (1) has been imitated all over the world (2) may have helped to perpetuate the British Empire before 1900 (3) has been strongly opposed by British royalty (4) has brought about the destruction of the British Commonwealth (5) may have caused arguments among the folk in distant corners of the Empire ....( )

b. We were about a quarter mile away when quiet swept over the colony. A thousand or more heads periscoped. Two thousand eyes glared. Save for our wading, the world's business had stopped. A

The title below that best expresses the ideas of this passage is:
1 Our shore birds
2 A quiet colony
3 Judgment day

thousand avian personalities were concentrated on us, and the psychological force of this was terrific. Contingents of homecoming feeders, suddenly aware of four strange specks moving across the lake, would bank violently and speed away. Then the chain reaction began. Every throat in that rookery let go with a concatenation of wild, raspy, terrorized trumpet bursts. With all wings now fully spread and churning, and quadrupling the color mass, the birds began to move as one, and the sky was filled with the sound of judgment day.

4 Waiting
5 An unwelcome intrusion upon a bird colony
.....................( )

The passage indicates that the writer (1)was a psychologist (2)observed the fear of the flying birds (3)was terrified at the sounds (4) crossed the lake by boat (5)went alone to the rookery ....( )

According to the passage, when they first noticed the visitors, the birds of the colony (1)flew away (2)became very quiet (3)churned their wings (4)set up a series of cries (5)glared at the homecoming birds
.....................( )

c. If one is tempted to reflect on the type of language which is used in polite society, and, more particularly, if one is inclined to interpret it literally, one must conclude that social intercourse involves a collection of inanities and a tissue of lies. We say "Good morning" to the boss although the weather is foul and our temper is no better. We say "Pleased to meet you" when we really mean, "I

The title below that best expresses the ideas of this passage is:
1 The dishonesty of our daily language
2 The ceremonial use of language
3 Reflections on polite society
4 Primitive customs compared with modern customs

hope I'll never see you again in my life." We chatter aimlessly at a tea about matters that are not fit to exercise the mind of a child of two.

To say "Pleased to meet you" or "Good morning" or to chatter at tea are examples of the ceremonial function of language. Language used in this way is not informational. It simply celebrates whatever feelings are responsible for bringing men together in social groups. It is said that the custom of shaking hands originated when primitive men held out empty hands to indicate that they had no concealed weapons and were thus amicably disposed. In the same way, when we say "How do you do," or "Good morning," we perform a sort of ceremony to indicate community of feeling with the person so addressed.

d. Today in America vast concourses of youth are flocking to our colleges, eager for something, just what they do not know. It makes much difference what they get. They will be prone to demand something they can immediately use; the tendency is strong to give it to them: science, economics, business administration, law in its narrower sense. I submit that the shepherds should not first feed the flocks with these. I argue for the outlines of what used to go as a

5 The value of language in winning social success ....( )

The chief purpose of the author seems to be to (1) ridicule society (2) amuse the reader (3) express a grudge against society (4) explain the basis of social conversation (5) explain the origin of language as used in daily life ....( )

The author refers to the original custom of shaking hands as (1) an indication of friendliness (2) a gesture of surrender (3) a well-concealed threat (4) a social lie (5) a gesture without special meaning ....( )

The title below that best expresses the ideas of this passage is:
1 Why pupils go to college
2 Foreign languages for culture
3 The need for vocational training
4 The shepherd and his student flock
5 The importance of a liberal education( )

liberal education—not necessarily in the sense that young folks should waste precious years in efforts, unsuccessful for some reason I cannot understand, to master ancient tongues; but I speak for an introduction into the thoughts and deeds of men who have lived before them, in other countries than their own, with other strifes and other needs. This I maintain, not in the interest of that general cultural background, which is so often a cloak for the superior person, the prig, the snob and the pedant. But I submit to you that in some such way alone can we meet and master the highpower salesman of political patent medicines.

One purpose of a college education should be to help students to (1) achieve political wisdom (2) become good salesmen (3) develop their talents (4) find their individual interests (5) become future leaders ....( )

Many students entering college desire to study (1) other countries (2) history and law (3) cultural subjects (4) "practical" subjects (5) too many subjects ....( )

The writer stresses the study of (1) other cultures (2) foreign languages (3) politics and medicine (4) business administration (5) general culture ....( )

e. If Shakespeare needs any excuse for the exuberance of his language (the high key in which he pitched most of his dramatic dialogue), it should be remembered that he was doing on the plastic stage of his own day what on the pictorial stage of our day is not so much required. Shakespeare's dramatic figures stood out on a platform-stage, without background, with the audience on three sides of it. And the whole of

The title below that best expresses the ideas of this paragraph is:

1 The scenery of the Elizabethan stage

2 The importance of actors in the Shakespearean drama

3 The influence of the Elizabethan stage on Shakespeare's style

4 The importance of words

his atmosphere and environment had to come from the gestures and language of the actors. When they spoke, they provided their own scenery, which we now provide for them. They had to do a good deal more (when they spoke) than actors have to do today in order to give the setting. They carried the scenery on their backs, as it were, and spoke it in words.

5 Suitable gestures for the Elizabethan stage ....( )

In comparison with actors of Shakespeare's time, actors of today (1) carry the settings in their words (2) pitch their voices in a lower key (3) depend more on elaborate settings (4) have to do more to make the setting clear (5) use many gestures ....( )

The nature of the stage for which Shakespeare wrote made it necessary for him to (1) employ only highly dramatic situations (2) depend on scenery owned by the actors themselves (3) have the actors shift the scenery (4) create atmosphere through the dialogue (5) restrict backgrounds to familiar types of scenes ....( )

ANSWERS TO SET A: a. 4, 2; b. 5, 2, 2; c. 2, 4, 1; d. 5, 1, 4, 1; e. 3, 3, 4.

SET B

a. Your mind, like your body, is a thing whereof the powers are developed by effort. That is a principal use, as I see it, of hard

The title below that best expresses the ideas of this passage is:

1 "Knowledge is power"

work in studies. Unless you train your body you can't be an athlete, and unless you train your mind you can't be much of a scholar. The four miles an oarsman covers at top speed is in itself nothing to the good, but the physical capacity to hold out over the course is thought to be of some worth. So a good part of what you learn by hard study may not be permanently retained, and may not seem to be of much final value, but your mind is a better and more powerful instrument because you have learned it. "Knowledge is power," but still more the faculty of acquiring and using knowledge is power. If you have a trained and powerful mind, you are bound to have stored it with something, but its value is more in what it can do, what it can grasp and use, than in what it contains; and if it were possible, as it is not, to come out of college with a trained and disciplined mind and nothing useful in it, you would still be ahead, and still, in a manner, educated.

2 How to retain and use facts
3 Why acquire knowledge
4 Physical and mental effort
5 The trained mind..( )

The author emphasizes that many of the facts you acquire by hard study (1) deal with rules of health (2) will be forgotten (3) are of questionable value (4) will be very useful to you in later life (5) will help you to understand the meaning of life..........( )

The man leaving college with a disciplined mind (1) is certain to succeed (2) is likely to be a poor athlete (3) has finished his education (4) is educated (5) can grasp any problem ....( )

b. The total impression made by any work of fiction can not be rightly understood without a sympathetic perception of the artistic aims of the writer. Consciously or unconsciously, he has accepted certain facts, and rejected or suppressed other facts, in order to

The title below that best expresses the ideas of this paragraph is:
1 Unity in disunity
2 The tolerance and impartiality of Nature
3 The novelist's failure
4 Understanding fiction

341

give unity to the particular aspect of human life which he is depicting. No novelist possesses the impartiality, the indifference, the infinite tolerance of Nature. Nature displays to us, with complete unconcern, the beautiful and the ugly, the precious and the trivial, the pure and the impure. But a writer must select the aspects of Nature and human nature that are demanded by the work in hand. He is forced to select, to combine, to create.

5 Nature, the true novelist
.....................( )

A novelist chooses for his story material which will (1)prove his impartiality (2)further his general purpose (3)completely copy Nature (4)create a beautiful effect (5) display his unconcern( )

A reader must (1)detect trivialities (2)understand all aspects of Nature (3)discover the aim of the novelist (4) maintain a tolerant attitude (5)reject certain facts ....( )

c. Solitude is a great chastener when once you accept it. It quietly eliminates all sorts of traits that were a part of you—among others, the desire to pose, to keep your best foot forever in evidence, to impress people as being something you would like to have them think you are even when you aren't. Some men I know are able to pose even in solitude; had they valets they no doubt would be heroes to them. But I find it the hardest kind of work myself, and as I am lazy I have stopped trying. To act without an audience is so tiresome and profitless that you gradually give it up and at

The title below that best expresses the ideas of this paragraph is:
1 Carelessness in clothes
2 Acting without an audience
3 Discoveries through solitude
4 Showing off to best advantage
5 Being a hero to yourself
.....................( )

A desire to appear at your best is a trait that (1) goes with laziness (2) may disappear when you are alone (3)depends last forget how to act at all. For you become more interested in making the acquaintance of yourself as you really are, which is a meeting that, in the haunts of men, rarely takes place. It is gratifying, for example, to discover that you prefer to be clean rather than dirty even when there is no one but God to care which you are; just as it is amusing to note, however, that for scrupulous cleanliness you are not inclined to make superhuman sacrifices, although you used to believe you were. Clothes, you learn, with something of a shock, have for you no interest whatsoever. . . . You learn to regard dress merely as covering, a precaution. For its color and its cut you care nothing.

primarily on clothes (4) is inhuman (5) is evil ....( )

In solitude, clothes (1) constitute one item that pleases the valet (2) make one careless (3) are part of acting (4) are valued for their utility only (5) are tiresome ....( )

The desire to appear well-dressed usually depends upon (1) an audience (2) industriousness (3) personal pride (4) the need for cleanliness (5) a fondness for acting ....( )

The activities of everyday life seldom give us the chance to (1) learn our own peculiarities (2) keep our best foot forward (3) impress people (4) dress as we would like (5) be immaculately clean ....( )

d. It is no secret that I am not one of those naturalists who suffer from cities, or affect to do so, nor do I find a city unnatural or uninteresting, or a rubbish heap of follies. It has always seemed

The title below that best expresses the ideas of this paragraph is:
1 The spirit of the city
2 Advantages of a city home

to me that there is something more than mechanically admirable about a train that arrives on time, a fire department that comes when you call it, a light that leaps into the room at a touch, and a clinic that will fight for the health of a penniless man and mass for him the agencies of mercy, the X ray, the precious radium, the anesthetics and the surgical skill. For, beyond any pay these services receive, stands out the pride in perfect performance. And above all I admire the noble impersonality of civilization that does not inquire where the recipient stands on religion or politics or race. I call this beauty, and I call it spirit—not some mystical soulfulness that nobody can define, but the spirit of man, that has been a million years a-growing.

3 Disagreement among naturalists
4 Admirable characteristics of cities
5 Tolerance in the city
.... ( )

The services rendered by city agencies are given (1) only for pay (2) on time (3) only to people having a certain political allegiance (4) to everybody (5) to the spirit of man .... ( )

The author makes a defense of (1) cities (2) prompt trains (3) rural life (4) nature (5) free clinics .... ( )

The aspect of city life most commendable to this author is its (1) punctuality (2) free benefits (3) impartial service (4) mechanical improvement (5) health clinics .... ( )

The author implies that efficient operation of public utilities is (1) expensive (2) of no special interest (3) admired by most naturalists (4) mechanically commendable (5) spiritual in quality .... ( )

344

SET C

The paragraphs that follow were taken from various examinations offered by the United States Civil Service Commission. Continue to use the elimination process to guide you in making the proper choices from among the possibilities.

1. "The application of the steam engine to the sawmill changed the whole lumber industry. Formerly the mills remained near the streams; now they follow the timber. Formerly the logs were floated downstream to their destination; now they are carried by the railroads."

What besides the method of transportation does the quotation indicate has changed in the lumber industry?
a. speed of cutting lumber
b. location of market
c. type of timber sold
d. route of railroads
e. source of power .... ( )

2. "More patents have been issued for inventions relating to transportation than for those in any other line of human activity. These inventions have resulted in a great financial saving to the people and have made possible a civilization that could not have existed without them."

Select the alternative that is best supported by the quotation. Transportation
a. would be impossible without inventions
b. is an important factor in our civilization
c. is still to be much improved
d. is more important than any other activity
e. is carried on through the Patent Office .... ( )

345

3. "There exists a false but popular idea that a clue is some mysterious fact which most people overlook, but which some very keen investigator easily discovers and recognizes as having, in itself, a remarkable meaning. The clue is most often an ordinary fact which an observant person picks up—something which gains its significance when, after a long series of careful investigations, it is connected with a network of other clues."

According to the quotation, to be of value, clues must be
a. discovered by skilled investigators
b. found under mysterious circumstances
c. discovered soon after the crime
d. observed many times
e. connected with other facts ....( )

4. "Just as the procedure of a collection department must be clear-cut and definite, the steps being taken with the sureness of a skilled chess player, so the various paragraphs of a collection letter must show clear organization, giving evidence of a mind that, from the beginning, has had a specific end in view."

The quotation best supports the view that a collection letter should always
a. show a spirit of sportsmanship
b. be divided into several paragraphs
c. express confidence in the debtor
d. be brief, but courteous
e. be carefully planned ....( )

5. "The likelihood of America's exhausting her natural resources seems to be growing less. All kinds of waste are being reworked and new uses are constantly being found for almost everything. We are getting more use out of our goods and are making many new byproducts out of what was formerly thrown away."

The quotation best supports the statement that we seem to be in less danger of exhausting our resources because

a. economy is found to lie in the use of substitutes
b. more service is obtained from a given amount of material
c. more raw materials are being produced
d. supply and demand are being controlled
e. we are allowing time for nature to restore them ....( )

6. "Probably few people realize, as they drive on a concrete road, that steel is used to keep the surface flat and even, in spite of the weight of busses and trucks. Steel bars, deeply imbedded in the concrete, provide sinews to take the stresses so that they cannot crack the slab or make it wavy."

The quotation best supports the statement that a concrete road

a. is expensive to build
b. usually cracks under heavy weights
c. looks like any other road
d. is used exclusively for heavy traffic
e. is reinforced with other material ....( )

7. "The countries in the Western Hemisphere were settled by people who were ready each day for new adventure. The peoples of North and South America have retained, in addition to expectant and forward-looking attitudes, the ability and the willingness that they have often shown in the past to adapt themselves to new conditions."

The quotation best supports the statements that the peoples in the Western Hemisphere

a. no longer have fresh adventures daily
b. are capable of making changes as new situations arise
c. are no more forward-looking than the peoples of other regions

347

d. tend to resist regulations

e. differ considerably among themselves .... ( )

8. "The coloration of textile fabrics composed of cotton and wool generally requires two processes, as the process used in dyeing wool is seldom capable of fixing the color upon cotton. The usual method is to immerse the fabric in the requisite baths to dye the wool and then to treat the partially dyed material in the manner found suitable for cotton."

The quotation best supports the statement that the dyeing of textile fabrics composed of cotton and wool

a. is less complicated than the dyeing of wool alone

b. is more successful when the material contains more cotton than wool

c. is not satisfactory when solid colors are desired

d. is restricted to two colors for any one fabric

e. is usually based upon the methods required for dyeing the different materials .... ( )

9. "Every language has its peculiar word associations that have no basis in logic and cannot therefore be reasoned about. These idiomatic expressions are ordinarily acquired only by much reading and conversation although questions about such matters may sometimes be answered by the dictionary. Dictionaries large enough to include quotations from standard authors are especially serviceable in determining questions of idiom."

The quotation best supports the statement that idiomatic expressions

a. give rise to meaningless arguments

b. are widely used by recognized authors

c. are explained in most dictionaries

d. are more common in some languages than in others

e. are best learned by observation of the language as actually used .... ( )

10. "The telegraph networks of the country now constitute wonderfully operated institutions, affording for ordinary use of modern business an important means of communication. The transmission of messages by electricity has reached the goal for which the postal service has long been striving, namely, the elimination of distance as an effective barrier of communication."

The quotation best supports the statement that
    a. a new standard of communication has been attained
    b. in the telegraph service, messages seldom go astray
    c. it is the distance between the parties which creates the need for communication
    d. modern business relies more upon the telegraph than upon the mails
    e. the telegraph is a form of postal service ....(   )

ANSWERS: 1. e, 2. b, 3. e, 4. e, 5. b;   6. e, 7. b, 8. e, 9. e, 10. a.

Score 2 points for each correct answer. You did well if your total was 16 or better.

SET D

The College Entrance Examination Board is a membership organization consisting of 205 colleges, 34 secondary schools and other educational associations. It prepares the Scholastic Aptitude Test and other examinations that are taken every year by thousands of students who are planning to enter college. The Scholastic Aptitude Test measures various kinds of ability in two broad areas, Verbal and Mathematics. It is significant to note that about 50 per cent of the time devoted to the verbal part of the test concerns reading comprehension. You should find it interesting to test your skill with the typical examples of reading questions that follow. They are reprinted from *A Description of the College Board Scholastic Aptitude Test.* Incidentally, should you desire a complete explanation of the SAT, plus valuable suggestions for handling various types of questions, you can obtain this booklet by writing to the College Entrance Examination Board, P.O. Box 592, Princeton, New Jersey; or P.O. Box 27896, Los Feliz Station, Los Angeles 27, California.

Good evidence that full comprehension is the essence of superior reading ability is found in that portion of the College Board booklet which explains the types of questions asked:

"Reading comprehension is tested at several levels. Some of the questions depend simply on the understanding of the plain sense of what has been directly stated. To answer other questions, you must be able to interpret and analyze what you have read. Still other questions are designed to test your ability to recognize reasonable applications of the principles or opinions expressed by the author. And some of the questions require you to judge what you have read—to observe good and bad points in the presentation, to recognize how far the author has supported his statements by evidence, to recognize and evaluate the means used by the author to get his points across, and so on."

Directions: Each passage in this section is followed by questions based on its content. After reading a passage, choose the best answer among the five suggested answers to the question.

Talking with a young man about success and a career, Doctor Samuel Johnson advised the youth "to know something about everything and everything about something." The advice was good—in Doctor Johnson's day, when

350

London was like an isolated village and it took a week to get the news from Paris, Rome, or Berlin. Today, if a man were to take all knowledge for his province and try to know something about everything, the allotment of time would give one minute to each subject, and soon the youth would flit from topic to topic as a butterfly from flower to flower, and life would be as evanescent as the butterfly that lives for the present honey and moment. Today commercial, literary, or inventive success means concentration.

55. The author implies that a modern scientist
    A. makes discoveries by accident
    B. must bend his mind in a specific direction
    C. is able to contribute only if he has a background of general knowledge
    D. must be well-versed in the arts
    E. must be successful, whatever the cost ....( )
56. According to the passage, if we tried now to follow Dr. Johnson's advice, we would
    A. lead a more worth-while life
    B. have a slower-paced, more peaceful, and more productive life
    C. fail in our attempts
    D. hasten the progress of civilization
    E. perceive a deeper reality ....( )
57. Why does the author compare the youth to a butterfly?
    A. Butterflies symbolize a life of luxury and ease.
    B. The butterfly, like the youth, exhausts a present source of energy.
    C. The butterfly, like the youth, has no clear single objective.
    D. The butterfly, like the youth, is unaware of the future.

E. The butterfly lives but a short time and thus
retains the innocence of youth ....( )
58. In which one of the following comparisons made by the
author is the parallelism of the elements least satisfactory?

A. Topics and flowers
B. The youth and the butterfly
C. London and an isolated village
D. Knowledge and province
E. Life and the butterfly ....( )

Birds always seem intensely alive because of their
high body temperature and the agility that comes of
flight. But being intensely alive does not necessarily mean
being intensely intelligent, as we know from human examples. In respect to their minds just as much as their
bodies, birds have developed along other lines than
mammals. Mammals have gradually perfected intelligence
and the capacity for learning by experience until this
line has culminated in that conscious reason and in
that deliberate reliance upon the accumulated experience
of previous generations which are unique properties
of the human species. Among mammals the level of intelligence has gradually risen, and simultaneously the
power and fixity of instincts has diminished. Birds, on
the other hand, have kept instinct as the mainstay of
their behavior, although, like all other backboned animals,
they possess some intelligence and some power of profit-
ing by experience. These are subordinate, however, used
merely to polish up the outfit of instincts which is
provided by heredity without having to be paid for in
terms of experience. Indeed, the anatomist could support these observations by comparing the brains of birds
and mammals. For whereas in mammals we can trace a

steady increase in the size and elaboration of the cerebral hemispheres, the front part of the brain which we know to be the seat of intelligence and learning, this region is never highly developed in any birds, but remains relatively small without convolutions on its surface. Other parts of the brain which are known to be the regulating machinery for complicated but more automatic and more emotional actions are in birds relatively larger than in the four-footed creatures.

59. The intelligence of birds is inherently limited by their
    A. small cerebral hemispheres
    B. extreme agility
    C. well-developed instincts
    D. small range of experience
    E. high body temperature ....( )

60. It can be inferred from the passage that the degree of activity in a given animal is related to
    A. size of cerebral hemispheres
    B. number of cerebral convolutions
    C. accumulated experience
    D. body temperature
    E. lack of intelligence ....( )

61. According to the author, instinctive action in birds is
    A. unaffected by learning
    B. independent of conscious reason
    C. dependent upon intelligence
    D. a measure of their intelligence
    E. controlled by the cerebral hemispheres ....( )

62. The words *accumulated experience,* as used in the fourth sentence, could properly imply all of the following EXCEPT
    A. language
    B. science
    C. manual dexterity

D. social organization

E. legal codes .... (   )

63. An ambiguity exists in the last sentence because the author fails to consider the fact that

A. mammals are also emotional creatures

B. not all four-footed creatures are mammals

C. some birds do not need a regulating machinery

D. small birds have relatively smaller regulating centers

E. mammals also carry on automatic actions ....(   )

Most professional economists today would agree that the primary purpose of economics is analytical, to *discover what is*. Whatever other aims some of them may have, their chief concern is to establish the principles upon which the present economic system works. There is a school of thought which regards economics as capable of becoming as exact and as "universally valid" as the physical sciences, and which denies, by implication, its essentially social and historical nature. These views, however, are put forward only on the occasion of methodological discussion and do not seem to affect the scope of the bulk of the work of members of this school: they are still mainly interested in the working of present-day capitalism.

The general public is very rarely aware of this positive and analytical purpose which the professional regards as the paramount, or even as the only legitimate one. The public knows that it can justifiably demand of the economist a statement of how the system works (though its faith in the explanation which is forthcoming is seldom great); but it generally wants to know also what is the right thing to *do*. Economists cannot always shirk this question; and when they answer they reveal more far-reaching differences of opinion than any that arise in the positive analysis upon which they all claim to base their advice.

78. The passage implies that economists try to avoid answering the question
    A. What is the right thing to do?
    B. How can a positive analysis be made?
    C. What is the purpose of economics?
    D. What is actually true?
    E. How does the economic system work? ....( )

79. It can be inferred from the passage that the author believes economics to be
    A. an exact science
    B. social and historical in nature
    C. a highly methodological discipline
    D. primarily capitalistic in function
    E. basically altruistic ....( )

80. In which one of the following would the "school of thought" in the third sentence be most likely to find expression?
    A. Radio round-table discussions
    B. Government bulletins
    C. Political speeches
    D. Popular magazines
    E. Professional journals ....( )

81. The passage implies that the opinions of economists differ most with respect to the
    A. basic facts with which economics should deal
    B. basic purpose of economics
    C. means for achieving social goals
    D. methods by which facts are to be gathered
    E. positive analysis upon which economic advice is taken ....( )

The best excuse that can be made for avarice is that it generally prevails in old men or in men of cold tempers, where all the other affections are extinct; and the mind, being incapable of remaining without some passion or pursuit, at least finds out this monstrously absurd one, which suits the coldness and inactivity of its temper. At the same time, it seems very extraordinary that so frosty, spiritless a passion should be able to carry us further than all the warmth of youth and pleasure. But if we look more narrowly into the matter, we shall find that this very circumstance renders the explication of the case more easy.

When the temper is warm and full of vigor, it naturally shoots out more ways than one and produces inferior passions to counterbalance, in some degree, its predominant inclination. It is impossible for a person of that temper, however bent on any pursuit, to be deprived of all sense of shame or all regard to sentiments of mankind. His friends must have some influence over him; and other considerations are apt to have their weight. All this serves to restrain him within some bounds. But it is no wonder that the avaricious man, being, from the coldness of his temper, without regard to reputation, to friendship, or to pleasure, should be carried so far by his prevailing inclination and should display his passion in such surprising instances.

We find no vice so irreclaimable as avarice and for this reason I am more apt to approve of those who attack it with wit and humor than of those who treat it in a serious manner. I would have the rest of mankind at least diverted by our manner of exposing it; as indeed there is no kind of diversion of which they seem so willing to partake.

82. The author implies that most people are *not* avaricious
because avarice
    A. can easily be detected by observers
    B. is an absurd pursuit
    C. rarely leads to success
    D. can be prevented by even a small sense of shame
    E. can be cured by persistent and witty attacks
    .... ( )
83. In the last sentence of the second paragraph, *coldness*
is used to mean
    A. senility
    B. anger
    C. irascibility
    D. stupidity
    E. callousness ....( )
84. The author observes that men generally are willing to
look at avarice in order to
    A. admire its surprising success
    B. enjoy criticizing it
    C. imitate it
    D. profit by its errors
    E. guard against it ....( )
85. The author would disapprove of those who seriously
attack avarice since they
    A. waste their efforts
    B. unconsciously increase its importance
    C. do not really understand its origin
    D. do so only to entertain and not to reform
    E. use methods which are too mild ....( )

ANSWERS: 55. B, 56. C, 57. C, 58. E, 59. A;   60. D, 61. B,
           62. C, 63. B, 78. A;   79. B, 80. E, 81. C, 82. D,
           83. E;   84. B, 85. A.

58. The least satisfactory comparison is E. What the author really means is that human life would be like the *life* of a butterfly—aimless and evanescent—not that human life would be like the butterfly itself.

61. The answer is B, since the author says that conscious reason is unique to the human species—possessed by humans alone. A is incorrect because the author says that birds do learn (profit by experience) and that the learning polishes up the outfit of instincts.

63. The answer is B. The author begins by comparing mammals with birds. But when he varies his vocabulary with *four-footed creatures,* his statement becomes unclear; there are some four-footed creatures that are not mammals (lizard, turtle, etc.).

80. The answer is E because "methodological discussion" suggests that when one economist talks to another, through the medium of a professional journal, he is likely to advance theories that he would not necessarily proclaim to the general public. All the remaining possibilities refer to areas in which the public would be the principal audience.

81. The answer is C because the key phrase in the passage here is "wants to know also what is the right thing to *do.*" This is another way of saying that information is desired regarding the means of achieving social goals.

84. The answer is B because the author says that in so far as exposing avarice is concerned "there is no kind of diversion of which they seem so willing to partake."

85. The first sentence in the last paragraph is the key to answer A because the author states that "no vice [is] so irreclaimable as avarice." Obviously it would be wasted effort to attempt to influence seriously a characteristic that is almost impossible to change.

If you were able to answer 14 or more of the questions correctly, you can congratulate yourself on having done well on this set. It is important to point out that if you were able to handle the SAT passages satisfactorily you proved to yourself that you are capable not only of picking out main ideas and details in your reading but also of using judgment and analysis—both so necessary for full comprehension!

Appendix II

Vocabulary Review

The paragraph tests below will give you the opportunity to review the words presented in the two lists found in Chapter IX. The words are taken in order, in groups of 10. In each exercise try to match the words given below the paragraph with the definitions inserted next to the spaces.

SECTION 1

Paragraph 1

With an _____ (nimble, spry) leap, the officer seized one of the men engaged in the _____ (dispute) and shouted an _____ (warning) to the other to withhold his advance. Although it appeared impossible to introduce _____ (friendship) between the two, stopping the argument was necessary before the situation became _____ (worsened). All who _____ (detest) quarrels will _____ (agree) in the idea that to hold anger in _____ (suspension) and to _____ (reduce, diminish) the force of conflict can best be accomplished by one who acts with _____ (briskness) as a wall between belligerents.

aggravated   agile
alacrity   admonition
abate   amity
altercation   acquiesce
abeyance   abhor

Paragraph 2

Peering through the _____ (opening) in the cracked wall, Bart observed with _____ (anxiety) that his _____ (opponent) had taken on the appearance of an _____ (ghost). The evil old man had covered his _____ (stern) face with a white hood, and the flowing robes he already wore completed the _____ (shocking) picture. Ordinarily such a display would have been greeted with laughter or _____ (boredom), but the _____ (intense, fierce) efforts of this villain to _____ (increase) the fears of Lydia would be successful unless some way were found to _____ (ease, lessen) her grief and make her face the realities of the situation.

appalling   assuage
aperture   apathy
augment   austere
apprehension   antagonist
apparition   ardent

Paragraph 3

_____ (greed) is often the basis for the actions and attitudes of a _____ (intolerant individual). So eager is this _____ (impulsive) wretch to prevent any challenge to his status that he welcomes the _____ (raging fires) of hate enkindled by his _____ (rough) disregard of human values. One need not be _____ (capable of seeing into the future) to predict what ultimately happens when such persons gain control. The world has witnessed repeatedly how unspeakable _____ (destruction) is brought about by men who _____ (agree) in the idea that mutual understanding must be _____ (hidden) away with the other outmoded beliefs of democratic living. We are fortunate that their efforts have invariably led them not only to _____ (disappointment) but to total defeat.

cached	conflagrations
chagrin	avarice
brusque	clairvoyant
bigot	capricious
carnage	concur

Paragraph 4

It was an amazing _____ (gadget). With his usual _____ (proper behavior) young Peters had requested an opinion from his _____ (fat) employer. The latter could hardly control the look of _____ (greed) that crept into his face as he envisioned _____ (plentiful) profits resulting from the sale of an automatic tire patcher. Mr. Worton was not one to _____ (think, guess) about his being held _____ (blameworthy) of a misdeed if he took advantage of his assistant. _____ (lessened in value) assets meant a _____ (dead) company unless Worton could so successfully _____ (diminish) the marketability of the mechanism that Peters would sell gladly and cheaply.

culpable	conjecture
depreciated	cupidity
contrivance	deprecate
copious	defunct
decorum	corpulent

Paragraph 5

The _____ (small in stature) student seemed _____ (deeply dejected) as he faced the faculty committee. He knew that the _____ (scorn) with which he had greeted the previous warnings would be a _____ (hindrance) to his receiving any mercy. Above all, he was about to _____ (waste away) all the hopes of his parents by his _____ (contemptible) conduct, and he could think of no reason why he should not be called _____ (neglectful) of his duty. By some _____ (irregular) means, he hoped to make of his case such a _____ (puzzle) that the final judgment would be difficult. Thus he began his defense by saying, in a _____ (modest) way, that it was all a complete mystery to him.

devious	diminutive
diffident	despicable
detriment	derision
disconsolate	dissipate
derelict	dilemma

Paragraph 6

To say that _____ (odd) Mr. Force would be sympathetic toward the _____ (very thin) young man before him seemed _____ (doubtful). Ordinarily, the _____ (boldness) of the strange applicant for a job would have _____ (drawn) a rebuke from the _____ (noted) banker. For some reason, however, the well-fed figure behind the desk decided that a refusal at this time would be like an _____ (tomb inscription) on the hopes of the now _____ (gentle) stranger who had burst into the office. Finally Mr. Force said, "I shall _____ (clear) you from the charge of forced entry and will refer you to our personnel manager."

364

The _____ (lifted spirits) caused by this announcement filled the room with warmth.

epitaph   exonerate
eccentric   elicited
docile   dubious
emaciated   effrontery
eminent   elation

Paragraph 7

It was considered _____ (desertion of faith) in that devastated land to talk of defeat. The _____ (deceit, cunning) of the enemy was feared almost as much as his _____ (stealthy) attacks. But the _____ (drawn thin) faces of the villagers showed the great _____ (courage) with which they had met the _____ (threatening) forces massed before them. _____ (economical) days were ahead for the inhabitants and _____ (silly) remarks about lean stomachs could not hide the _____ (excessive) demands that would be made upon their energies before the crisis was over. Fortunately, reasoning based on force is _____ (liable to error), and this was the weak link in the armor of the oppressors.

frugal   heresy
fallible   furtive
facetious   formidable
guile   haggard
fortitude   exorbitant

Paragraph 8

When two people become _____ (unable to be reconciled) enemies, each seems _____ (impenetrable) to reason. Any attempt to remove their _____ (unfriendly) attitudes by discussing forgiveness is bound to lead to an _____ (blind alley). Since both had probably been _____ (headstrong) in arriving at their state of _____ (senseless) animosity, the major _____ (obstacle) in the path of reconciliation was the removal of the idea that pride must be maintained in the face of any _____ (threatening) threat to its destruction. Sometimes such a situation becomes _____ (very funny), especially when a well-wisher seeks to escape with _____ (safety) from his efforts to create good will.

inane	hilarious
implacable	impasse
impunity	impediment
impervious	hostile
impetuous	impending

Paragraph 9

The _____ (clever) talents of Hollywood producers have made the adventures of _____ (unconquerable) Western heroes and _____ (brave) heroines the most popular of pictures. Nothing excites an audience so

much as seeing an _____ (needy) young man, with
_____ (unreadable) expression and quick fingers,
pursue the villains with _____ (unforgiving) zeal.
Even when the _____ (ceaseless) efforts of his enemies threaten to _____ (engulf) him with misfor-
tune, everyone knows that these _____ (periodic)
attacks will be defeated and the bad men made to look
_____ (out of place) as they grovel in the dust like
sandworms.

inexorable	indigent
incessant	ingenious
inundate	intrepid
indomitable	inscrutable
intermittent	incongruous

Paragraph 10

George was _____ (happy) when he learned that
his _____ (illness) was more the result of physical
_____ (sluggishness) than some organic disorder.
The doctor was rather _____ (brief) with his advice.

"Get out of the _____ (ghastly pale) atmosphere
of night clubs and into the sunshine," he said.

This was indeed a _____ (praiseworthy) suggestion. The patient had been so busy following his
_____ (profitable) profession of gossip columnist
that his only recreation had been watching the _____

(silly) antics of the ＿＿＿＿＿ (unchangeable) drinkers who frequent the various clubs. The ＿＿＿＿＿ (contradiction) of it all was that George had once been a prominent athlete.

lucrative	lethargy
irony	jubilant
laudable	inveterate
malady	laconic
lurid	ludicrous

Paragraph 11

Some people believed that the ＿＿＿＿＿ (wealth) of John Ford was partly the product of ＿＿＿＿＿ (nightly) prowling, a habit he had ＿＿＿＿＿ (trained) in his younger days. The more ＿＿＿＿＿ (simple), however, were quite ＿＿＿＿＿ (fawning, overly attentive) in his presence and made ＿＿＿＿＿ (a bow) to his every demand. He was ＿＿＿＿＿ (gloomy) by nature and could be ＿＿＿＿＿ (soothed) only by obedience and ＿＿＿＿＿ (very careful) attention to his ego. The amusing thing was that wealth had given him a false air of ＿＿＿＿＿ (universal knowledge).

mollified	omniscience
nurtured	obeisance
nocturnal	naïve
opulence	obsequious
morose	meticulous

Paragraph 12

Those men will be remembered by _____ (succeeding generations) who have labored long to conquer _____ (injurious) diseases that leave their marks in the _____ (pale) faces of their victims. Indeed we must praise their _____ (prematurely bright) efforts to use science to combat the _____ (lies) of fakers who create a _____ (wild noise) of publicity to cover _____ (noticeable) falsehoods in their claims. Sometimes the genuine research technician is accused of _____ (delaying) and finds himself in the _____ (dangerous) position of producing results quickly so that his critics will be forced into _____ (sorrow for sins) for their rash charges.

procrastinating   pallid
posterity   penitence
pernicious   precocious
precarious   perceptible
pandemonium   prevarications

Paragraph 13

As an escape from the _____ (ordinary) affairs of daily life, some people resort to _____ (recalling former times). During such moments, they fancy themselves performing _____ (amazing) feats, masterfully handling _____ (complaining) women with _____ (sticking out) tongues, providing _____ (return) for those who have been swindled, and being _____ (precise) in observing the laws of _____ (good behavior). This _____ (pause) from boredom may, however, create _____ (bitterness) in their hearts since they must soon face reality.

punctilious   reminiscence
rancor   prosaic
restitution   propriety
prodigious   querulous
protuberant   respite

Paragraph 14

With _____ (trumpetlike) tones, the watchman called for help. The warehouse had been reduced to a _____ (mess) by the _____ (stealthy) prowler who had broken in. When the officer arrived, he surveyed the scene with a _____ (superior) air, vowed _____ (revenge) upon the thief, and with great _____ (wisdom) suggested ideas that made us _____ (optimistic) about the prospects of catching the intruder. In these _____ (tight) circumstances, no one could afford to be _____ (shy, silent) about

his whereabouts the previous hour if he wished to avoid the
_____ (mark of disgrace) of suspicion.

sagacity	sanguine
stigma	reticent
stentorian	shambles
supercilious	surreptitious
retribution	stringent

Paragraph 15

The king was _____ (capable of being wounded).
He believed in the _____ (truthfulness) of his
_____ (poisonous) ministers and would not believe
the _____ (passionate) pleas of the queen that his
advisers were plotting to _____ (unseat) his power.
He claimed that circumstances would _____ (sustain)
his faith and marveled at his wife's _____ (stubbornness) in expressing her anxiety.

"Yours are the _____ (stale) fears of a woman
who lifts _____ (very loud) cries to support ground-
less suspicions. I shall not _____ (waver) in my
course of maintaining national unity," he said.

tenacity	vindicate
vacillate	vociferous
vulnerable	veracity
usurp	trite
venomous	vehement

ANSWERS TO SECTION 1 (given in the order of the appearance of the words in the paragraphs):

Paragraph	Word Order
1	agile, altercation, admonition, amity, aggravated, abhor, acquiesce, abeyance, abate, alacrity
2	aperture, apprehension, antagonist, apparition, austere, appalling, apathy, ardent, augment, assuage
3	avarice, bigot, capricious, conflagrations, brusque, clairvoyant, carnage, concur, cached, chagrin
4	contrivance, decorum, corpulent, cupidity, copious, conjecture, culpable, depreciated, defunct, deprecate
5	diminutive, disconsolate, derision, detriment, dissipate, despicable, derelict, devious, dilemma, diffident
6	eccentric, emaciated, dubious, effrontery, elicited, eminent, epitaph, docile, exonerate, elation
7	heresy, guile, furtive, haggard, fortitude, formidable, frugal, facetious, exorbitant, fallible
8	implacable, impervious, hostile, impasse, impetuous, inane, impediment, impending, hilarious, impunity
9	ingenious, indomitable, intrepid, indigent, inscrutable, inexorable, incessant, inundate, intermittent, incongruous
10	jubilant, malady, lethargy, laconic, lurid, laudable, lucrative, ludicrous, inveterate, irony
11	opulence, nocturnal, nurtured, naïve, obsequious, obeisance, morose, mollified, meticulous, omniscience

12	posterity, pernicious, pallid, precocious, prevarications, pandemonium, perceptible, procrastinating, precarious, penitence
13	prosaic, reminiscence, prodigious, querulous, protuberant, restitution, punctilious, propriety, respite, rancor
14	stentorian, shambles, surreptitious, supercilious, retribution, sagacity, sanguine, stringent, reticent, stigma
15	vulnerable, veracity, venomous, vehement, usurp, vindicate, tenacity, trite, vociferous, vacillate

SECTION 2

Paragraph 1

Czechoslovakia has achieved _____ (self-ruling) status after each great war. Yet the _____ (boldness) of her neighbors has brought to an abrupt end the _____ (favorable) start this nation has made toward democracy and has submerged her under the _____ (disdainful) rule of dictators who, rather than observe international _____ (courtesies), have cast _____ (slanders) upon her courage. Only the _____ (mental sharpness) of wise men in world affairs and the _____ (firm) refusal of the Czech people to submit will bring about an _____ (lightening) of this dreadful political _____ (wearing away) that has weakened a brave country.

arrogant   alleviation
autonomous   audacity
auspicious   amenities
attrition   aspersions
acumen   adamant

Paragraph 2

The _____ (main, chief) principles of success

of a _____ (faker) are the presentation of a

_____ (mild, kindly) look and the perfection of a

_____ (smooth) manner. In this way he is able

to withstand the _____ (slander) of such of his

victims as have been dragged down into a financial

_____ (disaster, flood), and are therefore eager

to bring a _____ (crippling disease) upon his plans.

These verbal _____ (blows) do not make him

_____ (become pale) since he is already busy en-

ticing others into a _____ (swamp) of deceit.

cataclysm   bog
benign   blight
cardinal   calumny
bland   charlatan
buffets   blanch

Paragraph 3

The _____ (deserved) reward for nations who

reach agreements at _____ (secret) meetings is the

treachery and deceit that are frequently _____ (accompanying elements) of _____ (agreeable) attitudes. Indeed, one must _____ (sympathize) with smaller nations who find the search for _____ (kindness, mercy) from big powers a _____ (small job) beyond their abilities. Undoubtedly _____ (secret plotting) of such a nature _____ (curbs) the spirit of international accord. The United Nations should _____ (force) all countries into observing Wilson's principle: "Open covenants, openly arrived at."

chore	collusion
clemency	coerce
condign	clandestine
commiserate	chastens
complaisant	concomitants

Paragraph 4

The _____ (sour realist) looks upon questions of _____ (worldwide) agreement as a problem that will continue to _____ (confuse) our best minds. Of course, his viewpoint is supported by the _____ (puzzling) phrases frequently found in _____ (agreements), and even a _____ (rapid, glancing) inspection of these meaningless words is enough to convince the most _____ (believing) that perhaps the snarling philosopher is right. However, some would call this a

_____ (cowardly) approach since it requires courage to hold up the prospect of peace as the _____ (center of attraction) of all hopeful people. It would be wrong to _____ (forgive) any effort to run away from a problem.

condone	cynic
cryptic	covenants
cynosure	confound
cosmic	cursory
credulous	craven

Paragraph 5

Clayton's ability to make _____ (belittling) remarks while exhibiting a _____ (polished) manner frequently fooled people into ignoring the _____ (harmful) effect his behavior might have. It took the efforts of a _____ (modest) young guest at a party to deflate his _____ (stretched out) ego. When he insisted upon treating her like a common _____ (heavy laborer), she calmly and with apparent _____ (respect) remarked,

"Your _____ (reverent) interest in yourself is exceeded only by the _____ (aimless) regard you display toward your closest friends. I could use _____ (delaying) verbal tactics with you, but I prefer to say simply that you are an insufferable boor."

deletrious devout
distended dilatory
derogatory debonair
demure drudge
desultory deference

Paragraph 6

The _____ (learned) old professor showed great _____ (uplifted spirits) when the Egyptian bones were finally _____ (dug up). Here, he thought, was material that would lead to the _____ (clearing up) of a thousand-year-old problem, and would serve for the _____ (instruction) of future scientists. The effort to get to the tomb had so _____ (weakened) most of the party, however, that several looked upon the whole affair with _____ (boredom) and would have welcomed an _____ (proclamation) to abandon their _____ (unsteady) journeys into the desert. On this point there would have been little _____ (quibbling) at the moment.

enervated ennui
equivocation erudite
edification erratic
edict exhilaration
exhumed elucidation

Paragraph 7

It was going to be difficult to _____ (disentangle) himself from the _____ (emergencies) of this situation. Brawley's efforts to _____ (steal) the gems had turned into a _____ (total failure) and now he would need all his intellectual _____ (good spirits) to avoid being made to _____ (pay for) his crime in the _____ (foul-smelling) confines of the county jail. A man of such _____ (difficult-to-please) habits could hardly compare iron bars to the _____ (strange, foreign) charm of a winter spent on the Riviera. Perhaps he would be able to dream up some _____ (excusing) circumstances for his presence in the room where he had been surprised.

fastidious	extenuating
extricate	expiate
exotic	filch
fiasco	exuberance
exigencies	fetid

Paragraph 8

To be a successful actor, one must be _____ (sociable) by nature, _____ (talkative) by impulse, and _____ (sinless) in manner and dress. Also, one needs the ability to run the _____ (range) of emotions and undertake the _____ (dangerous) task of being a different person every other night, even in the face of possible _____ (disgrace) at the hands of critics who consider it a _____ (wicked) crime if an artist uses _____ (bizarre) gestures in the effort to create realism. Perhaps the most necessary qualification is the luck of _____ (heedlessly) stumbling upon a producer who is seeking success through the _____ (happening by chance) circumstance of a likely play and a particular actor.

heinous	gregarious
fortuitous	gamut
inadvertently	garrulous
ignominy	grotesque
impeccable	hazardous

Paragraph 9

To _____ (recline lazily) about on the beach is more than relaxing. It enables one to watch the ever-changing picture of mankind. There is the _____ (easily angered) father chasing a youngster who has developed the _____ (harmless) habit, so he thinks, of tossing handfuls of sand at people, who regard this _____ (unfriendly) act with _____ (unspeakable) rage. Then, of course, there is the old gentleman who looks somewhat _____ (unsuitable) in his bathing suit of the 90's. We have the charmer who attempts to use his _____ (deadly) smile as a cloak over his _____ (inherent) worth and _____ (potential) villainy, and is successful only with those whom he can _____ (mislead by trickery) into accepting his oily words.

inimical	latent
irascible	lolls
ineffable	inveigle
incongruous	intrinsic
innocuous	insidious

Paragraph 10

The speedometer needle _____ (vibrated, swung) between 60 and 70 miles an hour. This _____ (showy) bravado was typical of the driver with _____ (ordinary) talents who suddenly became an important man behind the wheel. His _____ (unconcern) about excessive speed would not _____ (lessen) the blame should a blowout call for the powers of the _____ (mysterious) to avoid a serious accident. If you asked this foolhardy car owner why he took chances, he would probably offer _____ (unclear, cloudy) reasons, perhaps implying that his _____ (aggressive) attack upon the
380

road relieved him of _____ (everyday, ordinary) cares and helped him escape the _____ (tearful) expression of those who are bored.

occult	lugubrious
ostentatious	oscillated
militant	mundane
nonchalance	nebulous
mediocre	mitigate

Paragraph 11

It was rather a _____ (contradiction) that the old _____ (elder, chief), who had once been accused of _____ (unauthorized copying), should now offer his _____ (ridiculous) ideas as a _____ (cure-all) for the world's ills. How could one _____ (predict) a change in the _____ (stubbornness) with which nations cling to the concept of force as a bargaining point. It was a _____ (loose, casual) disregard for the truth and silly enough to send even the most _____ (sluggish) into _____ (seizures) of laughter.

promiscuous	paradox
paroxysms	preposterous
plagiarism	phlegmatic
patriarch	panacea
prognosticate	pertinacity

Paragraph 12

Judging from the _____ (harsh, loud) cries of the mob, the village _____ (scoundrel) could expect little mercy for his _____ (rebellious) attitude toward the importance of _____ (proper behavior) in public. Some shouted that he should be _____ (banished) to a distant island, others that his _____ (payment) be solitary confinement. Instead of attempting to _____ (mutually interchange) for the many kindnesses shown him, he had disgraced the town. No one suggested a _____ (pardon) since it would not have been _____ (appropriate) to the issue to claim that he had been ignorant of the laws. In fact, local merchants who had been forced to _____ (cut back expenses) in the face of poor business were inclined to blame him for their troubles.

retrench   reprobate
relevant   reprieve
raucous   recalcitrant
relegated   recompense
reciprocate   propriety

Paragraph 13

Much _____ (vulgar) comment greeted the _____ (winding) movements of the dancer. Instead of applause, there were _____ (grossly offensive) remarks, which indicated that the audience was well aware of Ramona's efforts to _____ (undermine) the minds of her countrymen at a time when _____ (treason) could have been a death blow to victory. Actually, this outburst, when viewed in _____ (backward look), was a _____ (concise) acknowledgment that her attempts to win good favor again would be no _____ (easy job). Many in the crowd hoped she would be forced into a more _____ (inactive) occupation, preferably one that would develop within her a _____ (silent) nature and prison pallor.

sinecure	ribald
taciturn	sedition
scurrilous	sinuous
retrospect	sedentary
subvert	succinct

Paragraph 14

Although his struggle against the _____ (unexpected changes) of life had been a _____ (brave) one, he realized now that his situation was _____ (equivalent) to failure. His once _____ (green) hopes had been destroyed, partly because of his own _____ (belligerent) attitude and rather _____ (changeable) temperament, and partly because he had never developed the ability to show _____ (oily) regard

for his _____ (ever-present) supervisors who, despite

their _____ (polished, suave) manner, betrayed a

_____ (greedy, hard to satisfy) appetite for ad-

vancement at the expense of those who didn't play the office

game properly.

unctuous

verdant

truculent

valiant

volatile

vicissitudes

urbane

ubiquitous

tantamount

voracious

Paragraph 15

In days of _____ (old), _____ (dried

out) sea captains commanded sailing vessels that responded

easily to every _____ (mild breeze). On those oc-

casions when a storm arose and the ship began to _____

(steer wildly) in the wind, it sometimes became necessary

to _____ (remove by force) the wheel from an over-

_____ (eager) pilot who might become upset and

give in to the _____ (uncontrolled) surge of the

waves. It was then that the _____ (shrewd) captain

would reach the _____ (topmost point) of his skill.

Casting a sort of _____ (harness) over the steering

mechanism, he would allow the craft to ride out the swells.

yaw	zenith
yore	wrest
yoke	zealous
wily	wizened
zephyr	wanton

ANSWERS TO SECTION 2 (given in the order of the appearance of the words in the paragraphs):

Paragraph	Word Order
1	autonomous, audacity, auspicious, arrogant, amenities, aspersions, acumen, adamant, alleviation, attrition
2	cardinal, charlatan, benign, bland, calumny, cataclysm, blight, buffets, blanch, bog
3	condign, clandestine, concomitants, complaisant, commiserate, clemency, chore, collusion, chastens, coerce
4	cynic, cosmic, confound, cryptic, covenants, cursory, credulous, craven, cynosure, condone
5	derogatory, debonair, deleterious, demure, distended, drudge, deference, devout, desultory, dilatory
6	erudite, exhilaration, exhumed, elucidation, edification, enervated, ennui, edict, erratic, equivocation
7	extricate, exigencies, filch, fiasco, exuberance, expiate, fetid, fastidious, exotic, extenuating
8	gregarious, garrulous, impeccable, gamut, hazardous, ignominy, heinous, grotesque, inadvertently, fortuitous
9	loll, irascible, innocuous, inimical, ineffable, incongruous, insidious, intrinsic, latent, inveigle

10	oscillated, ostentatious, mediocre, nonchalance, mitigate, occult, nebulous, militant, mundane, lugubrious
11	paradox, patriarch, plagiarism, preposterous, panacea, prognosticate, pertinacity, promiscuous, phlegmatic, paroxysms
12	raucous, reprobate, recalcitrant, propriety, relegated, recompense, reciprocate, reprieve, relevant, retrench
13	ribald, sinuous, scurrilous, subvert, sedition, retrospect, succinct, sinecure, sedentary, taciturn
14	vicissitudes, valiant, tantamount, verdant, truculent, volatile, unctuous, ubiquitous, urbane, voracious
15	yore, wizened, zephyr, yaw, wrest, zealous, wanton, wily, zenith, yoke

FINAL READING INVENTORY

No Roadblocks!

Stretched Recognition Span!

Speed Adjusted to Purpose and Material!

Full Comprehension!

Enlarged Vocabulary!

Skimming, When Necessary!

Extensive Reading of Varied Materials!